Carl Jung

Titles in the series Critical Lives present the work of leading cultural figures of the modern period. Each book explores the life of the artist, writer, philosopher or architect in question and relates it to their major works.

In the same series

Carl Jung

Paul Bishop

REAKTION BOOKS

Published by Reaktion Books Ltd
Unit 32, Waterside
44–48 Wharf Road
London N1 7UX, UK

www.reaktionbooks.co.uk

First published 2014
Transferred to digital printing 2019
Copyright © Paul Bishop 2014

Printed and bound in the USA by University of Chicago Press

A catalogue record for this book is available from the British Library
ISBN 978 1 78023 267 6

Contents

God speaketh once, and repeateth not the selfsame thing the second time.
By a dream in a vision by night, when deep sleep falleth upon men, and they are
sleeping in their beds: Then he openeth the ears of men, and teaching, instructeth
them in what they are to learn. That he may withdraw a man from the things he
is doing, and may deliver him from pride. Rescuing his soul from corruption:
and his life from passing to the sword.

Job 33:14–18, DRV

Only the gaze turned backwards can take us forwards, for the gaze turned
forwards leads backwards.

Novalis, *Fragments* – General Draft, §31

Carl Jung, 1960.

Abbreviations

CW   C. G. Jung, *Collected Works*, ed. Sir Herbert Read, Michael Fordham, Gerhard Adler, and William McGuire, 20 vols (London, 1953–83)

PU   C. G. Jung, *Psychology of the Unconscious: A Study of the Transformations and Symbolisms of the Libido: A Contribution to the History of the Evolution of Thought*, trans. Beatrice M. Hinkle, intro. William McGuire (London, 1991)

RB   C. G. Jung, *The Red Book: Liber Novus*, ed. Sonu Shamdasani, trans. Mark Kyburz, John Peck and Sonu Shamdasani (New York and London, 2009)

SNZ   C. G. Jung, *Seminar on Nietzsche's 'Zarathustra': Notes of the Seminar given in 1934–1939*, ed. James L. Jarrett, 2 vols (London, 1989)

L   C. G. Jung, *Letters*, ed. Gerhard Adler and Aniela Jaffé, trans. R.F.C. Hull, 2 vols (London, 1973–5)

MDR   Aniela Jaffé, ed., *C. G. Jung: Memories, Dreams, Reflections*, trans. Richard and Clara Winston (London, 1983)

SE   Sigmund Freud, *The Standard Edition of the Complete Works of Sigmund Freud*, general eds J. Strachey and A. Freud, 24 vols (London, 1953–74)

F/J   *The Freud-Jung Letters: The Correspondence between Sigmund Freud and C. G. Jung*, ed. William McGuire, trans. Ralph Manheim and R.F.C. Hull (Cambridge, MA, 1988)

GE   *Goethe Edition = Goethe's Collected Works*, ed. Victor Lange, Eric A. Blackall and Cyrus Hamlin, 12 vols (Boston, MA, and New York, 1983–9)

HA   Goethe, *Werke* [*Hamburger Ausgabe*], ed. Erich Trunz, 14 vols (Hamburg, 1948–60; Munich, 1981). Cited as *Werke* [HA]; *Briefe*, ed. Kurt Robert Mandelkow, 4 vols (Hamburg, 1962–7). Cited as *Briefe* [HA]

WA   Goethe, *Werke* [*Weimarer Ausgabe*], ed. on behalf of Großherzogin Sophie von Sachsen, 4 parts, 133 vols in 143 (Weimar, 1887–1919). Cited as *Werke* [WA]

Introduction: Biography and/as Poetry/Truth

To write a 'critical life' of any major thinker might seem a hazardous enterprise, especially if the subject of that 'critical life' is a psychologist. Just as we might feel uncomfortable to discover that our neighbour at a dinner party or on a long train journey is, in fact, a psychoanalyst, so one feels a certain reluctance to speculate about the desires and ambitions of someone whose job, after all, had been to speculate exactly about such things.

The problem of writing a 'critical life' (in this case of himself) posed a problem for Carl Gustav Jung, too, who observed in a text called *Memories, Dreams, Reflections* (1961), presented as his autobiography: 'I have neither the desire nor the capacity to stand outside myself and observe my fate in a truly objective way.'[1]

Nevertheless, the difficulties attendant on writing autobiography have never prevented great minds from writing one, and *Memories, Dreams, Reflections* – to the extent that it contains material contributed by Jung – can be read in the tradition of such works as the *Confessions* of St Augustine (in the fourth century) or of Jean-Jacques Rousseau (in the eighteenth), the life-histories of, say, Benvenuto Cellini (written *c.* 1570 and published in 1728), Benjamin Franklin (published 1791) or Casanova (published 1826), or, to come closer to Jung's linguistic-cultural background, of Goethe's *Dichtung und Wahrheit* or Nietzsche's *Ecce Homo*.

Memories, Dreams, Reflections

In the prologue to *Memories, Dreams, Reflections*, a work that is presented as having been written by Carl Gustav Jung and edited by Aniela Jaffé, the text is frankly offered as an explicit exercise in mythopoesis. In its prologue, we are invited to imagine how Jung has sat down and undertaken, in his 83rd year, to tell his 'personal myth'. We are warned that he can only 'tell stories', and whether they are 'the truth', we are told, is not the problem. 'The only question is: whether what I tell is *my* fable, *my* truth.'[2] Or, to put it another way, Jung's question might be: is it *meine Dichtung, meine Wahrheit*? Perhaps, too, Jung's words are intended to echo Goethe's in his xenium entitled 'The Motto':

> Truth, I tell you, truth and only the truth, of course:
>   My truth, for there is no other I know.[3]

In *Memories, Dreams, Reflections*, the criterion of factual accuracy comes to be replaced by one of existential authenticity. The only events of which we will learn are the only ones 'worth telling' – those moments 'when the eternal world erupted into the transitory one'.[4] Thus the moments of which the text will speak are 'inner experiences', for these constituted the 'primary material', the *Urstoff*, of Jung's scientific work.[5] These experiences were 'like the fiery-liquid igneous rock, out of which the stone, which had to be worked, was crystallized'.[6] The antithesis in this opening passage between the 'eternal' and the 'transitory' recalls one of Goethe's maxims that reverses the traditional (Platonic) order and prioritizes the 'transitory' over the 'eternal':

> I feel sorry for those people who make a lot of fuss about the transience of things and lose themselves in the contemplation of earthly vanity. After all, we are here precisely to make what is

transitory eternal; but that can only happen, when one knows how to appreciate both.[7]

This idea is repeated in the first section of Goethe's *Zahme Xenien*: 'Nothing of what's past / However it happened! / To make ourselves eternal / Is why we are here'.[8]

Hence to write a 'critical life' of Jung is, in a sense, to examine how Jung, in Goethe's words, *made himself eternal*. Or, to put it another way, it is to examine why Jung (still) matters. There already exist a good number of introductory works on Jung's life and thought, so why another? Because Jung's significance is ongoing and continually changing; it is, in other words, undergoing a continual process of *metamorphosis*. In his 'Observation on Morphology in General' (1817), Goethe defined morphology as including 'the principles of structured form, and the formation and transformation of organic bodies'; but what made it new, he added, was not its 'subject matter', but its 'intention and method'.[9] In 'The Purpose Set Forth', he highlighted the fact that 'the Germans have a word for the complex presented by a physical organism': namely, 'structured form' or *Gestalt*. 'But', he went on, 'if we look at all these *Gestalten*, especially the organic ones, we will discover that nothing in them is permanent, nothing is at rest or defined – everything is in a flux of continual motion'. And 'this is why', Goethe concluded, the German language 'frequently and fittingly makes use of the word *Bildung*' – meaning 'shaping', 'formation', and, in other contexts, 'education' – 'to describe the end product *and* what is in the process of production as well'.[10]

This developmental aspect is as important to *Memories, Dreams, Reflections* as is its awareness of the problems of autobiography, which comes to the fore when it focuses on its own intentional specificities as a text. Correspondingly, Jung's life is explicitly presented, not simply as a 'story', but as a particular kind of story – 'a story of the self-realization of the unconscious'.[11] Moreover, the unconscious as conceived here is something essentially *dynamic*, and hence the individual is conceptualized as something essentially *morphological*, something undergoing change and becoming: 'Everything in the unconscious', we read, 'seeks outward manifestation' – or in the words of the original German, it seeks to become real, *will Ereignis werden* – and thus 'the personality' (a word used here in the technical, Jungian sense) 'too desires to evolve out of its unconscious conditions' or to unfold itself, *sich entfalten*, 'and to experience itself as a whole', *sich als Ganzheit erleben*.[12] To fulfil this ambition, however, a particular kind of discourse is required, and the discourse of science is, we are told, not adequate to this task, because Jung 'does not experience [himself] as a scientific problem' and nor, for that matter, does anyone else.

What, then, remains instead of science? What tools are available, if a scientific discourse – or a strictly historical, 'biographical' discourse – is not? For Jung, there is an alternative to science, to *Wissenschaft*, to *logos*: it is called 'myth', but it is interesting to note how this concept is introduced. Because myth is presented, not simply as something fictional or religious, but as a means of expressing 'what one is to the inner vision', of giving expression to 'what the human being appears to be *sub specie aeternitatis*'.[13] Each of these two clauses is a gloss on the other: the 'inner vision' is the individual seen from the perspective of eternity, and the 'perspective of eternity' is accessible from the 'inner vision'. Moreover, precisely this phrase, *sub specie aeternitatis*, is famously used by the Dutch philosopher Baruch de Spinoza (1632–1677) in his *Ethics* (1677), in the context of introducing his notion of a 'third kind' of knowledge, or what he calls *scientia intuitiva*.[14] In a later chapter in *Memories, Dreams, Reflections* these themes are echoed when we are told that the decisive question of the human individual is: 'Are you related to something infinite or not?', and in another famous passage in his *Ethics* Spinoza tells us that we know – indeed, that we *experience* – that we are 'eternal'.[15]

It is *this* dimension of life, then, that 'myth' is supposed to express and which necessitates a particular narrative strategy. Jung has 'undertaken', so we are to understand him as saying, to 'tell' his 'personal myth', a strategy that involves 'making direct statements' or simply 'telling stories' (*Geschichten erzählen*).[16] Are these stories true? For Jung (and for some of his followers, if not for scholars and historians), whether or not the stories are 'true' is not at issue. What matters, rather, is their existential validity, whether the tale that is told is really Jung's tale: is it *his* 'fable' (*Märchen*), is it *his* 'truth' (*Wahrheit*)?

To express this dimension of the eternal as the quintessential quality of life itself – hence a *vitalist eternal dimension* – Jung uses a curiously precise and striking image: the rhizome. What is a rhizome? As any keen gardener will be able to explain, a rhizome is a horizontal plant stem, often (but not always) running underground, consisting of a series of nodes from which roots or shoots are sent forth. (Subsequent thinkers, notably the French philosophers Gilles Deleuze (1925–1995) and Félix Guattari (1930–1992) used the term 'rhizome' as a substitute for – in their eyes – the logocentric notion of the 'root', opposing the horizontality of their postmodern approach to the supposed verticality of classical metaphysics.[17] So it should not come as a surprise to learn that, as Christian Kerslake has demonstrated, Deleuze in his early years was in fact a reader and a reviewer of Jung.[18])

In a magnificent passage of botanical rhetoric, *Memories, Dreams, Reflections* describes 'life' as 'like a plant that lives on its rhizome', inasmuch as 'its true life is invisible, hidden in the rhizome'. Thus 'the part that appears above ground lasts only a single summer', then 'withers away – an ephemeral apparition' (much as the Psalmist laments that while 'man's days are as grass, as the flowers of the field so shall he flourish'; the famous biblical motif, in other words, that 'all flesh is grass').[19] What is true of the individual is also true of civilizations, and in *Memories, Dreams,*

Reflections Jung is presented as filled with 'an impression of absolute nullity' when contemplating 'the unending coming-into-being and decay of life and cultures'.[20] Yet there is something *subterranean* that *persists*, 'a sense of something that lives and endures beneath the eternal flux' is said always to have been present to Jung.[21] What persists and endures for Jung is what he called the *archaic*.[22] In a sense, Jung's position is an eminently logical one; after all, as Dilthey argued, 'the present never *is*; what we experience as present always contains the memory of what has just been present'.[23]

Subsequent texts authored by Jung return to this image of the rhizome. In his lectures delivered in 1937 at Yale University on 'Psychology and Religion', he remarked that 'the symptom is like the shoot above the ground, yet the main plant is an extended rhizome underground', and it is this rhizome that 'represents the content of a neurosis', being nothing less than 'the matrix of complexes, of symptoms, and of dreams'.[24] Then again, in the foreword to *Symbols of Transformation* (1952), the revised edition of his first major publication, *Transformations and Symbols of the Libido* (1911–12), Jung wrote that 'individual consciousness is only the flower and the fruit of a season, sprung from the perennial rhizome beneath the earth', arguing that, as a consequence, 'it would find itself in better accord with the truth if it took the existence of the rhizome into its calculations': or, in other words, if it reminded itself of the need to see itself *sub specie aeternitatis*. For, as Jung puts it, alluding to the *Tao Te Ching*, chapter 52, 'the root matter is the mother of all things'.[25] And in *Memories, Dreams, Reflections* itself, Jung's earliest memories are described as 'like the individual shoots of a single underground rhizome, like the stations on a road of unconscious development'.[26]

The idea behind the image of the rhizome – the notion of a perennial or eternal dimension to the psyche – is a constant theme in Jung's writings. In 1927 Jung delivered a lecture in Karlsruhe that was subsequently published as 'Analytical Psychology and "Weltanschauung"'. Here he presented analytical psychology as 'a reaction against an exaggerated rationalization of consciousness', which, 'in its endeavour to produce directed processes', thus 'isolates itself from nature' – never a good thing, in Jung's view – 'and so tears humankind from its own natural history'.[27] What happens when we are ripped from our own 'natural history' is portrayed by Jung in terms of an unbearable, claustrophic sense of oppression – an oppression from which, thus its hope and its promise, his psychology aims to liberate us.[28]

In a lecture given in 1932 to the Alsatian Pastoral Conference in Strasbourg, later published as 'Psychotherapists or the Clergy', Jung explained that his own therapy is intended to assist and accompany his patient through the experience when – 'it is like an inspired moment' – 'something Other rises up from the dark realm of the psyche and confronts him'.[29] This moment, Jung assured his audience, marks 'the beginning of the cure', even though 'this spontaneous activity of the psyche often becomes intense to the point where an inner voice or visionary images are perceived' – phenomena described as 'a true primordial experience of the spirit'.[30] For Jung, the primordial is not, as Freud suspected it of being, something infantile and hence problematic; rather, it is the solution to the problem of modernity.

In another short essay from around the same time, Jung contrasted his own position with that of his fellow analysts, Sigmund Freud (1856–1939) and Alfred Adler (1870–1937). Here he speaks of the libidinal drives (be they erotic, as Freud believed, or power-orientated, as Adler did), as coming into collision with spirit, with *Geist*.[31] Although Jung does not shy away from the fact that he cannot say exactly what *Geist* is, he clearly regards it as a liberating force, as a means of escaping what he called 'the inexorable cycle of biological events' or, as he strikingly described it, 'the fleshly bond leading back to father and mother or forward to the children that have sprung from our flesh – "incest" with the past and "incest" with the future, the original sin of perpetuation of the "family romance"'.[32] From such shackles, Jung wrote in a passage laden with salvific vocabulary, only *Geist* can free us, and he insisted on the need for an 'authentic-experience-of-the-primordial', for *Urerfahrung*. 'We moderns are faced with the necessity of rediscovering the life of the spirit: we must experience it anew for ourselves [*Urerfahrung machen*]', he declared, for 'it is the only way in which to break the spell that binds us to the cycle of biological events'.[33]

Thus a return to the 'archaic' and to the 'primordial' is also a way forward to the future: we need to rediscover how, in Goethe's words, 'the sensation of past and present being one' can introduce a new dimension to the present.[34] Indeed, many of his works, Goethe maintained, reflected this sensation, 'even though the sensation, at the moment when it was aroused directly by life, or in life itself', seemed 'strange' or 'inexplicable', even 'unpleasant'.[35]

In addition to the autobiographical work, *Memories, Dreams, Reflections*, there are three other major sources of information about Jung's life. First, there is correspondence, of which only a portion has been published. While the two-volume selection of Jung's letters remains an invaluable source of information, and some of his correspondences – such as with Freud (published 1974), Sabina Spielrein (1980), Hans Schmid-Guisan (1982), Wolfgang Pauli (1992), Emil Medtner (1994), Eugen Böhler (1996), Ernst Bernhard (2001), Victor White (2007) and James Kirsch (2011) – have established themselves as classic epistolary exchanges of notable intellectual-historical value, they remain, as things currently stand, an incomplete source of information. Their great value, however, derives from allowing us to see how Jung adapted his ideas to the assumptions of his various correspondents, be they fellow analysts, or philosophers, theologians, or members of the general public.

Second, there are the numerous biographies of Jung, several major ones having appeared within the last decade or so. Across this plethora of biographies, a certain trajectory can be detected. (For an account of some of these biographies and an analysis of their methodology, see Sonu Shamdasani's study of 2005.[36]) Perhaps inevitably, the earlier biographies tend to be hagiographical in their style and approach: as the titles of these biographies suggest, Jung is seen in them as in some sense a representative figure, a symbol of a particular historical-cultural juncture. Nor are these authors slow to embrace the notion, explicitly adulatory and only implicitly critical, that a mythical status may be ascribed to Jung.

Right back in the 1970s, however, the foundations were also laid for a critical, scholarly approach to Jung, in the form of the chapter devoted to Jung by Henri F. Ellenberger in his work *The Discovery of the Unconscious* (1970). This groundbreaking publication constitutes, in Shamdasani's eyes, nothing less than 'a watershed in Jung studies' and 'the inception of the field of Jung history as a distinct domain'.[37] Other critical or independently minded biographies began to emerge, and by the late 1990s a number of professional biographers had begun to turn their attention to Jung and, building on the work undertaken by Brome, produced some of the most comprehensive, if still not complete, accounts to date.[38]

In this same period, an entirely different – and highly critical, even hostile –version of Jung's life and work was offered by Richard Noll, a clinical psychologist and historian of science, in *The Jung Cult* (1994) and *The Aryan Christ* (1997). Although Noll's account, understandably enough, has been vigorously rejected by practitioners of analytical psychology, and some of its assumptions and conclusions questioned, his historical contextualization of Jung's work in relation to Ernst Haeckel and evolutionary biology, to the Nietzschean matriarchalism of J. J. Bachofen and Otto Gross, and to the project of cultural renewal embodied in the Stefan George circle, underscores how deeply and profoundly Jung belongs to a broader stream of thought in German culture.

Each of these accounts has its strength and its weaknesses: the hagiographical accounts offer an insight into the genuine charisma possessed by Jung, but lack the critical distance properly to appreciate the extent of his intellectual achievements. And his critics are sometimes too swift to condemn, or to judge Jung in terms other than those in which he was trying to operate. Most problematic of all, however, is that none of them had access to the Red Book (or *Liber Novus*), a work that absorbed Jung's attention for a period of some fifteen years, and that must have occupied hundreds of hours of his life, yet – with the Red Book being inaccessible to scholars – without his biographers having any sense of what it could have involved.

So with the publication in 2009 of a scholarly edition of the Red Book, together with a full interpretative apparatus, a new period of Jung studies has begun. With the ongoing work of the Philemon Foundation, there is also the prospect that more and more primary Jungian material will be made available.[39] Yet has the publication of the Red Book really brought about a sea change in Jung studies? Is it asking too much of the Red Book to expect it to do so? Or should one look elsewhere for new directions in scholarship on Jung?

For, in addition to his correspondence (insofar as it has been published) and the various biographical accounts of his life, there exists a third source of information: his library, which documents his passion for reading over many decades.[40] A yearning for a well-stocked library had always been characteristic of Jung since he was young, but a recurring dream he had in the 1920s indicates the *symbolic* importance of the library as a site for intellectual innovation. In this dream, 'large, fat folio volumes' adorned the walls, including 'a number of books embellished with copper engravings of a strange character'; these 'medieval incunabula and sixteenth-century prints', with their 'alchemical symbols', represented 'a part of [Jung's] personality, an aspect of [him]self'.[41] In fact, it was from his researches into mythology, folklore and religion that Jung came to develop his notion of the collective unconscious, which might even be understood, as Shamdasani has suggested, as a kind of 'library within'.[42]

But as well as reading books and writing them, when in 1913 Jung commenced work on his own unusual bibliophilic project in the form of the Red Book, he incorporated motifs both from world mythology (such as Izdubar, or Gilgamesh) and from the banality, commonplaceness, and trashiness of popular culture. Thus the composition of the Red Book gave Jung 'a new understanding of how to read', and Shamdasani has rightly noted that 'Jung's self-experimentation was largely undertaken while seated in his library'.[43] The significance of this key insight into Jung's working methods cannot be sufficiently emphasized, for it reveals the significance of analytical psychology as a cultural project.

Because it was 'nourished by his classical education', the personal mythology confected by Jung in his Red Book was 'syncretic, freely elaborating figures from classical myth', but works in the German tradition played a central role as well: notably, Faust and Zarathustra – from the celebrated works by Goethe and by Nietzsche – turned out to be 'key exemplars' of the self.[44] Because he was steeped in literature, Jung could include in *Psychological Types* (1921), his second great foundational monograph, a discussion of the type problem in poetry, and throughout his life he enjoyed connections of one kind or another with the literati of his age, such as Hermann Hesse, Gustav Meyrink, Thomas Mann and James Joyce.

When, in 1928, Jung received from the Sinologist Richard Wilhelm (1873–1930) a copy of the ancient Chinese text *The Secret of the Golden Flower*, this simultaneously initiated his interest in *I Ching*, the ancient Chinese oracle text, and in alchemy. Inspired by Mary Anne Atwood's *A Suggestive Inquiry into the Hermetic Mystery* (1850) and Ethan Allen Hitchcock's *Remarks on Alchemy and*

Richard Wilhelm.

the Alchemists (1857), as well as by Herbert Silberer (1882–1923) and Théodore Flournoy (1854–1920), Jung embarked on an activity he called 'treasure hunting': filling eight copybooks with excerpts sourced directly from ancient alchemical texts (to which he compiled an index volume). These alchemy copybooks constituted 'a remarkable scholarly apparatus', one that was capable of generating an 'endless series' of works: and, in the form of *Paracelsica* (1942), *Psychology and Alchemy* (1944), *The Psychology of the Transference* (1946) and *Mysterium coniunctionis* (1955–6), it did.[45] On the face of it, these works might have very little in common with Goethe, but we should remember that Goethe, too, had been nourished by such authors as Paracelsus (1493–1541), Basilius Valentinus (the pseudonym of a fifteenth-century Benedictine monk and alchemist from Erfurt), Georg von Welling (1652–1727), Johann Baptist van Helmont (1577–1644), and George Starkey (1628–1665), during his own period of crisis in Frankfurt from 1768 to 1770.[46]

In all Jung's changing interests, from alchemy in the 1920s to his lectures at the ETH in Zurich between 1933 and 1941, and his contributions throughout the 1930s and '40s to the Eranos Conferences in Ascona, organized by Olga Fröbe-Kapteyn (see the Conclusion pages 207–17), we find both innovation and continuity: we find, in other words, *metamorphosis*. Jung was always able to relate the new to the old, the unfamiliar to the familiar or even the East to the West: in his preface to an introduction to Zen Buddhism by D. T. Suzuki, translated by Heinrich Zimmer (both fellow Eranos lecturers), for instance, Jung noted how 'the tragedies of Goethe's *Faust* and Nietzsche's *Zarathustra* [. . .] mark the first glimmerings of a breakthrough of total experience in our Western hemisphere'.[47]

In other words, there is good reason to be more interested in the *textual* Jung, in the Jung that expressed itself through texts (in the form of the *Collected Works*, in lectures, seminars and correspondence) and that arose *through* encounters with texts, than in the *biographical* Jung, whose historical details must always remain a matter of conjecture and controversy, both because the requisite documentation is not always available, and because of the very nature of historical writing itself. The figure of Jung to which we nevertheless have access – and the figure of Jung that really *matters* – is the Jung whose story is sketched in the pages that follow, which constitutes, in a specific sense, a biography of Jung in books.

So this 'critical life' of Jung, which would like to belong to the tradition of introductory guides to Jung's life and thought to which others have also contributed, aims to be both 'critical' and 'appreciative', mindful of the historical juncture at which it is being written. For whatever the validity of such 'signature concepts' as the archetype or the collective unconscious, Jung's eminently *synthetic*, in the sense of *synthesizing*, approach to culture marks him out, not simply as one of the most important and influential intellectual figures of the twentieth century, but also – when much around us is (economically, politically, culturally, educationally, aesthetically) in a state of decline or collapse – as a thinker whose real time is perhaps yet still to come.

1

A Child of Goethe

In 1793 Goethe was caught up in the military campaign against France, centred on the city of Mainz. In the previous year he had been a witness to the battle at Valmy where, after a ferocious cannonade, he had told the troops, 'From this time and place a new epoch is beginning, and you will be able to say that you were there!'[1] Now, after a visit to Pempelfort, close to Düsseldorf, to his friend the philosopher Friedrich Heinrich Jacobi (1743–1819), he travelled, via Duisburg and Münster, back to Weimar, the capital of Sachsen-Weimar-Eisenach, where he held an important position as a minister in the provincial administration. After Christmas in Weimar he set out in May 1794 for Mainz, where the occupied city was being besieged by the coalition. The siege ended in the defeat of the French occupiers: on 23 July 1793 the destroyed city was handed back and Goethe entered Mainz on 26 July. After passing through Mannheim, Heidelberg and Frankfurt, he returned to Weimar on 22 August.

During his visit to Mannheim, or perhaps at some stage in his adopted home town of Weimar, Goethe met Sophie Ziegler, the wife of Franz Ignaz Jung (1759–1831), who was associated, along with her sister, with the Mannheim Theatre, and frequented the city's literary and cultural circles. Goethe met her, and had an affair with her, resulting in the birth of an illegitimate child. Being illegitimate, the child's paternity could never be disclosed, but the boy was named after his ostensible legal father, and called Carl Gustav Jung.

Johann Heinrich Lips (1758–1817), *Johann Wolfgang Goethe*, 1971, engraving.

The boy's mother retained a connection to Goethe, however; she became a good friend of Charlotte Kestner, the daughter of Charlotte Kestner née Buff, one of Goethe's earliest and most intense loves – and, scandalously, the model for the figure of Lotte in Goethe's novel *The Sorrows of Young Werther*. In turn, this younger Charlotte maintained the link between Goethe and his illegitimate son, Carl Gustav Jung, whom she frequently visited, until she finally moved to Basel, where the Jung family lived.

This Carl Gustav Jung had three marriages: first, to Virginie de Lassault (1804–1830); then, to Elisabeth Catherine Reyenthaler; and finally, to Sophie Frey (1812–1855), to whom in 1842 a son, called Johann Paul Achilles Jung, was born. Johann Paul Achilles became a Protestant pastor and married Emilie Preiswerk. The couple had two children: a boy, also called Carl Gustav, born in 1875, and his younger sister, Gertrud, born in 1884. This Carl Gustav went on to establish himself as one of the most prominent, and hence also one of the most controversial, thinkers of the twentieth century: C. G. Jung, the great analyst. And he used to enjoy it when, as often happened, the legend was told of how his great-grandfather was really Goethe. True, he used to protest, describing the story as 'annoying' or 'in bad taste'. 'Listen', he would say, 'the world's already full of all too many fools who tell tales about the "unknown father" – they need a good dose of psychoanalysis!'

Johann Paul Jung with his wife Emilie, March 1876.

Yet it has also been reported that Carl Gustav could not suppress 'a certain gratified amusement' when the tale was told.[2] Perhaps he thought: 'if people are stupid enough to believe it – then let them!'

The problem with the story of Carl Gustav Jung's descent from Goethe is this: there is not a scrap of evidence for it. Neither the archives of the Goethehaus in Frankfurt am Main, nor the baptismal register of the Jesuitenkirche in Mannheim, contain any records that support the claim. Nor, indeed, is it likely that they would; after all, the boy born in 1784 was an illegitimate child: a bastard. So why would the boy's grandson, two generations later, be willing to entertain the idea that Goethe was his (illegitimate) great-grandfather?

There may have been many reasons. For a start, Carl Gustav Jung had a complicated attitude towards paternity and the figure of the Father. This was also true of his biological father, Johann Paul Achilles Jung (1842–1896), the pastor of Kesswil, a small town on the Swiss shores of Lake Constance; then of Laufen, another small town, above the Rhine Falls. Jung's father cuts a sad figure. After his studies in Oriental languages in Göttingen, and his dissertation on the Arabic version of the biblical Song of Songs, he became a county parson. Like Eduard Mörike (1804–1875), a Swabian pastor from about the same time who penned verses of exquisite, if melancholy, beauty, Johann Paul Achilles discovered that country life was far from the idyll it was imagined to be. Nor was he even a poet. Still smoking the same kind of long pipe he had enjoyed as a student, he fell into a sort of sentimental idealism and tried to escape the pressures of his duties as a pastor; and as a husband, for his marriage was not going well; this did not escape the attention of his son. Above all, this son came to realize that his father, the local pastor, had, in reality, lost his religious faith. Struck with despair at the decline in his fortunes since his golden years as a student, Johann Paul Achilles wasted away in his miserable depression, became bedridden, and died in 1896 at the age of 52. His son, Carl Gustav, had barely turned twenty.

A church in Laufen, Switzerland.

Equally, Carl Gustav Jung had a complex relation to God the Father. According to a famous story, as a schoolboy Carl Gustav was one day contemplating the brightly glazed tiles on the roof of Basel Cathedral when, caught up in the beauty of the sight, he was suddenly struck by a terrible thought: a thought so terrible, he dared not think it: God was in Heaven, but . . . was all right with the world? This thought took the form of an obscene and disgusting image: the defecating deity. In the Old Testament, Moses was privileged to be given a view of the backside of God, but Carl Gustav was granted a vision of God's dark, terrible and disgusting aspect: a cloacal deity, sitting on his throne, that unleashed a giant turd that smashed the roof and destroyed the walls of the cathedral.[3] In the Book of Job, Jung would have found a text that spoke to his experience in its line 'Yet thou shalt plunge me in filth', and Jung's later (and controversial) treatise *Answer to Job* (1952) speaks openly of 'the shattering emotion which the unvarnished spectacle of divine savagery and ruthlessness produces in us'.[4] But it was not through the Bible, but through the canonical text of German culture, Goethe's *Faust*, that Jung was first to approach the problem of the dual nature of God, of 'evil and its universal power' and 'the mysterious role it played in delivering man from darkness and suffering'.[5]

Neither the biological nor the divine Father were positive figures for Jung, and so it is not surprising that Jung – initially, at least – sought a symbolic Father in the figure of Sigmund Freud.[6] After Jung initiated contact by letter in 1906 with the man who was considered, by common consent, as 'the father of psychoanalysis', their formal exchange had been followed up with several meetings in Vienna and elsewhere, and quickly became an intensive exchange of interests, ideas, and emotions.[7] Freud and Jung soon engaged in the identification as father and son, which transmuted into an identification as Moses and Joshua, and eventually analyst and analysand.[8] Freud even played along with the idea that Jung was somehow related to Goethe, in one letter citing a line from *Faust*, Part One – 'You're on intimate terms with the devil, / And yet you still fear fire?' – and adding, 'your grandfather said something like that'.[9] For his part, Jung used Goethe to bolster the authority of his own ideas, telling Freud that, after seeing a performance of selections from *Faust* in Zurich, that he now felt 'more confident' of the value of his work on *Transformations and Symbols of the Libido* (the book that would lead to his split from Freud):

As the whole thing sprang into life before my eyes, all kinds of thoughts came to me, and I felt sure that my respected great-grandfather would have given my work his placet, the more willingly as he would have noted with a smile that

the great-grandchild has continued and even extended the
ancestral line of his thought.[10]

But as the intensity and productivity of their relationship declined,
and as the political complications in the early circles of psychoanalysis imposed themselves, six years after it had begun Jung
terminated his relationship with the psychoanalytic father through
a quotation from Nietzsche's *Zarathustra*, 'one repays a teacher
poorly if one always remains only a student'.[11] In some respects,
Jung's claim to a blood-relationship to Goethe can be seen as a
strategic move. Freud might be a devotee of Goethe, but Jung was –
literally – his (great-)grandson! Nor is the idea of karma as strange
as it might appear: after all, in the eighteenth century such topics
as reincarnation, the transmigration of souls and pre-existence were
hotly debated by authors associated with the classical tradition.

Given Jung's ambivalent attitude towards his biological, divine
and symbolic Fathers, the consistently insinuated claim to a relation
to Goethe invites a psychoanalytic reading, precisely of the kind
that Freud (and, subsequently, Jung) developed. In 'The Concept
of the Collective Unconscious' (1936) Jung took as his starting point
Freud's interpretation of Leonardo da Vinci's painting *Virgin and
Child with St Anne*, a work in which, so Freud argued, the motif of
the dual mothers reflected the biographical circumstances of
Leonardo's life – his own two mothers (his biological mother,
Caterina, and his stepmother, his father's wife, Donna Albiera).[12]
Although Jung had initially welcomed Freud's treatment of
Leonardo, telling Freud it was 'wonderful' and, in his introduction
to *Transformations and Symbols of the Libido* (1911–12), citing Freud's
essay on Leonardo as a methodological exemplar for his own study,
in this lecture he argued that the painting *Virgin and Child with St
Anne* should not be seen in the light of the personal circumstance
that Leonardo had, so to speak, 'two mothers' (his real mother and
a stepmother), but rather in terms of the archetypal motif of the

'dual mother'.[13] To this motif Jung links to another, the motif of 'dual descent': namely, the descent from both human and divine parents. Hence, Jung explained, the tradition of godparents, which is connected to the idea of baptism as a kind of 'second birth'.[14] As an example, Jung cites the case of Benvenuto Cellini (1500–1571), the great Florentine goldsmith and sculptor, whose autobiography Goethe had translated in 1796.

If Jung's theory of religion reinscribes the fantasy of the family romance that rejects the (real) parents and replaces them with fantastic – or archetypal – substitutes, so his own 'romantic' biography claims Goethe as a distant parent, but in order to make a cultural-political point. So the legend according to which Jung was distantly related to Goethe – indeed, was the grandson of one of his bastard offspring – is really hinting at something important: a deep affinity between the ideals of analytical psychology and the aims of German classicism; an affinity which is not biological but which is far more important: intellectual and *cultural*. Central to the aim of German classicism is a vision of wholeness, of complete-ness, of totality, achieved through a process of synthesis: and precisely such a goal and process of synthesis lies at the heart of Jung's project of analytical psychology.

Understanding this point helps to explain the insistence in *Memories, Dreams, Reflections* on the significance of Goethe. Here we learn that Goethe became, in Jung's eyes, 'a prophet'; that Jung's 'godfather and authority was the great Goethe himself'; and that Goethe's extraordinary dramatic poem, *Faust*, came to mean more to Jung than his 'beloved Gospel according to St John'.[15] This importance attached to *Faust* constitutes a leitmotif in *Memories, Dreams, Reflections*, and indeed in Jung's work as a whole. (That *Faust* could be used in this way tells a lot about Jung, but it also says something about Goethe's work.) One of the few critics who seems fully able to appreciate the sheer *strangeness* of Goethe's *Faust* is Harold Bloom, who has celebrated the text as the ultimate 'countercanonical poem'.[16] For Bloom, *Faust* is 'a banquet of sense, though doubtless too replete with scarcely healthy viands', while 'as a sexual nightmare or erotic fantasy, it has no rival'.[17] Indeed, for Bloom, Goethe transcends all conventional literary categorizations, and his poetry and prose alike 'are at once exemplary of a Classical, almost universal *ethos*, and a Romantic, intensely personal *pathos*'; indeed, Goethe's wisdom, Bloom contends, 'abides', but 'it seems to come from some solar system other than our own'.[18]

In the case of Jung, however, the influence was as profound as it was specific: Jung's first major work, as we shall see (in chapter Five), was marked by a 'clearly Faustian' motif – as, 'casting aside the constraints of Christianity, Jung meant to make a descent to the depths of the soul, there to find the roots of man's being in the symbols of the libido which has been handed down from ancient times' – and thus 'to find redemption despite his own genial psychoanalytic pact with the devil'.[19] Goethe's great text, *Faust*, in effect offered Jung a template for his own emerging theories and ideas.

A Child of Switzerland

So much for Jung's symbolic background: what of his real background as a child? The account given in *Memories, Dreams, Reflections* of Jung's life as a child includes, among his earliest memories, being shown the sight of the Alps, glowing in the deep red light of sunset; and the occasion when, on a visit to Thurgau and its castle, on Lake Constance, he looked at the water of the lake: and gazed and gazed, and could not be dragged away from the water; the sight of such an expanse of water is said to have been 'an inconceivable pleasure', 'an incomparable splendour'.[20] But not all the memories are by any means so idyllic; darkness intrudes in the form of violence. For example, there is his memory of blood and water trickling down an open drain from a wash house in which the corpse of a man drowned at the Falls had been placed.[21] And later, from the time after the family had moved to Kleinhüningen, just outside Basel, in 1879, Jung recalls, along with the green colour of the sky after the eruption of Krakatoa in 1883 and the sight of a comet in the sky, the corpses stuck in the sand when the river Wiese broke its banks and flooded the village; he was also fascinated by the slaughter of a pig.[22]

At a very early age Carl Gustav was attracted to women, fascinated by what he later called the *Anima*. He is said to have remembered, for instance, the black hair and olive complexion of the family maid: recollecting, in almost fetishistic detail, her hairline, her throat, with its dark-pigmented skin, her ear.[23] Then there was the memory of a young, pretty girl with blue eyes, fair hair, who led him, one beautiful autumn day, along the Rhine, below the Falls, near the castle of Wörth.[24] Or later, as a schoolchild, he encountered (during a visit to Flüeli and to the relics of Brother Klaus) a young, slender girl with blue eyes, dressed in local costume. As they walked back from the hermitage together, they talked, and as he told her of his plans to study at university, he noticed the mix of shyness and admiration on her face. As the girl played Gretchen to his Faust, Jung declined to play the role of Mephistopheles, and he decided not to share with her his intuitions into the darker side of life.[25] Yet such encounters may well have determined Jung's later attitude towards women at an unconscious level. In the case of his maid, Jung is said to have had a sense of strangeness, yet also a curious sense of familiarity: a characteristic that came to symbolize for him 'the whole essence of womanhood'.[26] What, he wondered, were 'the threads of fate that led from Brother Klaus to the pretty girl'?[27] And in the case of the young girl who took him by the hand and led him through the autumnal leaves near Wörth, she later became his mother-in-law . . .[28]

Other sources recall how Jung, when a boy, once saw 'a woman far advanced in pregnancy wearing hoops' (presumably some sort of support device), 'which were then in fashion'; this struck him as 'a comical sight', which led him to ask his mother 'whether the woman was wearing a little horse' – that is, 'one of those little horses that used to be worn at carnivals or circuses and were buckled to the body' – and thereafter, 'whenever he saw women in this condition, it reminded him of his childish hypothesis'.[29] Or how, in the house of a spinster aunt, Jung saw an engraving of his grandfather on his mother's side, Samuel Preiswerk (1799–1871), an *Antistes*, or sort of bishop, 'represented as coming out of his house and standing on a little terrace', down from which came 'handrails and stairs . . . and a footpath leading to the cathedral'. Every Sunday morning, when he visited the aunt, Jung would kneel on a chair and look at the picture: *until his grandfather came down the steps*. 'But, my dear', his aunt would exclaim, 'he doesn't walk, he is still standing there!' *But Jung knew that he had seen him walking down*.[30]

During Jung's childhood, self-destructive urges manifested themselves, too. As a child Carl Gustav was always falling over: once down the stairs, another time against the stove leg. And on another occasion – or so his mother is supposed to have told him – he nearly slipped through the rails of the bridge leading over the Rhine Falls to Neuhausen, but was saved in the nick of time by the dark-haired, olive-skinned maid. Terror took the form of God himself, or at least the figure of Jesus, as imagined by the Lutheran theologian and poet Paul Gerhardt (1607–1676) in a famous hymn, *Nun ruhen alle Wälder* ('Now all the woods are sleeping'), as the winged, bird-like protector of young children, who even ate the chick-like objects of his care, to prevent Satan consuming them first.[31] This frightening image merged in Carl Gustav's mind with the Jesuit-like robes of the local Catholic priest and fed into his dream, dated to when he was three or four years old, of something very strange lurking in the cellar of the vicarage near Laufen castle. Here, perched on a rich golden throne, was standing a huge, naked phallus, its tip replaced by a single eye, gazing motionlessly upwards. In his dream Carl Gustav heard his mother's voice cry out, 'That is the man-eater!': a fusion of the dark, child-eating Lord Jesus, the Jesuit, and phallus. True to its etymology, the phallus was shining brightly (φαλος): a 'subterranean god', a god 'not-to-be-named', an 'alien guest both from above and below', responsible for Jung's 'initiation into the realm of darkness'.[32]

This dream (or vision, or fantasy) is clearly rich in all kinds of sexual and religious symbolism, but its theological symbolism seems clear: it is a rejection of Yahweh's claim, made in Deuteronomy (4:39), that 'the Lord [. . .] is God in heaven above, and in the earth beneath, and there is no other', because what Jung (thought he) saw reveals that there *is* a realm where the Judeo-Christian God is not in charge, and that there *is* another deity: a chthonic, Dionysian alternative. Even if Jung only spoke about this ithyphallic vision when he was 65 years old, its theological conclusions informed his thinking from the very start.[33]

Given that he was dreaming about what was in the basement of the parsonage in Laufen, perhaps it is just as well that the family soon moved to Kleinhüningen, close to (and now part of) Basel, in

The parsonage in Laufen, Switzerland.

1879, when Carl Gustav was four years old. The eighteenth-century parsonage there had fine furniture and old paintings hung on the walls. In particular, Jung is said to have remembered an Italian painting of the biblical theme of David and Goliath, the encounter of the valiant youth and the Philistine giant.[34] This picture was a mirror-copy of a painting from the workshop of the Bolognese painter Guido Reni (1575–1642), whose work in Rome shows the influence of Carracci and Caravaggio, and who enjoys the status of one of the great exponents of classicism. (As Jung tells us, the original hangs in the Louvre; and a later version can also be found in the Uffizi.) Another painting he remembered was an early nineteenth-century landscape of Basel. Apparently Jung would spend hours in front of these pictures, gazing at and absorbing their beauty.

When he was about six, Carl Gustav went on a day trip with his aunt to Basel and visited one of the museums there. On the way out, he and his aunt passed through the gallery of antiquities. Jung was absolutely amazed by the extraordinary sculptures: 'utterly overwhelmed', in fact, and his eyes opened wide, for 'never had [he] seen anything so beautiful'.[35] But although he could not stop looking at the marvellous Greek classical statues, the aunt was tugging at his hand, pulling her nephew to the exit. *Abscheulige Bueb, tue d'Auge zue, abscheulige Bueb, tue d'Auge zue!* she cried, 'shut your eyes, you disgusting little boy!' And only then did he notice: wearing fig leaves, the figures were naked. What does this story tell us? Only in a repressive culture is nudity considered a problem: to the eye of the child nakedness is something beautiful. Once again, this early encounter with classical culture, the classicism of antiquity, left an impression that was to remain with him and inform his thinking much later on.

One gets the impression that, as a child, the experiences Jung craved were intensely visual. Hence his enthusiasm for readings from *Orbis Pictus*, a famous seventeenth-century children's book by the theologian and pedagogue Johann Amos Comenius

Jung at the age of six,
18 November 1881.

(1592–1670), with its rich illustrations. Goethe recalls reading this book in the library of his father, who owned both the 1746 and the 1755 editions. In particular, Jung was intrigued by such 'exotic' religions as Hinduism, with its depictions of Brahma, Vishnu, Shiva: figures which, so he is said to have felt, displayed an 'affinity' with that dark revelation he had experienced in his dream of the subterranean ithyphallus.[36]

Thus far we have hardly said anything about Jung's mother; that is, his biological mother, Emilie Jung née Preiswerk (1848–1923). If the notion of 'Father' was, according to *Memories, Dreams, Reflections*, associated for Carl Gustav with two (contradictory?) concepts, 'reliability' and 'powerlessness', the notion of 'Mother' was associated with 'innate unreliability'; hence also, perhaps we are invited to read, with 'great power'?[37] The basis for this assumption is Carl Gustav's memory, when ill, of his father carrying him in his arms, singing such old student songs as 'Alles schweige, jeder neige'. By contrast, his mother is remembered for her absence (due in turn to illness, which led to her hospitalization for a number of months), connected with problems in her marriage. Later on, the marital problems of his parents are alluded to again, in the context of memories of how Carl Gustav used to sleep in the same room as his father, while 'frightening influences' are said to have come from the door to his mother's room.[38] The German philosopher Alfred Baeumler (1887–1968) once observed that 'in the word *mother* is combined everything that Romanticism sought, desired, strove for', in the sense that 'the indissoluble combination of demonic sexuality with love of the night and the belief in spirits, fear of and longing for death, ancestral cult and submission to fate' was precisely what constituted Romanticism.[39] From this point of view, Jung's relationship to his mother was, in this sense, eminently Romantic. 'At night', one can read in *Memories, Dreams, Reflections*, 'Mother was strange and mysterious', and an occasion of strange visions and terrifying anxiety dreams.[40] Whereas, by day, Emilie was 'a loving mother', at night, by contrast, she seemed 'uncanny' (*unheimlich*), a word closely associated with German Romanticism, especially as interpreted by Freud.[41] In *Memories, Dreams, Reflections* we find the following remark attributed to Jung:

> In the course of my life it has often happened to me that I suddenly knew something which I really could not know at all. The knowledge came to me as though it were my own idea. It was the same with my mother. She did not know what she was saying; it was like a voice wielding absolute authority, which said exactly what fitted the situation.[42]

This observation points to a constant preoccupation in Jung's thinking: a conflict between authenticity and originality, resolved in the insight that, as Goethe once put, 'everything worth thinking had already been thought, what we must to do is try to think it once again'.[43] As we shall see, this problem recurs for Carl Gustav when at school in the accusation of plagiarism.

As if to underscore the link between his own thoughts or experiences and an anterior tradition, on the same page of *Memories, Dreams, Reflections* as the above paragraph we find a reference to an incident in a work by the Swiss (but Prussian-born) novelist and academic Johann Heinrich Daniel Zschokke (1771–1848), in whose autobiographical *Eine Selbstschau* (1842) there is an account of how the author once unmasked a young man as a thief because he saw the crime committed 'before his inner eye'.[44] A recurring interest in Jung's later life involved matters that would today be described as paranormal or occult, although such an interest was (as we shall see in chapters Three and Four) by no means so marginal in the late nineteenth century and early twentieth as it is considered now.

From the account of Jung's early years given in *Memories, Dreams, Reflections*, the following incidents also stand out as highly unusual; and again they are related to the question of (self-)perception and to the problem of identity. In a sequence of memories introduced with a literary allusion, Jung is said to have become aware that the dualism in the outside world – 'the beauty of the bright daylight world, where *goldenes Sonnenlicht durch grüne Blätter spielt* [golden sunlight played through green leaves]', set against 'an inescapable world of shadows filled with frightening, unanswerable questions' – corresponded to a 'splitting' (*Entzweiung*) within himself that even threatened his 'inner security'.[45] In fact, he began to think of himself as two different persons, as having two separate personalities, 'No. 1' and 'No. 2'.

Carl Gustav sensed this inner dichotomy when sitting on a stone that jutted out from the wall in the garden in Kleinhüningen.

He would play a thinking-game (*Gedankenspiel*), which went through the following stages:

> CGJ: 'I'm sitting on top of the stone, and it's underneath me'.
> The stone: 'I'm lying here on this slope, and there's someone sitting on top of me'.
> CGJ: 'Am I the person sitting on the stone, or am I' – because able to imagine what the stone is thinking – 'really the stone on which that person is sitting?'

Thirty years later, when standing again on the slope, Jung remembered the game he used to play and in that moment he saw, 'in a flash of lightning', 'the quality of eternity' in his childhood.[46] In some respects, Jung was re-enacting the iconic posture associated with the great medieval German poet Walther von der Vogelweide (*c.* 1170–*c.* 1230), and the subject of illuminated manuscript portrayals of this writer. One of Walther's poems begins with the line, 'I sat on a stone', and in this posture the poet plays his own kind of *Gedankenspiel* and considers how one should live in the world, and how one can simultaneously enjoy three things: honour, property and the grace of God.

Carl Gustav's intuition informs his later, more theoretical approach to the 'historical' remnants of the psyche, conceived, as in a lecture given in 1925 and subsequently reproduced in many primers of Jungian theory, in terms of a 'geology of personality'.[47] In *The Relations between the Ego and the Unconscious* (1928), Jung claims that there remains, hidden away, the idea of 'some kind of concretized god, who conforms exactly to our wishes and ideas'.[48] For Jung, the largest part of the psyche is something he calls 'sheer unconscious fact', something utterly Other, some Thing that is 'as hard and difficult, just as granite lies there unmoving and inaccessible, yet it can fall on us at any time in accordance with unknown laws'.[49]

This questioning of Jung's identity ties in with two further memories, both linked with a symbolic Father and a biological father. On doctor's orders, because of his health problems, Jung was sent when he was fourteen years old to a hotel-sanatorium in the Entlebuch, a region midway between Bern and Lucerne, now a UNESCO Biosphere Reserve. Here he met a chemist from Basel, a scientist – not a philologist and linguist, like Johann Paul Achilles Jung – with a doctorate, 'perhaps one of those who knew the secrets of stones'.[50] On one of their outings, the guests were taken to a distillery, where 'in literal fulfilment' of a verse from Karl Arnold Kortum's comic epic *Die Jobsiade*: '*Nun aber naht sich das Malör, / Denn dies Getränke ist Likör*' ('But now there comes a kicker, / This stuff, you see, is liquor') – Carl Gustav resolved the duality within him between inner and outer, between personalities No. 1 and No. 2, by getting 'shamefully, triumphantly, gloriously' drunk. Here Jung experiences a moment of Dionysian ecstasy, underscored by the ironic allusion to a biblical passage, in which 'the earth and the heavens, the world and everything that "creeps and flies", revolves, rises, or falls, had become one' – 'as if', in Nietzsche's words, 'the veil of *māyā* had been torn aside and were now merely fluttering in tatters before the mysterious primordial unity'.[51] It is not hard to imagine the 'rather woeful end' to which this experience came, but for all that it may have been compromised by his 'stupidity', it is recorded as being 'a discovery and intuition of beauty and meaning': *Schönheit, Sinn*, key Jungian concepts.

At the end of his stay in the Entlebuch, Carl Gustav's father came and took him to Lucerne, where they boarded a steamship. Arriving in Vitznau, father and son stood at the bottom of the Rigi, the huge mountain towering over the village. Stylishly equipped with a bamboo cane and an English jockey cap, yet from a background that meant they could not both afford to take the train trip to the summit, Carl Gustav climbed aboard – the father ceding place to the son – and he began his ascent up the mountain. As the locomotive chugged its way up the Rigi and 'new abysses and panoramas' opened themselves up in these 'dizzying heights', those old questions of identity imposed themselves again: 'I no longer knew which was bigger, me or the mountain!'; but then, the peak attained, Jung found an important resolution, as he looked out 'into unimaginable distances'.[52] 'Yes,' he is said to have thought, 'this is the real world', where 'one can simply be without having to ask'. 'Here I can be human, here I am allowed to be', Jung may have recalled from Goethe's *Faust*.[53] Or as Nietzsche's Zarathustra put it: 'One should live upon mountains'.[54]

2

Secrets: Manikins and Pencil-cases in the Loft

The body of C. G. Jung rests in the graveyard of the Swiss Reformed church in Küsnacht. Around five foot tall, inscribed with the heraldic arms of the Jung family, and bearing Jung's name as well as those of his father, mother, his sister Gertrud and his wife Emma, the dignified gravestone carries along its top and bottom borders a Latin adage, *Vocatus atque non vocatus Deus aderit* ('Called or not called, God will be present'), quoted by Erasmus, and along its side borders a quotation from St Paul, *Primus homo de terra terrenus, Secundus homo de caelo caelestis* ('The first man was of the earth, earthly: the second man from heaven, heavenly').[1] But what (or who) is the god to which (or to whom) the adage refers? And is the reference to the first man and the second man to be understood in a theological or in an alchemical sense?

Jung's relation to the Christian Church in general, and to the Swiss Reformed Church in particular, was always highly problematic. The account offered in *Memories, Dreams, Reflections* highlights his dissatisfaction with the faith of his father, yet also his strong sense of the *sacred*, to use the phrase coined by the theologian Rudolf Otto (1869–1937). This sense soon translated itself into a set of ritual practices: kindling a fire, sitting on his stone, and carving out a tiny manikin from the end of his wooden school-ruler. A manikin? A strange thing, surely, for a child to do, yet as Jung later realized, entirely consistent with the practice of ancient peoples, both those far away and those closer to home.

In Australia, the indigenous people of the Arrente were known for a practice that involved making a *churinga* (or *tjurunga*), an item of religious significance consisting of a piece of polished stone or wood. These sacred objects were of huge interest to such anthropologists and sociologists as Emile Durkheim (1858–1917), who suggested the term *churinga* meant 'most sacred', or T.G.H. Strehlow (1908–1978), who understood the term to mean something 'secret' or 'personal'.[2] But Jung would not have had to travel to the other side of the world to find such objects. In 1910 Fritz Sartorius-Preiswerk (1862–1935) had discovered in Arlesheim, a small town in the Swiss canton of Basel, not far from where Jung lived, a Neolithic burial site in a cave at the local hermitage. In this and surrounding caves, ancient cult artefacts, thought to date back to Celtic times, have been recovered: bowls, tools, and flintstones painted with ochre – the so-called 'soul-stones', believed to have been death masks, now housed in the Museum der Kulturen in Basel.

Painted stones from a cave near Basel, Switzerland.

Carving of the
Greek demi-god
Telesphorus,
discovered in 1884.

The discovery of these painted stones (or *galets coloriés*) was of
interest to Jung, who refers to them and to the Australian *churingas*
as analogues of his own sculpting, carving activities.[3] Other, more
classical analogues mentioned by Jung are the monuments carved
by the Greeks to Asclepius, the god of medicine and healing, on
which a tiny cloaked god, or Telesphorus, graces the work and
stands reading from a scroll; while in the cult of Demeter (the
goddess of the harvest) the Kabeiroi, the mysterious name of
an equally mysterious set of miniature deities, played a similarly
protective role.[4]

The attic where Jung hid his manikin, at the parsonage at Klein-Hüningen, now a suburb of Basel, Switzerland.

The manikin carved by Jung was about two inches long, dressed in 'a frock coat, a top hat, and shiny shoes'.[5] He coloured the figure black, sawed it off the rest the ruler and made a small coat for him from a piece of wool. To keep the manikin safe, Jung made a little bed for him in his wooden pencil-case, and hid him in the loft at the top of the house. Just as Jung had his stone on which he used to sit and think (see chapter One), so the manikin had one, too: a long, smooth, black stone from the Rhine, painted in different watercolours to divide the top from the bottom. Jung popped the pretty stone into the pencil-case, and left it for his manikin to enjoy. Every so often Jung would visit the loft and bring his manikin a tiny scroll bearing a message in a private language. It was all a secret. *His* secret. Jung enjoyed his visits to the loft.

As suggested by his reference to the indigenous Australian word *churinga*, or personal secret, Jung's early experiences provided him with an initiation into what one might, following the French philosopher and theologian Bertrand Vergely, call 'the dialectic of the secret'.[6] For a secret is, on the one hand, something one hides and keeps, well, secret. On the other hand, a secret is something one shares with someone else, with someone privileged to be told such a secret. In fact, the telling of a secret acquires significance precisely because it is not told to anyone else; the eloquence of the secret relies on the silence surrounding it on other occasions. Thus a secret might be said to *secrete* something, perhaps as a nectar secretes a perfume. While secrets often have to do with suffering (we don't want to reveal that or why we are suffering), not having a secret itself can also be a source of suffering. As Vergely explains, and as Jung also believed – it is a *lack* of secrets, the very absence of any secrets that can also make us cry out; or make us whisper . . .

Memories, Dreams, Reflections tells us Jung believed that the possession of a secret had been 'the essential thing' about his boyhood years.[7] But this interest in the ancient, the archaic and the secret clearly defined his later life as well. In England in the 1920s, and later in his garden in Küsnacht, Jung carved a figure out of wood, then stone: he called it (or rather, we are told, his unconscious named it) Atmavictu, or 'breath of life'. Throughout his life Jung concerned himself with artistic activity: working away in the years surrounding the First World War on his Red Book (see chapter Four), and carving a number of statues for his 'tower' in Bollingen (see chapter Six).

By the time Jung began to attend the Humanistisches Gymnasium in Basel he had already acquired a number of 'secrets': his dream of the ithyphallic god in the basement; the manikin in the pencil-case in the loft; soon to come, his vision of God and the besmirching of the roof of Basel Cathedral. What did the other boys say when Jung told them about his secrets? Of course, he said nothing; after all, they were secret. A passage from *Memories, Dreams, Reflections* suggests the vast, aching sense of loneliness that the possession of these 'secrets', which taken together all amounted to one *big* secret, awoke in Jung as he entered on his teens: 'My entire youth can be understood in terms of the concept of a secret . . . [E]ven today I am lonely, because I know things and must speak about things that other people do not know and mostly do not even want to know.'[8] As Jung discovered in the course of his life, one of the things that people do not want to know about is the divine: he once observed that in polite society it is more embarrassing to talk about God at a dinner party than it is to tell a risqué joke.[9] So what was, for Jung, the *divine*?

On the one hand, there was the figure of the divine as Jung knew it from his father's sermons: sermons which Jung no longer believed, and in which, he suspected, nor did his father.[10] These sermons spoke of a 'good' God, they spoke of God's love for humans and how humans should love God, too.[11] On the other hand, there was the divine as Jung began to intuit it: an entirely different sense of the divine. This divinity was different. He – or She, or It – was entirely Other. Even from the Judeo-Christian Bible itself, in which God not only ordered Abraham to sacrifice Isaac, but later allowed his own Son to be crucified, one could get a sense of how terrible this God was, and Jung's vision of Basel Cathedral had confirmed this revelation: to encounter this Other God was both a 'bloody struggle' and 'supreme ecstasy'.[12]

A bloody struggle and a supreme ecstasy: this is not, however, a description that one could apply to Jung's first experience of Holy Communion. Jung ate the bread; it was tasteless. He drank the wine; it tasted insipid and slightly sour. The congregation was remarkable, not for the depressing awareness of its sins or its joyous sense of redemption, but for its sheer indifference. Jung's sense of disappointment was overwhelming: this was the pinnacle of religious initiation according to the Church in which he had been brought up, and it had turned out to be a complete failure. Because of his awareness of God as Other, Jung believed that He could do 'things of fire and of supernatural light', but there had been no trace of these here. For Jung, God was not just a gracious God, he was a terrible God as well; He was 'annihilating fire and an indescribable grace', He was above all something 'real' (*wirklich*), something (as the German word suggests) that *had an effect*. By contrast, the God of the Church as experienced by Jung was 'an absence of God', and so the Church was a place he should no longer visit, because it did not offer life, but death.[13]

In this (late) account offered in *Memories, Dreams, Reflections* of Jung's (early) thinking, we find a typical logical structure of argumentation that we shall encounter in his mature writings. It goes in three steps. First, Jung makes a distinction between a traditional, or 'happy-clappy', Christian conception of God, and his own. Second, internal to this second conception of God, there is a polarity: bloody struggle versus supreme ecstasy, annihilating fire versus indescribable grace. The third step remained at this stage for Jung a question: how to conceive a response to a polaristic divinity within the tradition of Christianity? In other words, could a synthesis between the Christian God and the Other, between the 'good' God and the dualistic God, be achieved? And if so, how?[14]

Drawing on the evidence presented in *Memories, Dreams, Reflections*, it seems that Jung internalized this problem. Just as his conception of God was dualistic, so was his conception of himself. Jung felt himself to be 'two different persons'.[15] We have already seen such a sense of psychic splitting when Jung used to sit on a stone; as he grew up, this sense of division became more refined and more elaborate. We have also seen how *Memories, Dreams, Reflections* talks openly about two personalities, No. 1 and No. 2. One of them was a schoolboy growing up in late nineteenth-century

Switzerland. The other was an old man from eighteenth-century Germany, wearing buckled shoes and a white wig, who used to drive in an old-fashioned, eighteenth-century coach. (This fantasy was nourished by a real antique coach that, one day, had driven past the house in Kleinhüningen in which Jung lived.[16]) The one had to go to school and do his homework; the other was 'remote' from the human world but 'close' to nature in an almost cosmic sense.[17] Nothing so strange in this, perhaps; after all, many a child with a vivid imagination has played at living in another time or place. The problem is that, for Jung, there was a nagging sense that it was the eighteenth-century old man who was real, and the late nineteenth-century schoolboy who was not.

Memories, Dreams, Reflections insists on Jung's strong identification with the eighteenth century: with the coach that drove past his house, with the figure (familiar to Jung from an old terracotta statuette owned by one of his aunts) of Dr Stückelberger, a famous eighteenth-century doctor in Basel; and most likely, although Jung does not explicitly say so, with an even more famous eighteenth-century figure: Goethe.[18] The identification with Goethe is hinted at by Jung's difficulties with mathematics at school. Goethe was wont to disparage mathematics, and his suspicion of the subject – indeed, as Werner Heisenberg highlighted with reference to the preface to the *Farbenlehre*, of all 'abstraction' – was well known.[19] Similarly, for Jung, mathematics was 'a stupid trick to catch peasants out', and his objections to mathematics were, we are told, *moral* ones.[20] Nor was maths the only subject that he found difficult. Surprisingly, in view of his work producing his manikin and his later achievements in the Red Book, he was no good at drawing or art; he began to hate PE classes, too.[21]

In response to this situation at school, Jung began to develop fainting fits when he was twelve. *Memories, Dreams, Reflections* describes him as being timid and as having an ambivalent attitude to the world: as something 'beautiful and desirable', but also 'filled with vague and incomprehensible perils'.[22] After he was knocked over and almost knocked out by another pupil when he was twelve, the frequency of his fainting fits began to increase and he had six months off school. He regained his enthusiasm for drawing, cultivating a caricatural vision that stayed with him until old age. And Jung plunged, as *Memories, Dreams, Reflections* put it, into 'the world of the mysterious': into the world of nature (trees, water, swamps, stones, animals) and into the world of culture (above all, his father's library).[23] But he was not happy, and unconsciously he knew: 'I was fleeing from myself.'[24]

But as Goethe knew, 'you cannot flee yourself'.[25] Overhearing his father remark to a visitor who had enquired after his son's health, 'What is going to happen to him, if he can't earn a living?', Jung pulled himself together and set about his school work. Interestingly, Jung described the effect of 'this collision with reality' as having given him an insight into the nature of neurosis.[26] A neurosis?[27] Significantly, what really alarmed Jung was not his dream of the phallus in the basement; nor the manikin in his pencil-case, hidden in the loft; nor the vision of the divine excrement hitting the roof of Basel Cathedral: no, what alarmed him was the prospect of not earning his own living.

After he had taken the decision to force his way through his neurosis back to normality, Jung turned first of all to learning his Latin grammar.[28] Later, we learn from *Memories, Dreams, Reflections* that one of the few schoolteachers whom Jung later remembered with gratitude was his Latin teacher. He used to get Jung to fetch books for him from the university library, and Jung enjoyed dipping into the books he had collected while walking back with them. As we saw earlier (see chapter One), Jung had been impressed in the museum in Basel by the statues of Greek antiquity; now he was acquiring a knowledge of classical Latin literature.

The incident that induced Jung's fainting fits suggests that he may not have been a very popular boy at school. As well as being shy and timid, though, he could also be headstrong. *Memories, Dreams, Reflections* tells of a holiday spent with family friends on Lake Lucerne. Jung and the host's son were allowed to go boating on the lake, but were urged to exercise caution. Of course, Jung – used to steering the *Waidling* (a kind of flat-boat or punt) that his family kept by the Abbatucci-Schanze (a bridgehead constructed by General Abbatucci in the campaign conducted by France against Germany in 1796) – immediately stood on the stern of the rowing boat and pushed off with one oar into the lake. The father called them back and spoke sternly to Jung. Although Jung knew he had done something wrong, he inwardly railed at the fact that someone dared to insult *him*. But then Jung reflected: this is a rich, powerful man, and you are just a schoolboy: so just who do you think *you* are?[29] Who indeed: of course, part of him may even have believed, in the form of 'vague glimmerings and dreams', that he was none other than Goethe . . .

Further evidence for Jung's lack of popularity is found in his complaint that his teachers considered him to be lazy and stupid, and if anything went wrong at school, it seems he was always the first to be blamed. When he was fifteen, Jung discovered how hostile his fellow pupils were towards him. Once, seven of them lay in wait and attacked him.[30] Jung – large, strong and prone to sudden rages – fought back, swinging one of them round by both arms and knocking the others to the ground. He couldn't remember afterwards whether or not he was punished, but he did remember one thing: he was never attacked again.

On another occasion Jung was accused by a teacher of plagiarism. He had turned in an essay in the German composition class, but received no mark for it, because the teacher believed that Jung had copied it from somewhere. Understandably, Jung was upset because the work was his, and this experience of powerlessness and injustice provoked in him a sense of 'grief and rage' that threatened to get 'out of control'.[31] Then came a strange experience: in the midst of his emotional turmoil there was 'a sudden inner silence', 'a mood of cool curiosity', and *sine ira et studio* – 'without anger and fondness', the motto of the Roman historian Tacitus – Jung found himself able to examine the situation and reflect on the motives for the teacher's behaviour.[32] That sense of dual identity that characterized Jung as a boy here acquired a therapeutic aspect. Adopting the Spinozistic perspective of looking at things *sub specie aeternitatis*, seeing the world from the perspective of personality No. 1 rather than of personality No. 2, or thinking about things (in Goethean terms) from the perspective of thousands of years rather than of the day-to-day, had a positive effect: 'as though a breath of the great world of stars and endless space had touched me', or 'as if a spirit had invisibly entered the room', the spirit of 'someone who was long dead yet perpetually present in timelessness far into the future'.[33]

All of these experiences and reflections underscore the image of Jung in his early teens as a singular, if somewhat lonely, character. Nevertheless, *Memories, Dreams, Reflections* also relates from this time in Jung's life a moment when he had another 'important experience', which he describes as 'tremendously important and new'.[34] Walking to school along the road from Kleinhüningen to Basel, it is recorded that, for a moment, Jung had 'the overwhelming feeling' of having emerged from a dense fog and now knowing: 'Now I am who I am', or even more simply in German, *Jetzt bin ich*.[35] It would be no exaggeration to describe this moment, in the term employed by the French philosopher Michel Onfray, as a kind of *hapax existentiel* (or defining autobiographical moment).[36] The experience is described in a way that shows it was at once extremely simple and extremely complex: 'In that moment I *came to myself*. Previously I had also been there, but everything had simply happened. Now I knew: now I am *who I am*, now I am there. Previously things had happened to me, but now it was I who willed things.'[37]

Carl Lutherer, *Wilhelm Traugott Krug*, *c.* 1833–4. Krug was the author of the *General Dictionary of the Philosophical Sciences* (1820s/1830s) used by Jung.

The language is almost biblical in its emphasis: when He revealed himself to Moses in the burning bush, God named Himself as 'I AM WHO I AM'. Now Jung could forget about the manikin in the pencil-case in the loft, and begin to get on with being who *he* was.

Jung's Philosophical Education

Jung's discovery of his own identity – of how he embarked on the path, in Nietzschean terms, of becoming who he was – took place, as all self-discovery must, in a specific historical, geographical and cultural context: in his case, in late nineteenth-century bourgeois Switzerland. To be sure, there was an intellectual context, too: the eighteenth-century literary and philosophical tradition of German-speaking Europe. And this tradition can be summed up in three important names: Goethe, Kant and Schopenhauer. How did Jung orientate himself within this tradition?

He did so by using a book he had found in his father's library, the second edition of the *General Dictionary of the Philosophical Sciences* (1832) by the German philosopher Wilhelm Traugott Krug (1770–1842).[38] To begin with, Jung's chief interest had been to find out what the dictionary said about God. In Krug's dictionary he learned that 'God' was etymologically related to the idea of the 'good', or in technical terms: God is the *ens summum*, or the *ens perfectissimum*. Given his intuitions and visions, this all struck Jung as highly unlikely, and it seemed to him that Krug was playing an elaborate philosophical game. He also consulted *Christian Dogmatics* (1869) by the Swiss theologian Alois Emanuel Biedermann (1819–1885).[39] Here he found a more independent-minded (and therefore more congenial) thinker, who described God (in a manner surely influenced by the German philosopher Ludwig Feuerbach, 1804–1872) as a personality conceived after analogy with the human ego, only posited on a cosmic scale. This seemed right to Jung.

God; Evil; Grace; Salvation: these themes are the universal ones of human experience, and thus of literature as well. Using his father's library as a starting-point, Jung began to read the novels of Friedrich Gerstäcker (1816–1872), the author of numerous best-sellers informed by his global travels. He read (in translation) the great English novels, and despite the best efforts (then as now) of the education system to spoil them, the classics of German literature. Jung had a voracious bibliographical appetite: he read drama, poetry, history, science.

Of the philosophical tradition in a stricter sense, Jung felt himself attracted to the thought of the Presocratic philosophers: to Pythagoras (known as the 'first philosopher'), to Heraclitus, to Empedocles. From these philosophers, only mysterious, suggestive fragments of their thought survived. Jung was also attracted by the thought of Plato, although he found the form of Socratic argumentation 'long-winded'. Of the medieval philosophers, he felt 'the breath of life' in the theologian and mystic Meister Eckhart, although he was not sure that he had understood him (indeed, who has?). Not interesting at all to Jung were such scholastic thinkers as St Thomas Aquinas, the critical philosophers of the eighteenth century and, especially, Hegel.

Although Jung approached Immanuel Kant (1724–1804) after reading Arthur Schopenhauer (1788–1860), in intellectual-historical terms it was Kant who had provided the basis for the thought of Schopenhauer. So we shall examine Jung's reaction to Kant first. According to *Memories, Dreams, Reflections*, Jung found that reading Kant caused him 'considerable headaches', particularly in the case of Kant's first critique, the *Critique of Pure Reason* (1781).[40] This is no wonder: Kant's work, even today, can strike readers as 'a terrifying slab', arousing 'anxiety and respect in all those who hold it in their hands: because it is so heavy, in all senses of this term'.[41] At the centre of Kant's epistemological theory lies the idea of the *Ding an sich* – the 'thing-in-itself', or the noumenon – something we can never know, because all we know are phenomena (appearances, things-for-us).

Herein lies the essence of Kant's 'Copernican revolution': just as Copernicus taught that the sun does not revolve around the earth, but the earth around the sun, so Kant argued in the preface to the second edition (1787) (and this passage give us a sense of the style of Kant's writing):

Up to now it has been assumed that all our cognition must conform to the objects; but all attempts to find out something about them *a priori* through concepts that would extend our cognition have, on this presupposition, come to nothing. Hence let us once try whether we do not get farther with the problems of metaphysics by assuming that the objects must conform to our cognition, which would better agree with the requested possibility of an *a priori* cognition of them, which is to establish something about objects before they are given to us.[42]

In short: what we know about the world is how the world *appears*, but not what the world *is in-itself*. Indeed, Kant maintained that, by definition, we could never know the thing-in-itself, and even though Jung's Kantianism sometimes appears somewhat confused, it is evident that Jung understood *this* point very well.

Hence in his later years, Jung was entirely comfortable with a position he defined as 'epistemologically, taking a stand on Kant', and which in turn he interpreted as meaning that 'an assertion doesn't posit its object'.[43] And he even tried to assimilate some of the fundamental notions of analytical psychology to the key concepts of the critical philosophy of Kant, telling one correspondent: 'In a certain sense I could say of the collective Unconscious exactly what Kant said of the *Ding an sich* – that it is merely a negative borderline concept.'[44] The legitimacy of his claim to be a Kantian, and to have abandoned 'the heaven-storming pretensions of the Romantic intellect', remains a vigorously contested area of Jung's thought.[45]

Jung's attention may also have been caught by another intriguing passage in this second preface, where Kant writes: 'Thus I had to deny knowledge in order to make room for faith.'[46] Like the image of the Copernican revolution, this passage has caused a good deal of controversy, but it may provide a context for the moment when Jung, in his famous interview with John Freeman in 1959, replied, in response to a question about whether he believed in God: 'I *know*. I don't need to believe. I know.'[47]

It is common, and by no means entirely wrong, to read post-Kantian philosophy as a series of attempts to evade the restrictions Kant had placed on the knowledge of the noumenon. The concept of the absolute activity of the ego (*Ich*) found in Johann Gottlieb Fichte (1762–1814), the reciprocity of humankind and nature found in Friedrich Wilhelm Schelling (1775–1854) (who, incidentally, developed an important theory of mythology in which Jung was greatly interested), and even the conception of history as the self-expression of 'spirit' (*Geist*) in Hegel: all eroded the limitations so carefully placed around knowledge by Kant, and demonstrated the point made by Friedrich Heinrich Jacobi (1743–1819) that the *Ding an sich* was the idea needed to maintain Kant's system, and at the same time the idea to which it was impossible to subscribe.[48]

One of the most sustained attempts to work within the Kantian paradigm, yet nevertheless radically to alter its conclusions, can be found in the thought of Schopenhauer, who argued that we *can* know what the noumenon is. Just as, for Kant, we look within and find the moral law, so, for Schopenhauer, we look within and find: the *amoral will*. And as within, so without; outside, too, we look around us and find the evidence of the will. The will, in other words, is 'the *thing-in-itself* proper'.[49] Thus the world appears to us as the world, but the essence of the world is will. In the terminology of Schopenhauer's central philosophical text, it is a question of *the world as will and representation*.

In *Memories, Dreams, Reflections*, Jung describes Schopenhauer a s 'the great discovery of my researches'.[50] The description provided of the world as attributed here to the philosopher of pessimism faithfully captures the pathos of Schopenhauer's worldview. Schopenhauer was, we are told, 'the first person who spoke of the suffering of the world that visibly and persistently surrounds us; of confusion, passion, evil, which all the other seemed hardly to notice and always wanted to dissolve in harmony and comprehensibility'.[51] With Schopenhauer's analysis of the world as a place of great suffering, Jung was in enthusiastic agreement. But not with Schopenhauer's response to this analysis. Why not?

The crux of the disagreement was Schopenhauer's doctrine of the denial of the will. If the affirmation of the will involves suffering in the world, then to overcome suffering in the world, one has to deny the will. For Schopenhauer, we deny the will, but only momentarily, through art; we deny it, more permanently, through saint-like resignation. 'Such a man', Schopenhauer wrote, 'who, after many bitter struggles with his own nature, has at last completely conquered, is then left only as pure knowing being, as the undimmed mirror of the world'.[52] But can Schopenhauer's vision of the world survive critical scrutiny? Jung's critique (as we find it in the pages of *Memories, Dreams, Reflections*) is thoroughgoing and profound:

Arthur Schopenhauer
in 1845.

I was all the more disappointed by [Schopenhauer's] idea that the intellect had only to hold up to the blind will its own image, in order to bring about its reversal. How could the will see this image at all, since it was blind? And why, even if it could see it, should it be persuaded to reverse itself, since the image would only show it exactly what it wanted? And what was the intellect? It is a function of the human soul – not a mirror, but an infinitely tiny little mirror, held up to the sun by a child and expecting the sun to be dazzled by it. This seemed to me entirely inadequate. It puzzled me that Schopenhauer could have come up with such an idea.[53]

In part, Jung's rejection of Schopenhauer's key idea, the denial of the will, which forms the basis of Schopenhauer's ethics, is informed by their shared inclination, of a Neoplatonic kind, to see consciousness, not as a mirror, but as a light. In his work entitled 'On the Nature of the Psyche' (1947; publication of revised text, 1954), Jung develops the idea that both consciousness, and the unconscious function like a light.[54] On the animal, the primitive, and the infantile level, 'consciousness is not a unity', but 'like a chain of islands or an a rchipelago': we should, therefore, think of ego-consciousness as surrounded by 'a multitude of little luminosities'.[55]

The philosophy of German Idealism plays an important role in the history that Jung sketches of the concept of the unconscious. (Jung, in other words, is very clear about the historicity of his own thought: in a sense, the 'loss' of the unconscious in modern society is expressed by and finds compensation in his own psychology of the unconscious: or, as he powerfully and poetically put it, 'since the stars have fallen from heaven and our highest symbols have paled, a secret life holds sway in the unconscious', and 'that is why we have a psychology today, and why we speak of the unconscious').[56] In 'The Psychology of the Child Archetype' (1940), for instance, Jung distinguishes between 'the problem of the dark side of the psyche' as found in Gottfried Wilhelm Leibniz (1646–1716), Kant and Schelling, and the pivotal role played by Carl Gustav Carus (1789–1869) and Eduard von Hartmann (1842–1906), in the recognition of 'the unconscious as the essential basis of the psyche'.[57] Similarly, in *Aion* (1951), Jung distinguishes between, on the one hand, 'certain suggestive ideas' about the unconscious in Leibniz, Kant, Schelling and Schopenhauer, and, on the other, the 'philosophical excursions' of Carus and von Hartmann.[58] Meanwhile, in 'Transformation Symbolism in the Mass' (1942; 1954), he offers a third genealogical trail. On this account, the postulation of 'the existence of an unconscious psyche' begins in Leibniz and Kant, continues 'with mounting intensity' in Schelling, Carus and von Hartmann, before 'modern psychology' arrives, ' discard[ing] the last metaphysical claims of the philosopher-psychologists and restrict[ing] the idea of the psyche's existence to the psychological statement', that is, phenomenology.[59]

Elsewhere, in 'Theoretical Considerations on the Nature of the Psyche' (1946; 1954), Jung offers a thumbnail sketch of the development of German Idealism. The 'victory' of Hegel over Kant, he suggests, dealt 'the gravest blow to reason', and the 'forces compensating for this calamitous development personified them-selves partly in the later Schelling, partly in Schopenhauer and Carus': one line of development in post-Kantian thought, therefore, while a second line results in the 'bursting upon us' in Nietzsche of 'that unbridled "bacchantic God" whom Hegel had already scented in nature'.[60] It is interesting to note how Jung implicitly aligns himself with the forces of reason, associating himself with Kant and portraying Hegel in extremely negative terms as 'a psychologist in disguise who projected great truths out of the subjective sphere into a cosmos he himself had created'.[61]

As these passages show, Jung paid considerable attention – more than is paid today, at any rate – to the work of Eduard von Hartmann, a German philosopher who bridges the era of Idealism and the emergence of modern thought. According to *Memories, Dreams, Reflections*, Jung read Hartmann 'assiduously' and it is likely that Hartmann was one of the major sources of Jung's knowledge of Schelling.[62] For instance, on two occasions Jung highlighted Schelling's notion of an 'eternal unconscious' (*ewig Unbewusstes*), an idea proposed by Schelling in his *System of Transcendental Idealism* (1800), but which Jung probably found in von Hartmann's *Philosophy of the Unconscious* (1869).[63]

'As my Father I have already died, as my Mother I still love and grow'

This remarkable tribute paid by Nietzsche to his mother in *Ecce Homo*, his final work, invites a Jungian reading, in which Nietzsche casts off his masculine, patriarchal side and embarks on (or acknowledges) the discovery of the feminine, intuitive side of the self.[64] Moreover, consideration of this sentence prompts reflection on the role played in the development of Jung's thought by *his* mother. While it was in the library of his father that Jung discovered Biedermann's *Christian Dogmatics* and Krug's *General Dictionary*, as well as Kant's *Critique of Pure Reason* and Schopenhauer's *The World as Will and Representation*, it was thanks to his mother that he discovered Goethe. 'Suddenly and without further preamble', as we are told in *Memories, Dreams, Reflections*, Emilie (or her 'No. 2 personality', her timeless, archetypal side) told her fifteen-year-old son, 'You really should read Goethe's *Faust* one of these days'.[65] So he did; and the text poured into his soul, it is said, 'like a miraculous balm'.[66]

What might have attracted Jung to *Faust*? To begin with, the work has acquired an almost legendary significance as a masterpiece of German literature, indeed, of world literature (to invoke a category invented by Goethe himself). It is the *Ur*-text of German-speaking (and, through its various operatic adaptations, European) culture. An edition of Goethe's collected works used to be found on the bookshelves of every German-speaking bourgeois household, and so it was in Jung's house, too.

More specifically, Goethe's drama is based on the medieval legend, with its roots in Gnosticism, about a scholar or magician called Faust or Faustus. Although, etymologically derived from *felix*, his name means 'fortunate' or 'lucky', Faust feels himself to be neither; in his drive for knowledge and pleasure he forfeits his eternal salvation by entering into a pact with the devil (or, in his pseudo-Greek or pseudo-Hebrew appellation, Mephistopheles). In the traditional legend, the versions in the medieval chapbooks, in the seventeenth- and eighteenth-century puppet plays (whose influence Goethe acknowledged), and in its famous stage version by Christopher Marlowe (1564–1593), at the end of his life Faust is doomed to eternal damnation; in Goethe's version, however, in a radical departure from every version of the story up to that point in its development, Faust is ultimately redeemed. So while *Faust*, Part One, tells of the seduction of Gretchen, her abandonment and her condemnation to death, the second part tells of Faust's conjuring up of Helen of Troy, his murder of Philemon and Baucis, and his salvation culminating in his admission to a vision of the Magna Mater.

When Jung read this work, how did he respond to it? On the one hand, he found in the figure of Faust someone who took the devil seriously: by concluding his pact with Mephisto, Faust was reckoning with no less than 'the adversary, who has the power to thwart God's intention to create a perfect world'.[67] Yet the figure of Mephisto is even more complex than this: in Goethe's text Mephisto describes himself as 'the spirit which eternally denies', and says that 'sin, destruction – evil, in brief, / Are my true element-in-chief'.[68] Echoing the providentialist theology of Milton's *Paradise Lost*, in which Satan's malice 'serve[s] but to bring forth / Infinite goodness, grace, and mercy', Mephisto also identifies himself as 'part of that force which would / Do ever evil, and does ever good'.[69] On the other hand, then, Jung took issue with Goethe's decision to save Faust. He regarded the figure of Faust as 'long-winded', 'characterless', 'puerile' and ultimately undeserving of 'his initiation into the great mysteries'.[70]

Jung's attitude could perhaps best be described as one of fascinated ambivalence. Goethe understood 'evil', its 'global power', its 'secret role in the redemption of human beings from darkness and suffering'; but by getting rid of Mephisto in the final act with 'a mere trick', with 'a sleight-of-hand', with 'a bit of jiggery-pokery', Goethe's work became too 'frivolous', too 'irresponsible', too 'theological' (the ultimate insult!).[71] In other words, Goethe 'became a prophet' for Jung, albeit one whose testimony was crucially incomplete.[72]

In accordance with the ancient Hermetic principle 'as above, so below', Jung's attention was held not just by the climactic elevation of Faust's entelechy (or soul) to the vision of the Magna Mater – the Eternal Feminine – at the end of *Faust*, Part Two, but by the description – given by Mephisto in Part One – of what Faust would find if he chose to descend to the mysterious figures of the Mothers. Indeed Mephisto stood, Jung sensed, in some kind of a relationship to 'the mystery of Mothers', and investigating this particular mystery was going to occupy a good deal of Jung's time in the years to come.

Although Jung felt he was still underestimated at school, where he had been (falsely) accused of plagiarism, and where he found that his passion for learning was met with dismissive hostility; and although he was twitted by his contemporaries, who gave him the nickname 'Father Abraham', Jung had made his own identification with Faust by deciding to acquaint himself with the philosophical tradition. What he called his 'philosophical development' lasted from the age of seventeen into his twenties. Although there was a growing expectation on his mother's side of the family that he would go and study theology, Jung had begun to develop his own conception of 'God's world': 'a *cosmos*', 'an eternity, in which everything is born, and everything has already died'.[73] And, for Jung, 'God's world' went beyond the *cosmos* into the sublime: in it belonged 'everything "more-than-human", blinding light, the darkness of the abyss, the cold indifference of something with no borders of space and time, and the uncanny grotesquerie of the irrational world of chance'.[74] As Faust might have said: 'Das ist deine Welt! das heisst eine Welt!' ('That's your world! That's what I call a world!').[75]

3

Science or Spiritism?

Jung's reasons for deciding to study medicine (which he did, from 1895 to 1900) were certainly not identical to those of Freud, who, according to his own account, decided to study medicine after a public lecture at which he heard an eminent Austrian doctor and zoologist, Carl Brühl (1820–1899), read out an extract from 'On Nature', a short text attributed to Goethe; but they were nevertheless analogous. According to *Memories, Dreams, Reflections*, Jung could not make up his mind between studying science or studying the humanities. Given his interest in fossils, plants, and animals, Jung was clearly drawn towards science; but he was also fascinated by the civilizations of ancient Egypt and ancient Babylon, and he toyed with the idea of becoming an archaeologist. In 1895 Jung opted – nudged, so he believed, by his unconscious in the form of two dreams, one about the recovery of prehistoric bones, the other about a giant radiolarian – for medicine.

Freud, in his autobiographical study, associates his decision to study medicine explicitly with Goethe; in the case of *Memories, Dreams, Reflections* the connection is more oblique and is centred around the awkward question of how Jung's studies were to be financed. Unable fully to fund his son's studies, Johann Paul Achilles Jung applied to the University of Basel for a grant. The award of the money shamed Carl Gustav, who regarded himself, as we have seen, under two aspects: personality No. 1, the child of his age; and personality No. 2, 'a *vita peracta*, born, living, dead, everything in one; a total vision of life', 'in secret accord with the Middle Ages, as personified by *Faust*', identified as 'godfather and authority' with Goethe.[1] The mediation of the eternal with the temporal, the infinite with the particular, being Carl-Gustav-Jung while being/wanting to be Johann-Wolfgang-Goethe: the outer (financial) insecurity compensated by an inner (psychological) security: this delicate balancing act, as we saw at the end of the previous chapter, reflected his ambivalence towards *Faust*. For this text was now more important to Jung than the Gospel according to St John; yet the 'ludic down-playing' of the evil Mephisto, Faust's 'ruthless arrogance', and the murder of Philemon and Baucis: all this worried Jung deeply.[2]

In turn, this ambivalence is reflected in an elaborate image, described in *Memories, Dreams, Reflections* as a dream that Jung had at this time. It is night. Jung is struggling against a strong wind, trying to move forward. Everywhere, dense fog. But he is holding a tiny light. *Don't let it go out!* And then, *there's something behind me!* A huge black figure, *behind me!* But still: *don't let the little light go out . . .*

In interpreting this dream for its readers, *Memories, Dreams, Reflections* tells us that the large black figure should be understand as a *Brockengespenst*, an optical illusion observed in the Harz Mountains, when one's own shadow is projected by light onto the fog or mist around one. In other words, it is part of Jung himself. Equally part of Jung himself, however, is the tiny light: the light of consciousness. So what does the dream mean? That one's knowledge is the single greatest treasure one possesses: set against the forces of the darkness, it may be small and fragile, but it nevertheless remains a light; and one's sole source of light. (Far from revelling in the darkness of the unconscious, in other words, Jung's psychological system seeks to protect, preserve and foster the illumination of consciousness.[3])

This dream is described as 'a great illumination', and it functions as another *hapax existentiel*. It constitutes a metaphoric representation of Jung's theory of time and his image of the world. For the shadow is not simply Jung himself, but the *vita peracta*, that is, his other character or second life, or in other words (as we have seen) Goethe. Whereas personality No. 2 threatens to pull Jung back into the past, personality No. 1 has to strive forward against the storm: into 'study', 'money-making', 'dependencies', 'entanglements', 'confusions', 'errors', 'submissions' and into 'defeats'. Yet what is more present than the present moment is the past; the present is not real, the past is; to escape it, we press forward; yet escape from the past is ultimately impossible and we have to come to terms with it. Pulled in two directions, between the archetypal forces of the past and the demands and responsibilities of the present, no wonder Jung describes his intuition as a vision of the post-lapsarian world. Eden is nothing more – but also nothing less – than a spectre, and the stony field, waiting to be tilled by the sweat of our brow, the world of light – of consciousness, of reality – is awaiting us.

In order to engage with the world of light, Jung realized that he would have to come to terms with himself, or, as it were, with his selves, Nos. 1 and 2. Identifying more securely with his No. 1 personality, his temporal self, personality No. 2 became increasingly lacking in temporal location and individual identity to the point of complete autonomy and timelessness. Or in other words: the less Jung felt himself to be Goethe, the more he felt himself to be Jung.

Intriguingly, moreover, *Memories, Dreams, Reflections* interprets in retrospect Jung's personal experiences as reflecting collective developments: that is, his own development 'anticipated future events' and 'paved the way for modes of adaptation', adaptation, that is, to his father's 'religious collapse' as well as to 'the shattering revelation of the world as we see it today'.[4] In fact, this is an important, yet frequently overlooked, aspect of Jung's self-presentation and his self-understanding, that his experiences – like Goethe's, like Nietzsche's – are in some sense *representative*. The idea informing Jung's sense of self is very much akin to what Thomas Mann once wrote about the function of the writer or the philosopher as 'a reporting instrument, seismograph, medium of sensitivity'.[5] Fully aware, as always, of the historical dimension of his experiences and, indeed, that he was reworking some of the key topoi and motifs of Western culture, Jung liked to cite the following phrase from Augustine of Hippo (354–430): 'do not go abroad; return within yourself: in the inward man dwells truth'.[6]

The confidence with which Jung applies this text from St Augustine to himself bears out the impression one gains from *Memories, Dreams, Reflections* that Jung's days as a student at Basel from 1895 to 1900 were 'a wonderful time' for him.[7] In particular, he enjoyed his membership of the Zofingia or, to give it its full name, the Schweizerischer Zofingerverein, one of the oldest Swiss student fraternities. Founded in 1819, and refounded in 1867 after its fusion with another fraternity, the Helvetia, the Zofingia provided (as it still does) its members with a forum for debate and discussion, and it counts among its most prominent members the historian of art and culture Jacob Burckhardt (1818–1897), the novelist Jeremias Gotthelf (1797–1854), the poet Conrad Ferdinand Meyer (1825–1898), the theologian Karl Barth (1886–1968), as well as, of course, Carl Jung.

Memories, Dreams, Reflections recalls something of the intellectual atmosphere of the Zofingia, associating it with passionate arguments about Schopenhauer and Kant, intense conversations about the 'stylistic nuances' of Cicero, and lively discussion and debate about theological and philosophical matters. Indeed, Jung became chairman of the Basel section of the fraternity for one semester, and gave a number of lectures at the Zofingia Society's meetings on such themes as 'the border zones of exact science', 'the nature and value of speculative inquiry', and the interpretation of Christianity offered by the contemporary German theologian Albrecht Ritschl (1822–1889), a kind of Hans Küng of his day.[8] But one should not overlook the fact that another function of the society was not so much intellectual, as social; in this respect, according to his student colleague and lifelong friend, Albert Oeri (1875–1950), Jung was known to his drinking companions as 'the barrel': he was 'rarely drunk', we are told, 'but when so, noisy'.[9] Together with their mutual friend, Andreas Vischer, Jung and Oeri would chat over a glass (or two, or three . . .) of Markgräfler, the famous wine from Baden, in such pubs as the 'Breo' in Steinen, a suburb of Basel; or, over the border, the 'Hirzen' in Haltingen or the 'Adler' in Weil am Rhein, small towns in the south-western tip of Germany.[10]

Oeri tells the following tale about Jung's dislike of walking home alone through the Nachtigallenwäldchen or 'Nightingale Woods' and down to the Bottminger Mill. 'As we were leaving the tavern', Oeri recalls, Jung would begin to talk to one of his drinking companions about 'something especially interesting', luring one of them to accompany him, 'without noticing it', to his front door. As they walked, Jung would interrupt his discourse to point out, say, the spot where someone called Dr Götz had been murdered, or something similar. To his hapless companion, who now had to return through the woods alone, Jung would offer his revolver for the trip back. 'I was not afraid of Dr Götz's ghost, not of living evil spirits', remarks Oeri, 'But I was afraid of Jung's revolver in my pocket'.[11]

It is worthwhile recalling that Jung was a student in Basel at a time when the university city was bathed in the nostalgic light of glorious splendour: in the nineteenth century, this patrician city-republic had established a reputation associated with Jacob Burckhardt and three other thinkers: the jurist and classical philologist Johann Jakob Bachofen (1815–1887), the theologian Franz Overbeck (1837–1905) and the philosopher Friedrich Nietzsche (1844–1900). As Lionel Gossman observes in his indispensable study of nineteenth-century Basel, the city and the university provided nothing less than 'a sanctuary for intellectual practices that ran counter to the reigning orthodoxies of German scholarship'.[12] Finding the peace and security of their 'unseasonable thoughts', the work of these scholars constitutes, in Gossman's view, 'a formidable critique not only of *Wissenschaft*' – in other words, science and knowledge in general –'as it was understood in the late nineteenth century, especially in Germany, but of the optimistic, self-confident modernism of their time'.[13]

Without a doubt, Jung felt himself in tune with this intellectual vigour, and with the Baslerian critique of modernity, if one may categorize it as such. Especially in contrast to Zurich, Jung felt, so he is recorded as saying, 'a nostalgic weakness' for 'the rich background of culture' in Basel, recalling 'the days when Bachofen and Burckhardt walked in the streets, and behind the cathedral stood the old chapter house, and the old bridge over the Rhine, half made of wood'.[14] By virtue of seeing Burckhardt 'walking near the Cathedral coming from the University library', Franz Overbeck and Bachofen, Jung felt that he was 'not separated by cosmic distances from them', and they formed a human link to a figure in whom Jung took great interest: Nietzsche.[15] Although Jung recalled that, when he was a student, there had been 'quite a number of young people in Basel, even certain professors of the younger generation, who studied *Zarathustra* and made a cult of it',[16] it would be several more years before Jung actually tackled reading *Zarathustra*. And if Burckhardt was reportedly relucant to read it, Jung was even less keen to engage with this work.[17] But why?

According to *Memories, Dreams, Reflections*, Jung had a 'secret fear' that he 'might perhaps be like' Nietzsche.[18] More specifically, three reasons are given for his sense of affinity with Nietzsche. First, despite the overriding differences between them – Nietzsche was German, a professor who had written (in the years before his mental collapse) many books, spoke High German, and knew Latin and Greek (as well as French, Italian, and Spanish), whereas Jung was Swiss, did not yet have a career, and only spoke the Waggis-Basel dialect – they had one thing in common: Nietzsche, like Jung,

Friedrich Nietzsche, *c.* 1875 , photograph by F. Hartmann.

was the son of a clergyman. As such, Jung believed, he was 'his father's unrevealed secret'.[19] Second, just as Nietzsche had been 'isolated from his environment' because of his 'secret', that is, because of his 'inner experiences, insights which he had unfortunately attempted to talk about, and had found that no one understood him', so Jung, as we have seen, felt himself to be in possession of a number of 'secrets' – the subterranean phallus, the manikin in the pencil-case – and he, too, knew of 'that cold shadow of embarrassment and estrangement which passed over people's faces' whenever he mentioned anything to do with the 'inner realm'.[20] And third, this meant that Jung feared he was, as Nietzsche had been, *Auch Einer* ('another one'), an allusion to the title of the popular novel published in 1870 by the German philosopher and aesthetician F. T. Vischer (1807–1887).

So although *Memories, Dreams, Reflections* identifies the terror Jung experienced when reading Nietzsche's *Untimely Meditations* (1873–6), and then *Thus Spoke Zarathustra* (1883–5), with the fear of being 'morbid' or 'sick' (borne out by the fact that of his two friends who claimed to be followers of Nietzsche, both were homosexual, one committing suicide, the other 'running to seed'), the *arrheton* – the 'inexpressible', the 'unspeakable' or the 'unsayable', the 'thing-not-to-be-spoken-of' – was precisely this secret: the 'upper storey' (Vischer), the tragic view of life (Nietzsche), the archetypal dimension to existence (Jung). For someone who possessed such a secret, great care had to be taken. Nietzsche hadn't done this: as it turned out, this was a big mistake. And so Nietzsche 'fell – tightrope-walker that he proclaimed himself to be – into depths far beyond himself', he 'fell headfirst into the unutterable mystery and wanted to sing its praises to the dull, godforsaken masses'.[21] From Nietzsche, Jung learnt this lesson: he wasn't going to make the same mistake.

The exhilaration of Jung's time at university coincides with the death of his father early in 1896, when Jung was barely in his twenties. In his dreams his father would appear to him and Jung found himself prompted to ask, 'what does it mean that my father returns in dreams and seems so real?'[22] In *Memories, Dreams, Reflections*, his father's death is said to have forced Jung to think about the possibility of a life after death, and it is likely that the unexpectedly early death of his father may well have sparked Jung's interest in spiritism, ultimately reflected in his choice of subject for his medical dissertation, 'On the Psychology and Pathology of so-called Occult Phenomena' (1902). At the same time, one should remember that one of Jung's great intellectual heroes, Nietzsche, had lost his father even earlier in his life, when he was only five.[23] (After his father's death, Nietzsche had been sent to Schulpforta, with its emphasis on the study of theology, against which he was later so spectacularly to turn.) If, in Nietzsche's mind, the death of the father became caught up in the question of the death of God, for Jung the death of the father turned into the question, not just of 'life after death' (thus the title of a chapter in *Memories, Dreams, Reflections*), but of what it might mean to be truly alive in this present life.

At Basel Jung followed the standard preparatory courses for medical school, the *Propedeutica*, and after the first course he became a junior assistant to Friedrich von Müller (1858–1941), a professor at the Anatomical Institute.[24] Although the courses emphasized biology and anatomy, Jung took an especial interest in evolutionary theory, comparative anatomy and neo-vitalistic theories: in short, what he described (using a Goethean term) as 'the morphological point of view', in the widest sense of the phrase.[25] Another of his lecturers at Basel was Friedrich Zschokke (1860–1936), a professor of zoology and comparative anatomy, whose 'deeper sense for the mysteries of the evolution of life' may well, as Adolf Portmann (1897–1982) has speculated, have left its mark on Jung's thinking about the structure and function of the psyche.[26] After passing his exams in 1896 and 1897, in 1898 – in other words, two years after the death of his father – Jung was faced with the choice of specializing in surgery or psychiatry. Jung's inclination toward surgery was reversed by two sets of experiences, both of which introduced him to the mysterious world of the occult and the paranormal.[27]

First, in the summer vacation of 1895 Jung had begun attending the seances held in Kleinhüningen by his cousin, Hélène (or Helly) Preiswerk (1880–1911).[28] Jung had already participated with students from the Zofingia club in experiments with a Ouija board and table-tilting, and it would be no exaggeration to describe the background in which Jung had grown up as one of gross superstition. His mother believed herself to be possessed of the supernatural power of second sight; in the Jung household, visits from poltergeists were not uncommon. In a late essay written on the topic of flying saucers, it becomes clear just how much, for Jung, both pagan beliefs and medieval superstition were still very much alive.[29] Here he related how he once came across a book of spells in the house of a local rustic *Strudel* (the Bernese dialect word, Jung notes, for a wizard or magician), which contained the *Merseburger Zaubersprüche* (a famous collection of medieval spells) in modern German, and an incantation to Venus![30]

It is important, however, to note that Jung was by no means alone in his fascination with the occult. After all, Thomas Mann (1875–1955) demonstrated a preoccupation with occultistic phenomena; Rainer Maria Rilke (1875–1926) came into contact with the famous spiritist Baron Karl Ludwig August Friedrich Maximilan du Prel (also known more simply as Carl du Prel) (1839–1899), placing the search for an alternative to materialism, and for poetic inspiration, at the centre of his interest in spiritism; even Nietzsche once attended a séance.[31] In other words, the age of Neo-Kantianism – the age of the great philosophical schools of Marburg and Heidelberg that revitalized the thought of Kant – was also the age of spiritism, occultism and mystical revival. (In turn, this coincidence of the rational and the irrational – in the form of romanticism and the so-called 'covert Enlightenment' – points to an antinomy within the Enlightenment of the previous century itself.)[32] As we shall see in chapter Four, Freud, too, was remarkably sympathetic to the idea of parapsychological or telepathic phenomena; in other words, an interest in the occult was not just a characteristic of Jung.

Second, the goings-on in the rectory in Kleinhüningen under the direction of Helly Preiswerk found their counterpart, in the summer of 1898, in a series of occultistic phenomena experienced in broad daylight. One hot afternoon Jung was studying his textbooks – which ones, we shall see in a moment – when he heard a loud noise, like a pistol shot. Running into the dining room, he (together with his mother and his sister) were astonished to discover that a 70-year-old walnut dining table, inherited from his paternal grandmother, Sophie Jung-Frey, had suddenly split down the middle. Jung attempted to offer a rationalist explanation, describing it as an example of 'a curious accident'; his mother, however, took a darker line. 'This means something', she said, disconcertingly.[33]

A couple of weeks later, Jung came home to find the female members of the household (mother, sister and maid) in a state of considerable agitation. There had been another loud noise, this time from their early nineteenth-century sideboard. The piece of furniture seemed intact but, looking inside, Jung found that, next to the bread in the bread basket kept in the side cupboard, the bread knife had snapped in two.[34] In the 1930s Jung explained the circumstances in great detail in a letter to J. B. Rhine (1895–1980), an American botanist turned (para)psychologist who had begun to conduct experimental investigations into extrasensory perception.[35]

The significance of these events lies in the way they meshed with a second strand to Jung's private programme of reading undertaken when he was a student at university. In addition to Krug's *General Dictionary of the Philosophical Sciences*, and as well as Kant, Schopenhauer and Nietzsche, Jung had, toward the end of the second semester, come across in the library of the father of one of his college friends a small book, dating from the 1870s, on spiritism. This discovery's impact was probably all the greater in the light of his own father's recent death in the spring of 1896. Jung relates that, as a consequence, he began to read works by the German astrophysicist and spiritist Johann Karl Friedrich Zöllner (1834–1882), the English chemist and physicist Sir William Crookes (1832–1857), as well as Carl du Prel, the German philosophers Carl August von Eschenmayer (1768–1852) and Joseph Görres (1776–1848), the medical doctor Johann Karl Passavant (1790–1857), the Romantic writer Justinus Andreas Christian Kerner (1786–1862) and, last but by no means least, the Swedish scientist and mystical theologian Emanuel Swedenborg (1688–1772).[36] A propos of these writers, Jung quite rightly remarks, in *Memories, Dreams, Reflections*, 'I read virtually the whole of the literature on spiritism available to me at the time'.[37]

The accounts of spiritistic phenomena reminded Jung of the tales and legends he had heard during his childhood and, from the evidence presented in these books, he came to the astounding conclusion that 'the material was, without question, authentic'![38] For Jung, these accounts were to be the first instance of what he came to regard as proof of 'objective psychic phenomena' and, more important, he explained why he considered them so significant. Reading them made his life 'much more attractive' and 'the world gained depth and background'.[39] In other words, his study of occultism was driven by that quintessentially Jungian preoccupation with the question of *meaning*.

To these two strands of reading – philosophy and spiritism – Jung's medical studies now added a third: professional medical science, especially psychiatry. Above all, Jung's attention was captured (and his suspicions, which were to remain with him for the rest of his life, about psychiatry aroused) by a work written by

Richard von Krafft-Ebing (a German-born baron, 1840–1902, who studied medicine in Heidelberg, before establishing a reputation as a psychiatrist, hypnotist and sexologist, notably through his study *Psychopathia sexualis*, 1886, thanks to which the terms 'sadism' and 'masochism' became popular.)[40] In the foreword to the fourth edition (1890) of his *Textbook of Psychiatry*, Krafft-Ebing wrote that 'it lies indeed in the peculiarity of the subject-matter and its incomplete state of development that psychiatric textbooks are stamped with a more or less subjective character', and described clinical cases as 'diseases of the personality'.[41]

When reading these words, Jung experienced, 'in a flash of illumination', the same heart-pounding excitement that he had

Richard von
Krafft-Ebing,
1903.

experienced in his dream of the giant radiolarian (see page 64). Where could he find a unique combination of his interests: biology and spiritism? Where could 'the two currents' of his interests 'flow together' and 'in a united stream dig their own bed'? Where was 'the empirical field common to biological and spiritual [*geistig*] facts'? Where would 'the collision of nature and spirit, of *Natur* and *Geist*, become a reality?[42] Where else would Jung be able to fulfil the Faustian ambition to become 'twin natures blended' or 'united double nature', *geeinte Zweinatur*?[43] There was only one answer, it seemed: in psychiatry.

For psychiatry, as Jung understood it, not only embodied his life theme of the *coniunctio oppositorum*, the 'unification of the opposites', it also meant a fresh approach to medicine. Robbed, thanks to an error of hubristic oversight – he overlooked some moulds in a corner of a slide containing epithelial cells – in his pathological anatomy test, of the highest possible mark in the examination, Jung received the same mark as another candidate. Dismissively referring to this student as a 'loner' with a 'monomaniacal ambition' (Jung could almost be describing himself), he notes his colleague's obsession with 'facts' and his subsequent decline into schizophrenia. For his part, Jung would go on to write a book on schizophrenia (or *dementia praecox*), and later bypass schizophrenia himself (or so some have argued) by entering a state that might well be described as psychosis. His experiences, both as a doctor and as a borderline psychotic, would confirm his view of psychiatry in the broadest sense as 'a dialogue between the sick psyche and the "normal" psyche of the doctor' and as 'a coming-to-terms of the "sick" person with the equally subjective personality of the therapist'.[44] The delusions and hallucinations of the mentally ill were, he would try to demonstrate, not simply 'symptoms', but possessed 'a human meaning' (*einen menschlichen Sinn*).[45]

This search for meaning is evident in the choice of reward to which Jung treated himself when his exams were over: he decided to spend a week in Munich where, as Richard Noll puts it, Jung intended 'to indulge his passions for art and archaeology'.[46] Noll's account (conceived as an 'apocryphon' to the 'gospel' of *Memories, Dreams, Reflections*) conjures up well the sights and sounds of *fin-de-siècle* Munich as they must have appeared to Jung in that week in December 1900. Before setting off by train for Bavaria, Jung had permitted himself the luxury of going to the opera for the first time, and the melodies of Bizet's *Carmen* – a work about which Nietzsche, too, had been famously enthusiastic – would have accompanied him on his journey. In Munich, or so *Memories, Dreams, Reflections* records, Jung saw 'real classical art for the first time' (and, on this occasion, with no aunt to pull him by the hand and to remonstrate with him for looking at naughty statues).[47]

In the Glyptothek, Jung would have found himself 'in the presence of the gods', and definitely in the presence of statues of all manner of pagan deities: Assyrian, Egyptian, Greek, Etruscan, Roman.[48] In its Hall of Bacchus, he would have admired the notorious Barberini *Faun*, the statue of a drunken satyr resting with his legs akimbo; he will have come across 'compelling hermaphroditic figures and images of Dionysian orgies in which the god led swooning, dancing young mad women known as maenads in flowing, processional revelry'; and he will have found 'images of satyrs and the great satyr-god Pan' – in front of all this, Noll speculates, Jung 'with his small-town Protestant upbringing, could not but have felt that he was in the presence of something a bit obscene and forbidden – something Nietzschean'.[49] In Munich, too, Jung would also have seen an exhibition in the Neue Pinakothek of the recent work of the German Symbolist painter Franz von Stuck (1863–1928), including the famous painting *Sin*, to which he was to make reference more than a decade later in his ground breaking study of libidinal symbolism.[50] Noll suggests that Jung's fantasies were fuelled by this 'phantasmagoria of gods, nymphs, satyrs, and sin', then he forgot all about them.[51] But did he really forget them?

Burghölzli, Zurich

Toward the end of his week that had begun in Munich, Jung then
travelled to Stuttgart, where he paid a visit to his great-aunt,
Anna Reimer-Jung, the daughter of Carl Gustav Jung's first marriage
to Virginie de Lassaulx (1804–1840). This vivacious and intelligent
old lady, with her aristocratic air and flashing blue eyes, was
married to a psychiatrist, Hermann Reimer, the son of the Berlin
publisher Georg Andreas Reimer, and with this visit Jung saw
himself as taking leave (in the words of *Memories, Dreams, Reflections*)
of 'the nostalgia' – the *nostos algos*, the 'pain of homecoming' – of
his childhood.[52]

As one chapter ends, the next begins. Fresh from his journey
to Bavaria and Baden-Württemberg, Jung took up his post as an
assistant in the Burghölzli on 10 December 1900. Located on a
wooded hill (hence its name) in the Riesbach district in south-east
Zurich, the Burghölzli has been the psychiatric hospital attached
to the University of Zurich since its foundation in 1870, comparable
to the Maudsley Hospital in south London. Under the direction
of August-Henri Forel (1848–1931), the hospital began to gain a
reputation in the medical world, and its heyday was to come
under its fifth director, Eugene Bleuler (1857–1939), who was in
charge when Jung began working there.[53]

The move to the Burghölzli represented a shift in Jung's life in
several respects. He was no longer a student; he had embarked
on a professional career. He was no longer in Basel (where he was
'stamped for all time' as the son of Pastor Jung, as the grandson of
Professor Jung, and as the illegitimate great-grandson of Goethe),
but in Zurich (where he could be the legitimate, *spiritual* son of
Goethe). He had moved from 'the rich background of culture' (or,
to put it less positively, 'the pressure of tradition' and 'the brown
fog of the centuries') to a world, not so much of intellect, as of
commerce. And he had moved from the world of his mother,

Jung in Burghölzi, Zürich, *c.* 1909–10.

someone who remained 'always a stranger' to him, into the different world of what Lacan would call *le nom du père*, the world of 'intention, consciousness, duty, responsibility' or – in the curious phrase found in *Memories, Dreams, Reflections* – 'the monastery of the world'.[54] One senses that Jung did not quite feel at home in the Burghölzli, given the references to 'knowledge that shrank to ever small circles', to 'oppressively narrow horizons', and to 'the unending desert of routine'.

In the evenings, Jung read through all 50 volumes of the *Allgemeine Zeitschrift für Psychiatrie* to get himself up-to-speed on the subject of psychiatry; and to acquaint himself, as he put it, with 'the psychiatric mentality'.[55] For his professional colleagues seemed no less interesting that his patients (and perhaps, or so one wonders he might have thought, in greater need of treatment?). In order better to understand the 'mentality' of the psychiatric profession, and for his personal interest, Jung began to 'compile statistics' about the 'hereditary background' of his fellow psychiatrists. One suspects that Jung would have been the kind of colleague to keep an eye on.[56]

Thanks to Bleuler, several psychiatric terms entered the German language (and thence, into English): 'autism', 'ambivalence' and, above all, 'schizophrenia': the *skhizein* or 'splitting' of the *phrēn* or 'mind'. Previously this disorder had been known as *dementia praecox* (or a 'dementia' affecting the young), and Bleuler brought about nothing less than a revolution in its diagnosis and treatment. As a clinician at the Burghölzli, Jung treated numerous cases of schizophrenia, although Anthony Storr has suggested that, given the paucity of case-histories in the corpus of Jung's writings, he was 'not very much interested in neurosis as such'; indeed, Storr suspects that 'kind and compassionate though Jung was, he was always more interested in ideas than in people, and rapidly became bored with the unravelling of those emotional tangles within the family which constitute the bread-and-butter of the average psychotherapeutic practice'.[57] Nevertheless, Storr notes that a good deal of Jung's thought had its origin in his clinical experiences at the Burghölzli.

Memories, Dreams, Reflections mentions some of the cases with whose treatment Jung was charged. It is important to remember that these were highly disturbed individuals, whose mental and physical suffering was real. For instance, there was Babette S., a woman from the backstreets of Zurich's old town, whose father was a drunk and whose sister was a prostitute.[58] For the other doctors, she was a classic case of psychic disintegration; but for Jung, there was a method (so to speak) in her madness. If she said, 'I am Socrates' deputy', this meant she had (like Socrates) been unjustly accused. And if she said, 'Naples and I must supply the world with noodles', what she really meant was: 'I feel inferior

– and must compensate for this'. In other words, Jung became convinced that 'much of what [I] had hitherto regarded as senseless was not as crazy as it seemed', and even paranoid ideas and hallucinations 'contained a germ of meaning'.[59]

In presenting his patient's case in his clinical writings, Jung tried to convey a sense of 'the richness of her inner life', even though she was 'apparently so dull and apathetic', sitting in her room, darning her linen, and mumbling a few meaningless phrases. Accordingly, Jung invites us to discover in her 'baroque jumble of words' something different: namely, 'the fragments of an enigmatic inscription, bits and pieces of fairy-tale fantasies', which have 'broken away' from 'hard reality' and become 'a far-off world of their own', a place where (as Jung poetically describes it) 'the tables are ever laden, and a thousand banquets are held in golden palaces'.[60] For Jung, the unconscious psyche becomes a kind of permanent feast, where the task of the analyst is to study the menu and make sense of the various dishes and their ingredients.

Then again, there was the 75-year-old woman who had been admitted nearly half a century earlier.[61] She could not speak or eat solids, and made curious rhythmic motions with her hands. Everyone thought her case demonstrated a catatonic form of schizophrenia, but Jung was not so sure. Those hand gestures looked, to him, like the gestures made by a cobbler when stitching a pair of shoes. Sure enough, after her death Jung asked her brother at the funeral why she had lost her sanity. It turned out the woman had fallen in love with a shoemaker who had rejected her. In the movements of the woman's arms, Jung discerned a identification with her lover that had lasted to her death. At the core of a psychosis, he came to believe, lay a nexus of 'meaningful connections' (*Sinnzusammenhänge*), to the uncovering of which any effective therapy should be devoted.[62]

Finally, there was the case of the young woman admitted suffering from 'melancholy' and diagnosed as schizophrenic. Once again, Jung had his doubts, and thought her problem was depression. When dealing with her case, Jung made use of a technique that he had been developing under the direction of Bleuler: the word association test. This test had been invented by the Victorian polymath and eugenicist Sir Francis Galton (1822–1911), and adapted by the German psychologist Wilhelm Wundt (1831–1920).[63] Further work had been undertaken in Heidelberg by the psychiatrist Gustav Aschaffenburg (1866–1944) and Emil Kraepelin (1856–1926), but it was Jung who, in collaboration with his colleague Franz Riklin (1878–1926), refined the use of the test. (According to William McGuire, a word test administered to Jung by Ludwig Binswanger in 1907 reveals that Jung had a complex about Goethe.[64]) This very early work undertaken by Jung is frequently overlooked in accounts, because it is straightforward, hardcore empirical science; it suits neither the empiricists to admit that Jung discovered that their approach was inadequate to the matter at hand, nor are the Jungians always sufficiently proud of their founder's roots in evidence-based science.

Why did Jung become interested in word association? Originally, Jung had been interested in anatomical brain research and had been involved in preparing brain dissections in the Burghölzli. When Jung asked one of his colleagues, Alexander von Muralt, what a brain dissection could really reveal about a patient, he admitted it was useless. Von Muralt then turned to photography, and Jung decided it was time to move on from brain dissection, too.[65]

It seemed that word association tests could bring about real improvements in Jung's patients. Using word association with this young female patient, for instance, Jung discovered 'a dark and tragic story' behind her condition: her love for the son of a wealthy industrialist, his apparent indifference and her subsequent marriage to another man. Five years later a mutual friend told her that the industrialist's son had been shocked and disappointed by her marriage, a fact which had plunged her into depression and brought about a murderous negligence that led to the death of her four-year-old daughter. Jung, demonstrating a cavalier approach to the treatment of his patient – 'in general it may be said that unequivocal rules scarcely exist in psychology' – confronted her with the accusation of murder. Two weeks later, the woman was discharged: burdened with the conscious acknowledgement of what she had done, the rest of her life would be spent in atonement and expiation, but at least she had her life back.[66]

In *Memories, Dreams, Reflections* Jung draws the following conclusions from this episode, which offers an insight into what he believed therapy could offer:

> Therapy only really begins after the investigation of th[e] wholly personal story. It is the patient's secret, the rock against which he is shattered. If I know his secret story, I have a key to the treatment. The doctor's task is to find out how to gain that knowledge . . . In therapy the problem is always the whole person, never the symptom alone. We must ask questions which challenge the whole personality.[67]

As we have seen, Jung knew all about the importance of secrets. And in his work, as it began to take shape, he would ask questions that challenged not just the personality of his patients or clients, but the very conception of the personality itself.

The academic counterpart to Jung's clinical work on word association was his medical dissertation, submitted to the University of Zurich in 1901 and published in 1902, under the title 'On the Psychology and Pathology of so-called Occult Phenomena'.[68] As the word 'so-called' suggests, Jung's dissertation was – contrary, perhaps, to one's expectations – a sceptical one and thoroughly empirical in its approach. Jung investigated the formation of visions in somnambulistic states, with reference to the work on the implantation of suggestions in states of partial sleep undertaken by Alfred Binet (1857–1911), a French psychologist and inventor of intelligence tests, and Charles Féré (1852–1907), another French doctor, both of whom were members of the Salpêtrière School of Hypnosis around Charcot (see below). According to Binet's and Féré's research, stimuli on anaesthetic regions of the skin of hysterical subjects could result in visual images, or in vivid responses could be perceived as visual.

Jung's thesis included an extensive discussion of the seances conducted by his cousin, Helly Preiswerk, and the different personalities that manifested themselves in (and through) her mediumistic experiences. Although he claimed that 'books of a mystical nature' had never been allowed in the family, Jung had, for her fifteenth birthday, given Helly a copy of *The Seer of Prevorst* (*Die Seherin von Prevorst*, 1829), a work about a case of clairvoyancy by the German Romantic poet and doctor Justinus Kerner, and he referred to the work in his thesis.[69] Moreover, Jung telescoped the five or so years of Helly's activity into just two, and his account of the fantastic schemas elaborated and different personalities expressed during her semi-somnambulistic trances reads like a miniature version of the remarkable case of multiple personality disorder evinced in a medium in Geneva and recorded by the Swiss psychologist Théodore Flournoy (1854–1920) in *From India to the Planet Mars: A Case of Multiple Personality with Imaginary Languages* (1899).[70] Catherine Élise Müller, or Hélène Smith as Flournoy called her, claimed to be a reincarnation of Marie Antoinette, a fifteenth-century Indian princess and a visitor to Mars: she 'invented' a language called Martian, while speaking perfect French and Sanskrit in her other 'incarnations'.

One of Helly's personalities in the seances was called Ivenes, a woman who had apparently been a lover of Goethe: if Jung fantasized about being Goethe, Helly in turn projected *her* fantasies about *him* into this imaginary love affair in the past. Although Jung (doubtless wisely) omits this aspect of her fantasies from his thesis, in one passage he draws on an example of what Goethe meant by the use of the faculty of 'intuitive perception' (*Anschauung*), describing what he called 'these independent transmutations of simple stimuli' in Goethean terms as 'the primary phenomenon in the formation of somnambulistic dream'.[71] Jung noted that 'analogous phenomena' could occur even in conscious, waking states as well, albeit 'in exceptional cases', and he cited Goethe's account of how, 'when he vividly conjured up the image of a flower', he could see it 'undergoing changes of its own accord, as if entering into new combinations of form'.[72] The source for this account is given by Jung as the following passage from Goethe's review (1820) of *Contributions to the Knowledge of Seeing in a Subjective Respect* (1819) by the Czech doctor and natural scientist Johannes Evangelista Purkinje (1787–1869):

> I had the ability, with my eyes closed and my head lowered, to evoke the image of a flower in the centre of my organ of visualization; and to perceive the flower in such a way that it did not remain in its original form for a single moment, but spread out, and from within there unfolded again new flowers with coloured as well as green leaves. They were not natural flowers by any means, but products of the imagination.[73]

Goethe, then, was in the background to this dissertation in more ways than one. Elsewhere, Jung cited the similarity between a passage in Nietzsche's *Thus Spoke Zarathustra* and one in Kerner's *The Seer of Prevorst* as an example of another psychological phenomenon, cryptomnesia (the unrecognized return of a forgotten memory).[74]

Jung's decision to submit his dissertation to the Medical Faculty of the university in Zurich rather than Basel was a political or strategic one in several respects. For one thing, it marked his departure from Basel and his shift of domicile and intellectual allegiance to Zurich; for another, it kept it away from his relatives in Basel, one of whom, after all, he had in effect described as being mad. When it appeared in print these relatives were understandably annoyed; indeed, it has been suggested that it made Helly's sisters highly ineligible, and left most of them, in the end, unmarried.

In 1902 and 1903 Jung took a sabbatical from his work at the Burghölzli to spend the winter semester attending the lectures given in Paris by the French psychologist Pierre Janet (1859–1947). Janet, whose largely forgotten work has recently been hailed by Michel Onfray as providing the basis for a hedonist and materialist (as opposed to Freudian and 'idealist') psychoanalysis, had studied under the great French neurologist Jean-Martin Charcot (1825–1893), with whom Freud himself had studied in the winter semester of 1885 to 1886 at the Salpêtrière.[75] (In a letter to his wife-to-be, Martha Bernays, Freud described Charcot as 'one of the greatest doctors, a genial and serious-minded person', confessing that 'no one else has had such an influence on me').[76] What Charcot had been for Freud, Pierre Janet – along with Binet and Flournoy, the latter of whom Jung had visited in Geneva – was for Jung. Indeed, it has been argued by Sonu Shamdasani that a greater appreciation of the influence on Jung of nineteenth-century French psychology – as well as of William James (1842–1910), the American psychologist and author of the two-volume work *The Principles of Psychology* (1890) and of *The Varieties of Religious Experience* (1902), and of Wilhelm Wundt – might help move us away from the conventional and, in his view, 'Freudocentric' reading of Jung's work.[77] Nevertheless, the significance of Jung's relationship with Freud cannot be overlooked, and the existence of the (published) correspondence between Jung and Freud enables us to contextualize that relationship with considerable precision.

Nor were the only important relationships in Jung's life intellectual ones. In February 1903, at the age of 28, Jung married the nearly 21-year-old Emma Rauschenbach (1882–1955), the daughter of a wealthy industrial manufacturer and known as the second

Jung and Emma
Rauschenbach i
1903, the year tl
they married.

richest heiress in Switzerland. With his marriage to Emma, Jung
brought structure and regularity into his erotic life, a life charged
with rich and beautiful fantasy, as suggested by his memories of
the young, pretty girl with blue eyes and fair hair, who led him, one
autumn, along the Rhine, below the Falls, or of the young, slender
girl with blue eyes, dressed in local costume, whom he met visiting
the relics of Brother Klaus in Flüeli. Yet ultimately, not even the
beautiful and intelligent Emma Jung would be able to contain and
control the erotic impulses of her husband, although despite (or
because) of this, she became an important exponent of Jungian
psychology in her own right.[78] After living for a while in a flat in
the Burghölzli, below Eugen Bleuler and his wife Hedwig, and after
the birth of their daughters Agathe (in December 1904) and Gret
(in February 1906), and their only son Franz (in November 1908),

Küsnacht, Switzerland, 1905.

the Jungs moved in 1909 to Küsnacht, just outside Zurich, where they had two further children: Marianne (in 1910) and Helene (in March 1914). By the shores of Lake Zurich, a magnificent new house was built at Seestraße 228, where Jung was to spend the rest of his life.[79] Jung had a beautiful house; a beautiful wife; beautiful children; an exacting, but interesting, job. He had arrived; surely nothing could go wrong now?

Jung with Emma and four of their children in Switzerland 1917.

4

Occultism, Psychoanalysis and Beyond

Actually – and I confess this to you with a struggle – I have a boundless admiration for you both as a man and a researcher, and I bear you no conscious grudge. So the self-preservation complex does not come from there; it is rather that my veneration for you has something of the character of a "religious" crush. Though it does not really bother me, I still feel it is disgusting and ridiculous because of its undeniable erotic undertone. This abominable feeling comes from the fact that as a boy I was the victim of a sexual assault by a man I once worshipped.[1]

Or so Jung wrote to Freud. His statement gives us a good idea of the astonishing degree of confessional and personal intimacy achieved within a year-and-a-half of Jung sending Freud a copy of his *Diagnostic Association Studies* (1906) in April 1906. In his final paper in this collection, entitled 'Psychoanalysis and Association Experiments' (1906), Jung drew on Freud's famous case study of Anna O., published as 'Fragments of an Analysis of a Case of Hysteria' a year earlier in 1905. In his paper, Jung paid tribute to how Freud had 'for the most part abandoned the terminology that he had laid down in the *Studies on Hysteria*', a work co-authored with the physician and hypnotist Josef Breuer (1842–1925) and published in 1895, and had 'substituted for it a number of different and more fitting expressions'.[2]

Sigmund Freud, 1921, photograph by Max Halberstadt.

For Jung, it made strategic sense to ally himself with Freud, who had been making a name for himself in Vienna and had established his reputation with *The Interpretation of Dreams* (*Die Traumdeutung*) (published in 1899, but bearing the symbolically significant publication date of 1900). For his part, Freud saw an advantage in an alliance with Jung, who was not just Swiss and Protestant, but an Aryan, as he wrote to his fellow psychoanalyst (and Jew) Karl Abraham on 26 December 1908.[3]

The published correspondence between Jung and Freud provides fascinating testimony of the sheer intellectual excitement at the exchange of ideas that took place between the older analyst (who was in his fifties) and his younger correspondent (who was in his thirties), and their mutual identification as 'father' and 'son'.[4] Jung had a copy of Freud's photograph enlarged and sent it to his friends; when Freud addressed him as 'friend' (rather than 'colleague'), Jung responded with emotion to this 'token' of Freud's 'confidence': 'The undeserved gift of your friendship is one of the high points in my life'.[5] In Jung, Freud saw someone who would continue and develop his work, his 'successor and crown prince'.[6] What was going on? Taking his cue from Freud's letter to Jung of 4 October 1909 after their visit to America ('The day after we separated an incredible number of people looked amazingly like you; wherever I went in Hamburg, your light hat with the dark band kept turning up), the historian Richard Noll has pertinently observed, 'these guys were aware of the dynamics', 'they were Freud and Jung, they'd better know what was going on, right?'[7]

Sometimes Freud and Jung analysed each other's dreams, as when they discussed an example given in Jung's *The Psychology of Dementia Praecox* (1907), a study on psychosis. Here is the dream as recounted by Jung:

> I saw horses being hoisted by thick cables to a great height. One of them, a powerful brown horse which was tied up with straps and was hoisted aloft like a package, struck me particularly. Suddenly the cable broke and the horse crashed to the street. I noticed that the horse was dragging a heavy log along with it, and I wondered how it could advance so quickly. It was obviously frightened and could easily cause an accident. Then a rider came up on a little horse and rode along slowly in front of the frightened horse, which moderated its pace somewhat. I still feared that the horse might run over the rider, when a cab came

along and drove in front of the rider at the same pace, thus
bringing the frightened horse to a still slower gait. I then
thought now all is well, the danger is over.[8]

What does the dream mean? Over several pages Jung sets out his
interpretation of the dream, associating the motif of height with
work and ambition; the figure of the large horse with the idea of
the 'yoke of matrimony'; the image of the galloping horse with a
picture by the Swiss artist Albert Welti (1862–1912), *Mondnacht*
('Moonlit Night'), and hence sexuality; and the smaller horse with
a 'rocking horse' or pregnancy.[9] Jung concluded that the meaning
of the dream was 'perfectly clear', namely that 'the wife's pregnancy
and the problem of too many children impose restraints on the
husband'; it was a dream that outwardly showed 'the hopes and
disappointments of an upward-striving career' but inwardly
concealed 'an extremely personal matter which may well have
been accompanied by painful feelings'.[10]

In his study Jung attributed this dream to an unidentified
patient, but in his correspondence with Freud he revealed that he
knew the 'dream material' and the 'dream thoughts' in fact 'much
better' than he had said, for he knew the dreamer intimately: it was
Jung himself.[11] As one commentator has demonstrated, this dream
is susceptible to yet further interpretations for it also yields, given
the parallels between details in the dream and the parable of the
tightrope walker in the 'Preface' to *Thus Spoke Zarathustra*, a reference to Jung's attitude towards Nietzsche.[12] (In his reply to Jung,
however, Freud wondered whether Jung should have gone further
and stressed the predictable interpretation, 'log = penis'.[13])

On other occasions Freud and Jung compared notes on their
respective patients: for instance, on 23 October 1906 Jung told
Freud about a 'difficult case' with which he was dealing, that of
'a 20-year-old Russian girl student' who had been 'ill for 6 years',
following a traumatic experience when she was three or four years

old.[14] We now know that the patient in question was someone called Sabina Spielrein (1884–1942), the daughter of a family of Jewish professional doctors (her mother, a dentist; her father, a physician). Thanks to documents uncovered in the 1970s and published by an Italian Jungian analyst, Aldo Carotenuto, we also know that after, or during, her analysis with Jung she began a sexual liaison with him.[15] The case of Sabina Spielrein is but the first of many examples of 'boundary issues' that dog psychoanalysis and analytical psychology alike; when replying to Jung, Freud told him that he had nearly been in a similar situation a number of times but had always had a narrow escape, while he urged Jung to think of such instances of 'countertransference' as really a blessing in disguise.[16] In her turn, Spielrein began a correspondence with Freud, telling him how Jung had been her 'doctor', then her 'friend', then her 'poet, i.e., beloved'.[17]

Tipped off by an anonymous letter (now thought to have been penned by Emma Jung), her mother came to learn of the affair and responded by writing a letter to Jung, who in turn replied with an extraordinary letter pointing out that, while a doctor is paid a fee and knows his limits, a friend receives no fee (and by implication then there are no limits). 'Therefore I would suggest', Jung wrote to Frau Spielrein, 'that if you wish me to adhere strictly to my role as doctor, you should pay me a fee as suitable recompense for my trouble. In that way', he continued, 'you may be *absolutely certain* that I will respect my duty as a doctor *under all circumstances*'; his fee, he added was '10 francs per consultation'.[18] (Jung's letter, cited in this letter from Spielrein to Freud, shows an ungallant, even callous side to Jung; as John Kerr explains, however, Jung's behaviour is explicable, which does not mean defensible, as that of any man who has been caught out.[19])

During their liaison, Jung and Spielrein fashioned an erotic fantasy centred around a figure from the operas of Wagner: a love-child called Siegfried. Spielrein called it her 'Siegfried problem'.[20] For Richard Noll, this fantasy intersects both with Wagner's music and with Wagner's life: in her diary, Spielrein recalls how 'tears' came to Jung's eyes when she explained 'something about, for example, Wagner's psychological music', and Siegfried is the ultra-Germanic name of the great heroic figure in the third opera of Wagner's *Ring* cycle; while it was generally known that Siegfried Wagner had been born during Wagner's extramarital affair with Cosima, while she was still married to Hans von Bülow.[21] For Noll, 'the fantasy of the eventual triumph of the genius to win his mistress and sire a Siegfried' served as 'one of the scripts through which Jung and Spielrein enacted their relationship', and while Noll reduces Wagner's significance to a political one (as a path to *völkisch renovatio*), the mediation of their affair through the symbol of Siegfried could also be seen as an attempt to live out a strategy described by Goethe in *Dichtung und Wahrheit*.

In Part Three, Book 11, Goethe suggests that 'all people of good quality sense' – 'as they progress in their cultural development' – 'that they have a double role to play in the world, a real one and an ideal one'; moreover, Goethe adds, 'this feeling must be viewed as the basis of every noble impulse'.[22] (Here we find a psychological account for the outlook, associated in part with the classical culture of Goethe's and Schiller's Weimar, of *idealism*.) Solemnly Goethe proclaims that 'we learn only too clearly the real part assigned to us; as far as the other is concerned, we can seldom be certain of it'; but he also asserts that 'surely the youthful propensity for comparing oneself with characters in novels must be numbered among the most pardonable attempts to progress to something higher, to equate oneself with something higher', for 'it is very innocent, and very harmless, however much it is fulminated against'.[23]

To be sure, Jung's behaviour with Spielrein might strike us as anything but noble, but we are here to understand, not to moralize. Moreover, despite her experience with Jung (and, for that matter, with Freud), Spielrein went on to become a psychoanalyst in her own right and it would be entirely wrong to reduce her (as Jung did in his correspondence with Freud) to a clinical case or (as some feminist readings, which deny Spielrein any agency, might) to the status of a passive victim. In the meantime, Spielrein's writings have been published, and her seminal lecture to the Vienna Psychoanalytic Society on 29 November 1911, in which she proposes that the drive for procreation 'consists also psychologically of two antagonistic components, and hence is as much a creative as a destructive drive', anticipates both Freud's notion of *thanatos* (or 'death drive') and the central Jungian idea of transformation (or *Wandlung*).[24]

Although it has become conventional to emphasize the differences between Freud and Jung, they arguably had more in common than might appear at first sight. Following their exchange of letters, Jung (together with Emma) paid a visit to Freud in Vienna in March 1907. On a second visit to the Freud household in March 1909, according to *Memories, Dreams, Reflections*, Freud asked Jung to promise 'never to abandon' the sexual theory of the libido, and their conversation (reconstructed from this account) continued as follows:

> Freud: You see, we must make a dogma of it, an unshakable bulwark.
> Jung (*astonished*): A bulwark – against what?
> Freud: Against the black tide of – (*hesitates, then adds*) – of occultism.[25]

All too often Freud is presented essentially as a figure of the Enlightenment, as a scientist, a rationalist (and this is very much the image that the institutions of psychoanalysis have tried to cultivate); by contrast, Jung is presented as a Romantic, a dreamer, a mystic, an irrationalist (and this, too, is an image that the institutions of psychoanalysis have cultivated). But this obscures the remarkable amount of common ground between Freud and Jung as far as their attitude to 'occultism' is concerned: in other words, to parapsychology.

In his recent critique of psychoanalysis, the French philosopher Michel Onfray has waxed indignant about what he calls '*un monde de causalités magiques*' ('a world of magic causality'), in Freud's thinking[26] in 'Psycho-Analysis and Telepathy', a paper read by Freud to the Committee of the International Psychoanalytic Society in the Harz in September 1921, in which Freud took as his starting point the apparent fact that 'it no longer seems possible to keep away from the study of what are known as "occult" phenomena'.[27] Freud saw, on the surface, a certain similarity in the reception both occultism and psychoanalysis had garnered from conventional science, and on this basis Freud even suggested that 'alliance and co-operation between analysts and occultists might thus appear both plausible and promising'.[28]

In his correspondence one finds regular hints at telepathic or occult possibilities. Writing to Karl Abraham on 9 July 1925, for instance, Freud opened his letter by observing that Anna, his daughter, had, 'with her telepathic sensibility', recently remarked that Abraham had not been in touch, shortly before they received a letter from him.[29] Then again, writing to Eduardo Weiss on 24 April 1932, Freud confessed: 'I am, it is true, prepared to believe that behind all so-called occult phenomena lies something new and important: the fact of thought-transference, i.e., the transferring of psychical processes through space to other people', and that 'I know of proofs of this observation made in daylight and am thinking of expressing my opinion publicly about this'.[30] After all, as Freud further wrote to Weiss on 8 May 1932, 'a psychoanalyst's refraining from taking part publicly in occult studies is a purely practical measure, and only a temporary one, not at all an expression on principle', and 'contemptuous rejection of these studies without any experience of them would really be to imitate the deplorable example of our opponents'.[31] But Freud did also commit himself in print.

In *The Psychopathology of Everyday Life* (1901), Freud said of 'presentiments, prophetic dreams, telepathic experiences, manifestations of supernatural forces, and the like', that he was 'far from meaning to pass so sweeping a condemnation of these phenomena, of which so many detailed observations have been made even by men of outstanding intellect'.[32] Indeed, he even went so far as to posit that 'if the existence of still other phenomena – those, for example, claimed by spiritualists – were to be established, we should merely set about modifying our "laws" in the way demanded by the new discovery'.[33] Then again, in 1932 in one of his introductory lectures on psychoanalysis, Freud observed that 'not every case, of course, is equally convincing and in not every case is it equally possible to exclude more rational explanations; but, taking them as a whole, there remains a strong balance of probability in favour of thought-transference as a fact'.[34]

Now we should not overlook the fact that Freud – in common with Goethe, Thomas Mann and so many other German writers – was capable of writing in an ironic tone, in a way that tends to be (but is not entirely) absent in Jung. But Freud's interest in numerology attained an intensity that is entirely on a par with Jung's later astrological deliberations. Here the influence of Wilhelm Fließ (1858–1928), the German biologist and doctor who developed a theory of biorhythms based on cycles of 23 and 28 days (corresponding to one's physical and emotional states of well-being), can be clearly felt. In his letter to Fließ of 1 March 1896, Freud discerned a numerological relation between his wife's menstrual cycle and the birth of their daughter, Anna, and in his letter to Fließ of 22 June 1894 he explained his belief that he would die at the age of 51 as a 'compromise opinion', for which he had 'no scientific basis'.[35]

Some years later, in a letter to Jung of 16 April 1909, Freud wrote how he had discovered a numerological significance in his new telephone number (1 43 62), which gave rise in him to the fear that he would die when he was 62. For, as he told Jung: 'In 1899 when I wrote *The Interpretation of Dreams* I was 43 years old', and 'thus it was plausible to suppose that the other figures signified the end of my life'; Freud himself called this both 'a superstitious notion', evidence that 'the hidden influence' of Fließ was 'at work', as well as a confirmation of 'the specifically Jewish nature of my mysticism'.[36] Similarly, in *The Psychopathology of Everyday Life*, Freud cited his random choice of a number, 2467, as an example of how any set of numerals, while apparently plucked out of the blue, can actually conceal an important truth.[37] (In miniature, this corresponds to the entire principle informing the psychoanalytic endeavour: namely, that what might appear to be the contingent detail of everyday life is, in fact, replete with psychological significance.) Compared with these exercises in statistical signification, Jung's later work with the quantum physicist Wolfgang Pauli (1900–1958) on the 'cosmic number' (as it happens, 137, which is at once the 'fine structure constant' of light and the sum of the Hebrew letters of the word *kabbalah*) seems much less eccentric.[38]

On Jung's second visit to Freud in Vienna in March 1909, during which Freud issued his warning about 'the black tide of mud of occultism', something strange happened. If we are to believe the account in *Memories, Dreams, Reflections*, on the final evening their conversation had turned towards the occult. Freud was apparently dismissing parapsychology in general and precognition in particular (despite, as we have seen, his evident interest in these subjects, but in later years it suited Jung to emphasize the differences between him and Freud). As Freud talked, Jung became aware of a curious sensation: it felt as if his diaphragm had turned into iron and begun to glow red-hot. Suddenly there was a loud bang from a bookcase in the room, which startled them and made them fear it was about to fall over. But Jung kept his cool: 'There', he told Freud, 'that is an example of a so-called catalytic exteriorization phenomenon' (or, in other words, a physical effect caused by a mental thought). Freud's reaction was sceptical: *Das ist ja ein leibhaftiger Unsinn!* What nonsense! 'No, it isn't,' Jung insisted, 'and to prove my point I now predict that in a moment there will be another loud report!' And as if on cue: *bang!* Freud stared at Jung, we are told, 'aghast'.[39]

This account might be easily dismissed as yet further evidence, if it were needed, of the overactive imagination of the author of *Memories, Dreams, Reflections*. But in their correspondence both men referred to the events of this evening without any disagreement that they had taken place. On 2 April, Jung wrote to Freud of his feeling of dissatisfaction (literally: his *sentiments d'incomplétude*) after their final evening, fearing that his 'spookiness' had left a bad impression on Freud.[40] It took Freud several days to get round to replying, but when he did, he acknowledged that 'the knocking poltergeist' had made 'a deep impression' on him. He came up with two explanations. The first, that in one room a pair of heavy Egyptian stelae on a bookshelf caused a constant creaking sound, Freud dismisses: 'That is too easy to explain'. Instead, he proposes a second explanation: his own credulity, or at least his willingness to believe, depended on 'the magic' of Jung's 'personal presence'. And he turned the entire episode into a joke through a literary allusion, writing of how he, Freud, now contemplated his 'despiritualized furniture' in much the same way that Friedrich Schiller, in his poem 'The Gods of Greece' (*Die Götter Griechenlands*), contemplated 'undeified nature after the gods of Greece had passed away'.[41]

In other words, the difference between Freud's outlook and Jung's was, in important respects, a good deal less obvious than, in years to come (and for essentially political or strategic reasons), both of them were to claim it was. For instance, a number of passages found in

Freud's writings sound highly Jungian. In 'Leonardo and a Memory of his Childhood' (1910), Freud brought in numerous literary and mythological references to explain Leonardo's childhood fantasy of the vulture; no wonder Jung, in his letter to Freud of 17 June 1910, acclaimed the work as 'wonderful'.[42] In his 'Postscript' of 1912 to the Schreber case (published as *Psychoanalytic Notes on an Autobiographical Account of Paranoia (Dementia Paranoides)* (1911), Freud explicitly agreed with Jung's ideas, noting that his colleague had 'excellent grounds for his assertion that the mythopoeic forces of humankind are not extinct, but that to this very day they give rise in the neuroses to the same psychical products as in the remotest past ages', and concluding that:

> in dreams and neuroses . . . we come once more upon the *child* and the peculiarities which characterize his modes of thought and his emotional life . . . and we come upon the *savage* too . . . upon the *primitive* man, as he stands revealed to us in the light of the researches of archaeology and of ethnology.[43]

Then again, in 'Thoughts for the Times on War and Death' (1915), Freud used the notion that characteristics of the primitive mind could still manifest themselves (as a regression) to help explain the First World War.[44] By the same token, in a passage added to *The Interpretation of Dreams* in 1919, Freud acknowledged that dream analysis could provide knowledge of 'man's archaic heritage, of what is psychically innate in him', supporting this idea with reference to exactly the same passage from Nietzsche that Jung, in *Transformations and Symbols of the Libido*, had cited: 'In the dream this piece of primeval humanity continues to exercise itself'.[45] And as late as 'The Ego and the Id' (1923) and in 'An Outline of Psychoanalysis' (1930), Freud spoke of our 'archaic heritage' and of how some dreams had to be as 'part of the archaic heritage', adding that 'we find the counterpart of this phylogenetic material in the earliest human legends and in surviving customs' and concluding: 'Thus dreams constitute a source of human prehistory which is not to be neglected'.[46]

Above all, Freud's own approach to psychoanalysis made use of the very principle that he attributed to primitive societies: his interpretations of dreams, for example, read them in accordance with the principle of '*as if*'.[47] For instance, Freud recounts the following dream of a young woman suffering from agoraphobia as a result of fears of seduction:

> I was walking in the street in the summer, wearing a straw hat of peculiar shape; its middle-piece was bent upwards and its side-pieces hung downwards . . . in such a way that one side was lower than the other. I was cheerful and in a self-confident frame of mind; and, as I passed a group of young officers, I thought: 'None of you can do me any harm!'[48]

In his analysis of this dream, Freud does exactly the reverse of his famous remark to the effect that 'sometimes a cigar is just a cigar', suggesting that the hat represented 'a male genital organ, with its middle-piece sticking up, and its two side-pieces hanging down'.[49]

The hermeneutic approach adopted here can be met again in Freud's discussion of the primitive mind in *Totem and Taboo* (1912–13). Here he argued that 'the principle governing magic, the technique of the animistic mode of thinking, is the principle of the "omnipotence of thoughts"', because 'in primitive men the process of thinking is still to a great extent sexualized' and 'this is the origin of their belief in the omnipotence of thoughts, their unshakable confidence in the possibility of controlling the world'.[50] On the basis that 'similarity and contiguity' are 'the two essential principles of processes of association', Freud argues that 'the true explanation of all the folly of magical observances is the domination of the association of ideas', adding that magic's 'true essence' lay in 'the misunderstanding which leads it to replace the laws of nature by psychological ones'.[51] In this respect, Freud's (over)interpretation of his agoraphobic patient's dream would seem to be a perfect example of E. B. Tylor's definition (cited by Freud) of magic as 'mistaking an ideal connection for a real one'.[52]

Evidently Jung would push this argument much further than Freud wanted to do, and in 'primitive' culture, as Jung actually experienced it among the tribes of the Pueblo Indians of New Mexico and the Elgonyi in East Africa (see chapter Seven), he would find something that would bring him close to arguing for the superiority of 'primitive' culture over modern, post-Enlightenment culture.[53] Yet there are also important differences between Freud and Jung as regards their intellectual positions, and it would be unfair (and inaccurate) to collapse their respective psychoanalytic systems into something completely identical. So how did Jung complete his shift away from Freud?

The growing difference between the two men emerges very clearly from their correspondence, and in particular in Jung's letters to Freud in the period between 1909 and 1910. These documents reflect Jung's developing interest in mythological motifs, which crystallizes around the figure of the ancient god Dionysos. In his letter to Freud of 8 November 1909, for instance, Jung excitedly told Freud how his studies of the history of symbolism, particularly the four volumes of *Symbolism and Mythology of the Ancient Peoples* (1810–23) by the German philologist Georg Friedrich Creuzer (1771–1858) and *A Discourse on the Worship of Priapus, and its Connection with the Mystic Theology of the Ancients* (2nd edn, 1865) by the English classicist Richard Payne Knight (1750–1824), had revived his interest in archaeology. 'Rich lodes open up', as he put it, 'for the phylogenetic basis of the theory of neurosis'.[54] The sort of thing that had captured Jung's attention is the account of the ritual cults of Egypt given in the fifth century BCE by the Greek historian Herodotus, comparing them with Greek traditions.

In his *Histories*, Herodotus tells us what happened at the festival in honour of Artemis at Boubastis:

> Men sail with women, large crowds of them play together in each barge. Throughout the entire journey, some of the women play castanets, some of the men play flutes, and the rest of them, both men and women, sing and clap their hands. Whenever they approach some city along the way to Boubastis, they skirt the shore with their barge, and while some of the women continue as before, others shout at the women of the city, mocking and ridiculing them, and some dance, and still others stands up and lift their robes, exposing themselves.[55]

Herodotus also tells us about the festival in honour of Isis at Bousiris, and the cults in honour of Athena, Helios and Leo at Sais, Heliopolis and Bouto; but it was the cult of Ares at Papremis that Jung found particularly interesting:

> As soon as the sun goes down, a few of the priests attend to the sacred image, while many other priests stand at the entrance to the sanctuary holding wooden clubs; opposite them stands a crowd of more than 1,000 men who are fulfilling their vows, and who are also holding clubs. On the day previous to this, the sacred image is carried in a small gilded wooden shrine to another sacred building. And now the few priests left with the image pull a four-wheeled wagon containing both the shrine and the image inside it to the sanctuary. But those priests standing before the gates do not allow them to enter, and those who are bound by their vows assist the god by striking the others who resist them. The battle intensifies as they yield their wooden clubs; heads are bashed, and I think that many must die from their wounds, although the Egyptians deny that anyone actually dies.[56]

Why would anybody want to indulge in that kind of behaviour? In *Transformations and Symbols of the Libido*, Jung cited the passage above, and he noted Herodotus' explanation of this custom: 'According to the native Egyptians . . . the mother of the god Ares used to live in this sanctuary; and when Ares, who grew up apart from his mother, reached adulthood, he wanted to mingle with her', but 'his mother's servants, having never seen him before, warded him off and did not permit him to approach her', so 'he returned with a group of people from another city and, after beating up the servants, went in to be with his mother'.[57] But Herodotus' explanation is, in turn, in need of an explanation and Jung believed he could provide it: in this fantasy of the rape of the mother, we see a symbol of a psychological event – the return to the collective unconscious (or the Great Mother) and the rebirth of the heroic individual.[58]

Bust of Herodotus, Roman copy in marble, 2nd century AD, after Greek bronze original, 4th century BCE.

For Jung, however, Herodotus was too shy and retiring. 'It's a crying shame,' he told Freud, 'that already with Herodotus prudery puts forth its quaint blossoms', and 'on his own admission he covers up a lot of things "for reasons of decency"'; 'where' wondered Jung 'did the Greeks learn that from so early?'[59] Nevertheless, Jung found Herodotus' account of the festival of Dionysos especially absorbing. For 'the Egyptians', Herodotus wrote, 'celebrate the festival of Dionysos in nearly the same way as the Hellenes do, except they do not have choral dances':

And instead of phalluses they have their own invention – marionettes as tall as one and a half feet, which the women carry around through the villages; these marionettes have genitals that move up and down and are not much smaller than their entire bodies. A flute player leads the way, and the women follow, singing the praises of Dionysos. There is a sacred story which explains why the genitals are so large and why they are the only part of the marionettes that move.)[60]

'The dying and resurgent god' – the Orphic mysteries, Thammuz, Osiris, Dionysos, Adonis and so on – is 'everywhere phallic', Jung triumphantly concluded.[61] But why does any of this stuff about ancient cults and customs matter?

It matters because, as he told Freud on a letter begun on Christmas Day (!) and finished on New Year's Eve (!) 1909, Jung was 'turning over and over' in his mind 'the problem of antiquity' and finding it 'a hard nut to crack' (*ein schweres Stück*).[62] To be sure, antiquity reveals 'a lot of infantile sexuality' (and, to this extent, confirmed Freud's arguments), but 'that is not all'. Rather, or so it seemed to Jung, 'antiquity was ravaged by the struggle with *incest*, with which sexual *repression* begins' (or was it vice versa)? Here it was important to look at 'the history of family law' (much as, perhaps, Johann Jakob Bachofen had done?), for 'the history of civilization', or at least what remains of it, is 'too skimpy'.[63]

Because Jacob Burckhardt's *History of Greek Civilization* (1898–1902) remained, in Jung's view, 'wholly on the surface', he had set it aside and begun to immerse himself – thanks to *Psyche* (1890–94), the monumental study of Greek cultic practices and beliefs – in Greek daimonology – by the great German classicist Erwin Rohde (1845–1898). In particular, it seemed to Jung, Rohde's erstwhile friend Nietzsche had 'intuited a great deal' about Dionysos, and Jung was developing the idea that 'the Dionysian frenzy was a backwash of sexuality' whose 'historical significance [had] been insufficiently appreciated', although 'essential elements' of it had 'overflowed into Christianity but in another compromise formation'.[64]

A month or so later, inspired by an invitation from a chemist in Bern, Alfred Knapp, to join an International Fraternity for Ethics and Culture founded in 1908 by the Swiss psychiatrist and sexologist Auguste Forel (1848–1931), Jung outlined his vision for psychoanalysis in the following programmatic statement of 11 February 1910:

> I think we must give ΨA [psychoanalysis] time to infiltrate into people from many centres, to revivify among intellectuals a feeling for symbol and myth, ever so gently to transform Christ back into the soothsaying god of the vine, which he was, and in this way absorb those ecstatic instinctual forces of Christianity for the *one* purpose of making the cult and the sacred myth what they once were – a drunken feast of joy where man regained the ethos and holiness of an animal.[65]

In his reply, Freud – who, it must be remembered, had not exactly set it as his main task to serve 'the vital forces of religion' – responded that he could hear how 'the tempest is raging', coming across as 'a distant thunder'; while for his part he was not 'thinking of a substitute for religion', and certainly not organized religion, because instead he took the view that 'this need must be sublimated'.[66]

But by now there was no stopping Jung. In his letter to Freud of 8 May 1911, Jung described his investigations of mythology in his own mythical terms of a sojourn in a dark, sweet-scented land of magic, and by 23 June 1911 it had become clear to him that the symbolism of the incest fantasy had less to do (as Freud thought it did) with what happened between Oedipus and Jocasta (or, in other words, with real sexual desire), and more with the meaning of the mysterious Mothers whom Faust encountered in the celebrated scene of Part Two of Goethe's dramatic poem: 'Formation, transformation, / The eternal mind's eternal recreation'.[67] Not only was 'unconscious fantasy', Jung observed, 'an amazing witches' kitchen', but 'this is the matrix of the mind, as' – with a nod in the direction of his Goethean inheritance – 'the little great-grandfather correctly saw'.[68] So it is not surprising that, by 25 February 1912, Jung was actually speaking of his own research in terms of a descent to the underworld (or *katabasis*).[69]

What was at stake in this shift away from Freud? In essence, Jung was struggling to find a solution to a hitherto unsolved problem in psychoanalysis: what is the source of repression? In answering this question, Jung proposed a new understanding of 'introversion' as a positive, not just a retrograde, stage in the development of the human individual, and concomitantly a conception of the unconscious as an intelligent, not just an infantile, structure.[70] In his attempt to provide his own answer, Freud was to move away from a monolithic conception of the libido and introduce a variety of dyadic and triadic solutions, opposing 'pleasure principle' and 'reality principle'; 'id', 'ego' and 'super-ego'; and Eros and Thanatos. In *his* attempt to provide an answer, Jung essentially placed the problem within a Nietzschean framework. In a draft sent to Freud, Jung had posed the problems in terms of 'sexuality destroying itself', a phrase that provoked in Freud 'a vigorous shaking of the head' and which Jung himself described as 'an extremely paradoxical formulation'.[71] In line with his interest in Herodotus and antiquity, the debate was framed with reference to the cult of Mithras, the divine figure in an ancient Iranian religion that had been adopted by many in the Roman army.[72] (Jung's interest in Mithras has, in turn, been read by Richard Noll as evidence for Jung's supposed desire to found his own semi-religious cult.)

Within Mithraism, the central image in its iconography depicts the god (Mithras) in the act of sacrificing a bull (the tauroctony), while a dog and a snake reach up toward the blood, a scorpion attacks the bull's genitals, a raven flies around the scene, and corns of wheat emerge from the wounded bull. For Freud, this image symbolizes 'the killing of the animal ego by the human ego' as 'the mythological projection of repression' in which 'the sublimated part of the human being (the conscious ego) sacrifices (regretfully) its vigorous drives'; for Freud, sexuality is sacrificed for consciousness, and so that 'where id was, there shall ego be'. But for Jung, something else is going on, inasmuch as 'the symbol of fecundity, the useful and generally accepted (not censored) *alter ego* of Mithras (the bull) is slain by another sexual symbol'; for Jung, sexuality is sacrificing itself, but why? Jung sees something different, something darker going on, inasmuch as 'the self-sacrifice is voluntary and involuntary at once', and 'there is an evil necessity in it'.[73] There is, he argues, 'a conflict at the heart of sexuality itself', and the resolution of this conflict leads to an increase in abundance, in fruitfulness, in life.[74]

The structure of Jung's argumentation owes much to Nietzsche, and a link with Nietzsche's thinking can be found in an important passage in *On the Genealogy of Morals* (1887). Here Nietzsche undertakes to investigate what he calls the ascetic ideal. 'Such a self-contradiction as the ascetic appears to represent, "life *against* life", is . . . a simple absurdity', he writes, but only apparently so, for 'the ascetic ideal springs from the protective instinct of a degenerating life' or, in other words, 'the ascetic ideal is an artifice for the *preservation* of life'.[75] In an earlier work, *Thus Spoke Zarathustra* (1882–4), where the principle of the will-to-power is announced, Zarathustra creeps into 'the very heart of Life, and into the very roots of her heart', and Life herself tells him a secret: '"Behold," she said, "I am that which must always over-come itself ."'[76] One could well see in Nietzsche's interest in asceticism as a form of the will-to-power a radical extension of a complex and controversial notion found in Goethe, *Entsagung*: usually translated as 'renunciation' or 'resignation', but concep-tually related to the idea of self-sacrifice with an aim of greater fruitfulness.

In the Avesta, the main collection of the sacred texts of Zoroastrianism, the benevolent divinity of rainfall and fertility, Tishtrya, engages in a cosmic struggle with Apaosha, a drought-bringing daimon. In one of the hymns known as the Yashts, Tishtrya and Apaosha are presented as two mighty horses, one white and one black, who fight each other for three days and three nights. Apaosha wins, but Tishtrya appeals to Ahura Mazda, the supreme god, who sacrifices himself to Tishtrya, reinvigorating him so that he can finally triumph over Apoasha, vanquishing drought and restoring refreshing rain and fruitfulness to the earth. In his letter to Freud, Jung sees in this myth a representation of 'active libido' and 'resistant (incestuous) libido', and in turn a symbol of 'the dual aspect of Mithras as man's active and resistant libido (bull and serpent)'.[77] Later, in *Transformations and Symbols of the Libido*, where he meditated further on these themes, Jung saw in the legend of which this hymn speaks 'how libido is opposed to libido, will against will, the discordance of primitive man with him-self, which he recognizes again in all the adversity and contrasts of external nature'.[78]

From his interpretation of the Mithras cult, Jung drew four conclusions. First, a vitalist conclusion about the conflict internal to sexuality, 'the comforting and truly dithyrambic outcome of the self-sacrifice' as meaning: 'and *yet* we shall be fruitful again'.[79] Second, a cultural-historical point, to the effect that 'the sufferings of humanity must have been immense during the various attempts at "domestication"', in line with Nietzsche's argument in *On the Genealogy of Morals* (Part Two, §16). Third, an astonishing argument about the superiority of Mithraism over Christianity – 'in the Christ myth everything goes awry in the end: here no garlic sprouts from the bull's nostrils, no grain from his tail' – and an apologia for Emperor Julian the Apostate's attempt to replace Christianity with Mithraism.[80] And finally, an overwhelming conviction that there are deep psychological forces impelling us towards culture, as the adaptation of the Mithraic myth to the calendar reveals:

The *crab* that pinches the bull's testicles is the *scorpion* of the autumnal equinox, depriving the bull of its fruitfulness. The *bird* depicted on some of the monuments is the raven, messenger of the gods, which brings Mithras the command for self-sacrifice; the daimonion that stands warningly at man's side in his attempt at self-subjugation, in other words the *force compelling him towards culture*.[81]

Ultimately, what Mithras himself represents is 'the prototype of a hero who understands how to accomplish of his own free will what the repression is after', namely, 'temporary or permanent renunciation of fruitfulness . . . in order to realize the ethical ideal of the subjugation of instinct'.[82]

Gradually Jung found himself moving further and further away from Freud, who in turn must have become increasingly alarmed about the ideas proposed by his 'crown prince' and successor-to-be. As one would expect, dreams and parapraxes (slips-of-the-tongue

Left to right: Freud, A. A. Brill, Ernest Jones, G. Stanley Hall, Sándor Ferenczi and Jung at Clark University, Worcester, Massachusetts, 1909.

or *Ausrutscher*) accompanied their gradual intellectual drift apart. While waiting for the ship in Bremen that would take them over to America in September 1909, Jung began talking about the 'peat bog corpses' that could be found in parts of Northern Germany and Denmark, the bodies of prehistoric men who had drowned or been buried in the soft soil of that region.[83] 'Why are you so concerned with these corpses?', Freud asked, and in the course of one conversation Freud fainted.[84] Three years later, during the 1912 psychoanalytic congress held in Munich, Jung defended Amenhotep IV or Akhenaten, the pharoah who had tried to steer Egyptian religion away from polytheism by installing a cult of the sun (or Aten). As he did so, Freud suddenly fainted, whereupon Jung picked him up and carried him to the room next door and he laid him on a sofa. As Jung was carrying him, Freud half came to: *Memories, Dreams, Reflections* records that Jung would 'never forget the look' Freud gave him, while Ernest Jones's biography of Freud notes that on this (or a similar) occasion his first words when he revived fully were: 'How sweet it must be to die'.[85]

Finally, after Jung had told Freud on 25 February 1912 about his own *katabasis* (or 'descent to the underworld') – 'So what is keeping me hidden is the κατάβασις to the realm of the Mothers, where, as we know, Theseus and Peirithoos remained stuck, grown fast to the rocks. But in time I shall come up again' – and begged him to remain patient: 'So please do forebear with me a while longer. I shall bring all sorts of wonderful things with me *ad majorem gloriam* ψα'. When he did return it was (in a letter of 3 March 1912) to cite Nietzsche (or rather, given the context, practically to throw the quotation in Freud's face): 'Let Zarathustra speak for me: "One repays a teacher badly if one remains a pupil"'.[86] In the end Jung took offence when Freud made a trip to Switzerland to visit the analyst Ludwig Binswanger in Kreuzlingen (in the canton of Thurgau), but did not call in on Jung (in Küsnacht, near Zurich, some 40 km away). 'I understand the gesture of Kreuzlingen', he told Freud.[87] (What Jung didn't know was that Freud's visit was motivated by the fact that Binswanger was about to undergo an operation for cancer.) Thereafter relations between Jung and Freud were distinctly formal, sometimes frosty. In 1911–12 Jung published *Transformations and Symbols of the Libido*, first as two articles in the *Jahrbuch für psychoanalytische und psychopathologische Forschungen*, then as a book; Freud responded indirectly in 1913 in *Totem and Taboo*, and directly in 1914 in 'On the History of the Psychoanalytic Movement'.

In this latter work, Freud lambasted Jungian psychology for having abandoned the sexual theory of the libido: 'For sexual libido an abstract concept has been substituted, of which one may safely say that it remains mystifying and incomprehensible to wise men and fools alike'.[88] Along with the sexual theory of the libido, Freud wrote, Jung regarded the incest complex as 'merely "symbolic"'.[89] (Of course, for Jung it was precisely the symbolic dimension that mattered: there was no 'merely' about it.) In other words, Jung (like Adler) had tried to create 'a new religio-ethical system', which was bound to reinterpret, distort or jettison what Freud called 'the factual findings of analysis'.[90] The Jungian school, Freud insisted, was based on nothing less than a fundamental misunderstanding: 'The truth is that these people have picked out a few cultural over-tones from the symphony of life and have once more failed to hear the mighty and primordial melody of the instincts'.[91]

In recent years it has been suggested that it is 'a Freudocentric legend' to view Freud and psychoanalysis as the 'principal source' for Jung's work, leading to 'the complete mislocation of his work in the intellectual history of the twentieth century'.[92] Yet in a letter to Edith Schröder of 1957, Jung acknowledged Freud's significance as 'a cultural critic and psychological pioneer', adding: 'Without Freud's "psychoanalysis" I wouldn't have had a clue'.[93]

The Red Book

According to *Memories, Dreams, Reflections*, the parting of ways with Freud resulted in 'a period of inner uncertainty' for Jung.[94] That is a considerable understatement. To understand Jung's predicament, one must reflect, as *Memories, Dreams, Reflections* itself does, on his achievements up to that point; and on those achievements that still lay ahead of him. On the one hand, Jung believed that he now possessed 'a key to mythology' that would enable him to unlock 'all the gates of the unconscious psyche'.[95] On the other, however, something within him whispered the question: why *should* one unlock all the gates of the psyche? Or in other words: Jung may have written about the myths of *the past*, but what about the myths of *the present*? In the present, do we still have a collective myth? And, if not, then did Jung himself have a myth? Or in which myth did *he* live? As *Memories, Dreams, Reflections* puts it, at this point Jung's thinking simply came to a stop; he had reached a dead end.

From Freud, and from his own experiences with patients in the Burghölzli, Jung knew he should pay attention to his dreams. But what was he to make of three of these in particular? First, around Christmas 1912 he had dreamed he was in a magnificent Italian loggia, sitting on a splendid gold Renaissance chair. Sitting with his children (Franz, Gret and Marianne) at a bright green emerald table, he suddenly saw a small white bird descend and promptly turn into a little girl, who ran off into the castle with the others. Soon the girl returned and tenderly embraced him; turning back into the dove, she spoke to Jung: 'Only in the first hours of the night can I turn myself into a human, while the male dove is busy with the twelve dead.' And flew off.[96] Second, he dreamed he was in a place like Les Alyscamps, the ancient Roman necropolis just outside Arles in France. Amid the ancient sarcophagi, Jung saw a line of tombs on which lay a series of dead men, progressing back through time from a gentleman of the 1830s, then someone from the previous century, and so on down to a twelfth-century crusader knight in chain mail. Spooky enough, but even spookier was that, as Jung passed down the row, the dead men came alive! As Jung looked on, the dead began to unclasp their hands, and even to the left of the crusader knight a finger was beginning to stir.[97] Third came a dream where Jung is in Austria: bright sunshine shines down on two figures, an old Austrian customs guard and a medieval knight, bearing a Maltese Cross on his back. Both men are dead and yet they are both walking around at midday, while inside his head Jung hears a voice: 'It is all empty and disgusting'.[98]

Well, what was Jung supposed to make of these? As far as the first was concerned, Jung initially believed – or so he told his friend E. A. Bennet – that the twelve dead men referred to the twelve days of Christmas, 'for that is the dark time of the year, when traditionally

Hermes Trismegistus, illustration from Daniel Stolz von Stolzenberg's
Viridarium Chymicum (1624).

witches are about', and 'to say "before Christmas" is to say "before
the sun lives again", for Christmas Day is at the turning point of
the year when the sun's birth was celebrated in the Mithraic religion'.[99] (Jung was later to link the white bird of his dream with the
god Hermes and thus with 'the spiritual element', while the green
table represented the 'emerald tablet', or the *Tabula smaragdina*, of
Hermes Trismegistus. So on this account the dream foreshadowed
his interest in alchemy.[100]) As far as the first and second were concerned, they both featured the same fantasy: that something dead
was present, but this something was also still alive.[101] (Later, in
1925, Jung was to focus on the contrast in the third dream between
the Austrian figure, as a symbol of Freudian psychoanalysis, and
something older and other: the crusader, from the age of the late
thirteenth- and early fourteenth-century German mystic Meister
Eckhart, from 'the time of the culture of the knights', that is, a time

'when many ideas blossomed, only to be killed again, but they are coming to life again now'.[102])

Something dead . . . that was really alive . . . In Freud's writings, Jung had already encountered the view that the unconscious contains the vestiges of archaic experience.[103] But these dreams were telling him (or so he was subsequently to interpret them) something different: that the past is not dead, but is part of the living psyche.[104] Jung came to this conclusion on the basis of three things: his own dreams, his own research into psychiatry and, above all, his own direct experiences of the unconscious (as informed by his thinking and reading).

Those experiences now came to take two forms. First, when only around 37 or 38 years old Jung began to withdraw from public professional life. In 1913 he resigned his lectureship at Zurich University and in 1914 he resigned as president of the International Psychoanalytic Association. Recalling his games as a ten- or eleven-year-old child – building houses and castles from stones – Jung took the biblical injunction 'unless ye become as little children' quite literally, and on the shore of Lake Zurich by his house he began collecting stones and making constructions with them: some cottages, a castle, a whole village, in fact, with a church or, more precisely, a square building with a hexagonal drum on top and a dome. But where would he find the altar? One day, or so *Memories, Dreams, Reflections* records, he came across a red stone in a pyramid shape, about an inch and a half tall. Jung knew that, polished into this shape by the action of the water, the stone was in one respect 'a pure product of chance'.[105] In other respects, however, Jung at once knew what he had found: an altar! He carefully placed it under the dome, and as he did so, he recalled the subterranean phallus of his childhood dream, a connection that gave him 'a feeling of satisfaction'.[106] But was part of the satisfaction derived not merely from connecting with his own childhood, but from connecting with the childhood of Johann Wolfgang Goethe? After all, in one of the most famous passages of *Dichtung und Wahrheit*, Goethe brought the first book to a close with an account of how, as a seven-year-old child, he built an altar to the God of Nature: 'the God who is in direct contact with nature, who acknowledges and loves it as His work'.[107]

Jung believed that, as *Memories, Dreams, Reflections* puts it, he had 'no choice but to return to [his childhood] and take up once more that child's life with his childish games'.[108] He goes so far as to describe this moment as 'a turning point' or *ein Wendepunkt* in his fate, achieved only after 'the most extreme resignation' and as 'the painful experience of humiliation', for what could be more ridiculous and at the same time more serious than the realization that he could really do nothing other than play?[109]

So for Jung, as an adult, to re-establish contact with his earlier childhood life when he was eleven years old, he had to return to the games he had once played at that time. Now, after lunch, he would build with the stones until his patients arrived; and if they left early enough, he went back to playing with the stones. In the course of this play activity he found that his thoughts became clearer and that he was able to 'grasp the fantasies' he could 'intuitively feel' within him.[110] Subsequently, a number of psychologists and psychotherapists, including Donald Winnicott (1876–1971) and Jean Piaget (1896–1980), have emphasized the therapeutic uses of play. In particular, Dora Kalff (1904–1990), founder of the International Society for Sandplay Therapy, devised a technique of sandplay based on Jungian principles, which has become an expanding area of Jungian therapeutic practice.[111]

But one can also see in this development how Jung enacts the claim made by the German poet, playwright and aesthetic philosopher Friedrich Schiller (1759–1805) in his treatise *On the Aesthetic Education of Humankind* (1795), to the effect that 'the human being only plays when he or she is in the fullest sense of the word a human being, and a human being is only fully one when he or she plays'.[112]

Second, from the autumn of 1913 through to the spring and summer of 1914 Jung experienced (or so we are told) a startling sequence of vivid dreams and visions. In October 1913, in the middle of a train journey from Zurich to Schaffhausen, he was suddenly overcome by a vision of a monstrous flood destroying Europe and, particularly, Switzerland: giant waves swirled with 'the floating rubble of civilization' and thousands of drowned people, until the whole sea turned to blood.[113] (As Jung later recalled, at one point the train went through a tunnel and he entirely lost consciousness of time and place, awakening an hour later to hear the conductor announcing their arrival in Schaffhausen.[114]) It is no exaggeration to describe this vision as apocalyptic, and it is no wonder Jung was disturbed by it, especially when, two weeks later, the vision was repeated and he heard the words: 'Look at it, this is all real and it will take place; about that there is no doubt.'[115]

Then, in a thrice-repeated dream in April, May and June 1914, Jung saw an icy wave of Arctic air descend across western Europe, freezing the water, killing all plants with its frost, and leaving the entire region deserted by human beings.[116] Here the sequence seems the reverse of his earlier dreams, where *something dead* was really *something coming alive again*; on the occasion of this dream, however, something happened that has led the psychoanalyst John Gedo and the sociologist Peter Homans to argue that Jung saw himself as a prophetic figure: in the midst of the terrible chill, a solitary leaf-bearing but fruitless tree remains – 'my tree of life', Jung remarks – whose leaves are transformed by the effects of the frost into sweet grapes full of healing juices, grapes which Jung plucks and distributes to a large, waiting crowd.[117] If, in his letter to Freud, Jung had expressed the wish to 'transform Christ back into the soothsaying god of the vine, which he was', in this dream Jung himself actually *becomes* the divine Dionysos.[118]

Understandably, Jung feared that he was menaced by a psychosis and he interpreted the dreams as pointing to a revolution going on inside himself: the overthrow of his sanity, presumably. In the summer of 1914 Jung undertook a short lecture tour of the UK, giving a paper on 24 July 1924 to the Psycho-Medical Society in London with the title 'On Psychological Understanding' (subsequently published in the *Journal of Abnormal Psychology*), before hightailing it to Aberdeen and giving a paper on 28 July 1924 on 'The Importance of the Unconscious in Psychopathology' to a meeting of the British Medical Association in that city. The irony could not have been greater: here was Jung, preparing to give a lecture on schizophrenia, yet fearing that he himself was soon to be a fit subject for psychopathology. 'I kept saying to myself: "I'll be speaking about myself! Very likely I'll go mad after reading out this paper"', he later recalled.[119]

So when, after the assassination of Archduke Franz Ferdinand of Austria in Sarajevo on 28 June 1914, Austria–Hungary declared war on Serbia on 28 July, the German Empire began to mobilize on 30 July, then declared war on Russia on 1 August, and Great Britain declared war on Germany on 4 August, Jung's response was an odd one. When he read in the newspapers that war had broken out, 'nobody' (he recalled) 'was happier than I', because it became clear to him that his dreams *had* been prophetic, and that he was *not* threatened by schizophrenia or psychosis.[120]

Perhaps it is instructive to compare Jung's reaction to news of the war with those of, say, Franz Kafka or Thomas Mann. In his famous diary entry of 2 August 1914, Kafka recorded events as follows: 'Germany has declared war on Russia. In the afternoon, swimming lessons'; in his letter to his brother Heinrich, on 3 August 1914, when France had declared war on Germany, Thomas Mann wrote 'that one should be happy to be allowed to experience such great things', and promptly penned his *Thoughts during War*: 'War! What we experienced was purification, liberation, and a terrible hope'.[121] Similarly ecstatic responses came from such other leading academics and intellectuals as Max Weber, Werner Sombart, Georg Simmel, Ernst

Toller, Hermann Bahr, Ernst Troeltsch, Friedrich Meinecke and Friedrich Naumann.[122] (And lest one suspect it was the Germans alone who were bellicose, in France the enthusiasm for the Great War of the philosopher Henri Bergson displays a similar contour.)

Jung, however, had specific reasons for being pleased: 'I understood', he later recollected, 'that my dreams and my visions came to me from the subsoil of my collective unconscious', and so 'what remained for me to do now was to deepen and validate this discovery': a process that was to last for the next 40 years (and then another ten, for Jung would continue to live and work for almost a decade after he made this statement).[123] But Jung's method of deepening and validating his discovery was to be a highly unusual and very private, even secret, one.

For after the war had broken out, the visions did not cease: on the contrary, *Memories, Dreams, Reflections* speaks of the release of 'an incessant stream of fantasies' and of 'one thunderstorm follow[ing] another', experiences of a kind that had shattered the likes of Hölderlin and Nietzsche (to whom Jung, as we have seen, already felt uncomfortably similar).[124] During the season of Advent in 1913 (in fact, on 12 December 1913, if *Memories, Dreams, Reflections* is to be believed) Jung resolved upon 'the decisive step'. Sitting at his desk, thinking over his fears about whether and how to engage with these fantasies, he suddenly came to a decision: and 'then I let myself drop'.[125]

What this exactly means is hard to say, and how we should interpret what resulted from what ensued is equally controversial. According to *Memories, Dreams, Reflections*, and also to his 1925 seminar on Analytical Psychology, Jung embarked on a remarkable sequence of visions, which he transcribed into a set of small, black notebooks. He proceeded to work up their contents into an elaborated, 'aestheticized' form.[126] In the final stages of this complex process of transcription and elaboration, the visions were transferred, presumably by Jung, onto a series of parchment pages, inserted into a large folio volume of some 600 pages, bound in red leather, on the spine of which the title *Liber Novus* was inscribed. And so, in the immediate run-up to and aftermath of the outbreak of the war, but even when it was over, and for many years afterwards, Jung continued his work on what became known as the Red Book.

For many years, while the existence of the Red Book was acknowledged, only a very restricted number of people were invited to view it, even during Jung's lifetime, and following his death his heirs decided to shut the book away from prying eyes in a Zurich bank vault. While extracts did appear in a few places, it was not until 2010 that the Red Book was finally published, in a luxurious facsimile edition with copious editorial notes by Sonu Shamdasani. Within the confines of our brief study, it is impossible to do more than offer the briefest of outlines of its contents.[127]

The Red Book consists of three sections: 'Liber Primus', 'Liber Secundus' and a third section somewhat misleadingly translated as 'Scrutinies' (which detracts from the connotations in the original German, *Prüfungen*, of 'examinations' and 'trials'). Overall, the startling visual effects of the Red Book – both artistic and literary – confirm the truth of Hegel's assertion in his 'Jenaer Realphilosophie' that:

> the human being is this night, this empty nothing, that contains everything in its simplicity – an unending wealth of many representations, images, of which none belongs to him – or which are not present. This night, this interior of nature, that exists here – pure self – in phantasmagorical representations, is night all around it, in which here shoots a bloody head – there another white ghastly apparition, suddenly here before it, and just so disappears. One catches sight of this night when one looks human beings in the eye – into a night that becomes awful.[128]

There is indeed something truly aw(e)ful about Jung's Red Book.

If it is hard adequately to summarize the contents of the Red Book, it is even harder to give a succinct interpretation of their meaning or significance. Suffice it to say, however, that major significance accrues to the figure of Philemon, a pagan figure imbued with an Egypto-Hellenic atmosphere tinged with Gnosticism.[129] Thanks to Philemon, and the other figures in his fantasies (Elijah, Salome), Jung gained 'the crucial insight' that 'there are things in the psyche that I do not produce, but which produce themselves and have their own life'.[130] In other words, the psyche is something autonomous. In particular, Philemon represented 'a force which was not me'; thanks to him, Jung came to learn of 'psychic objectivity, the reality of the psyche [*die "Wirklichkeit der Seele"*]'; or, psychologically, Philemon represented 'superior insight'.[131] Many years later, in his correspondence with Father Victor White, Jung wrote that he had once had 'a real ghost-ly guru', describing it as 'a long and – I am afraid – exceedingly strange story', and *Memories, Dreams, Reflections* takes a similar view of Philemon as being what, in the Vedic tradition of India, is called a guru.[132]

However, two observations can be made that might help contextualize what Jung was undertaking in his Red Book. First, initially it is strange to hear of Jung talking with the figures of his imagination. But in *Dichtung und Wahrheit*, Goethe writes at length of his 'peculiar habit', as he calls it, of 'recasting even soliloquy as dialogue' and 'transform[ing] even solitary thinking into social conversation'.[133] How this worked in practice is set out by Goethe (writing about himself in the third person) in considerable detail as follows:

When he found himself alone, he would summon up in spirit some person of his acquaintance. He would ask this person to be seated, pace up and down by him, stand in front of him, and discuss whatever subject he had in mind. The person would occasionally answer him and indicate, with the customary gestures, his agreement or disagreement; and everyone has a particular way of doing this. Then the speaker would continue, and expand on whatever seemed to please his guest; or he would qualify what the latter disapproved of, and define it more clearly, and even finally be willing to abandon his thesis.[134]

Furthermore, there exists anecdotal evidence to suggest that Goethe was by no means exaggerating in this account. According to one source, when a visitor to Goethe's house in Weimar in 1813 heard a conversation going on, and asked whether Herr Geheimrat Goethe already had company, he was told by a servant: 'He's talking to himself'.[135] Could Jung's dialogues with his soul, with Elijah and Salome, and with Philemon, be seen as an extension of this Goethean dialogue with the figures of *his* imagination, as a kind of psychological equivalent of Goethe's literary version of an *exercice spirituel*? After all, further on in *Dichtung und Wahrheit* Goethe explains another aspect of what he calls his 'productive talent':

What I perceived while awake in the daytime, often developed into orderly dreams at night, and when I opened my eyes I would see either an amazing new whole or part for something already begun . . . As I reflected on this natural gift and saw that it was my very own possession, which no outside influence could either facilitate or hinder, I was glad to make it the philosophical basis for my whole existence.[136]

In an almost proto-Jungian fashion, this 'idea' transformed itself for Goethe into an 'image', which had a mythological quality to it: 'the old mythological figure of Prometheus'.[137] Understanding how, 'in order to produce something of significance', one 'had to isolate oneself', Goethe 'imitated Prometheus by separating [him]self from the gods', and he goes so far as to say: 'The myth of Prometheus came to life in me'.[138] Goethe's 'productive talent' might thus be seen as the forerunner of what Jung called 'active imagination'.[139]

A second contextualizing perspective is that, during the time Jung was working on his Red Book, he was also exposed once more to a major cultural influence on his life and thought: in other words, to Nietzsche. For, as Jung explained to the participants of his seminar on *Thus Spoke Zarathustra* at the session held on 21 November 1934, the time of work on the Red Book was the time of his re-engagement with Nietzsche:

> I read *Zarathustra* for the first time with consciousness in the first year of the war, in November 1914, twenty years ago; then suddenly the spirit seized me and carried me to a desert country in which I read *Zarathustra*. I did not understand really, but I made marks with my pencil at every place where I slightly stumbled . . . There are still those marks in my German edition, and invariably I have found that these places are things that grate, that don't go down really.[140]

A few months later, on 20 February 1935, Jung had this to say about his policy of annotating his copy of *Zarathustra* and the impact that reading Nietzsche had had on him:

> I read *Zarathustra* for the first time when I was only twenty-three, and then later, in the winter of 1914–1915, I studied it very carefully and made a lot of annotations. I was already interested in the concept of the self, but I was not clear how I should understand it. I made my marks, however, when I came across these passages, and they seemed very important to me.[141]

In other words, during precisely the period when Jung was working on his Red Book, he rediscovered Nietzsche: in particular, he engaged for the first time in any real depth with Nietzsche's masterpiece,

Zarathustra. So it is not surprising that in the Red Book we find numerous echoes, allusions and resonances that remind us of *Zarathustra*.[142] (Indeed, because he was so fascinated by *Zarathustra*, on one occasion Jung even went so far as to say that he 'could well have written a book "*Thus Spoke Philemon*"': and one could say that, in the Red Book, he did.) More important, it reminds us that the Red Book is not simply a direct transcription of his visions: it is a reworking, an interpretation and an 'aestheticizing elaboration' of them.

Leaving aside (for reasons of space) the complex and difficult question of whether Jung's undertaking in his Red Book was ultimately an artistic or a scientific exercise, it is surely right for *Memories, Dreams, Reflections* to describe his visionary experiences as 'the *prima materia* for a lifetime's work', and as a 'stream of lava', whose 'flames' contained a 'passion' that left his life 'reshaped and reordered': 'It was the primal material that brought this about'.[143] From now on, Jung saw his task in the following terms: 'to incorporate this incandescent material into the contemporary picture of the world'.[144] And, characteristically, this task of confronting the new with the old, the present with the past, the transitory with the eternal, is envisaged in alchemical terms, for 'the initial imaginings and dreams' were like 'the fiery liquid basalt', and 'out of these crystallized the stone that I could sculpt'.[145] This image of sculpting a stone demonstrates well how Jung stood at a crossroads between various philosophical and alchemical traditions; and how, as always, he took these traditions and reworked them for his own purposes.

5

Out with the New, in with the (Very) Old: From Psychoanalysis to Analytical Psychology

During his time at the Burghölzli (1905–9), Jung had also been appointed as a lecturer in the Medical Faculty of the University of Zurich (1905–13), but from 1909 onward he began to spend an increasing amount of time on his private practice. In 1913, the year of his break with Freud, Jung resigned his lectureship at Zurich and in 1914 he resigned as President of the International Psychoanalytic Association. Following his period of 'intensive introversion' or 'confrontation with the unconscious' (in the period from 1913 to 1919), Jung had, by the end of the 1920s, produced – in addition to a substantial number of papers on psychoanalysis and on experiments (conducted with Ludwig Binswanger) on word association – two major works. One of these, the Red Book, was unpublished (and, by its very nature, virtually unpublishable), and so it would remain for decades to come. The other was a monograph based on two major essays, originally published in volumes III (1911) and IV (1912) of the *Jahrbuch für psychoanalytische und psychopathologische Forschungen*, edited by Eugen Bleuler and Freud. These were published in book form in 1912 as *Transformations and Symbols of the Libido*.

The book was translated into English by Beatrice M. Hinkle (see below) and published in 1916 under the title *Psychology of the Unconscious*, retaining as a subtitle the book's original German title: 'A Study of the Transformations and Symbolisms of the Libido: A Contribution to the History of the Evolution of Thought'.

The book's English title can cause confusion, because a short study published by Jung in 1917 (and subsequently reissued and revised in 1918, 1926, 1937 and 1943) is entitled 'On the Psychology of the Unconscious', but this is a very different kind of work: short, schematic, programmatic. Furthermore, in 1951 Jung undertook a major revision of *Transformations and Symbols of the Libido* and republished it under the title *Symbols of Transformation* (1952). A comparison of the 1911–12 and 1952 editions of this work is instructive, revealing both the shifts in emphasis as well as the underlying continuity in Jung's thought. (The German original was reprinted in a handy paperback edition in 1991, and the English translation was reprinted in the same year as a supplementary volume to the *Collected Works* of Jung.) But what is *Transformations and Symbols of the Libido* about?

In his correspondence with Freud, Jung had shared his exploration of the culture of antiquity, but he had also confessed his concern that all he could offer was 'banalities'.[1] Was the fruit of his research into Herodotus, Friedrich Creuzer and Erwin Rohde nothing more than 'banalities or hieroglyphics'?[2] From its very first, triumphant sentences, however, *Transformations and Symbols of the Libido* exudes an exuberance and confidence that confirms the sense that its author has been on a journey and safely reached his final destination.[3]

Whereas Freud's own dreams had formed the central element of *The Interpretation of Dreams*, Jung's *Transformations and Symbols of the Libido* was presented as a detailed commentary on the visions, originally published in 1906 by Théodore Flournoy (1854–1920), of a female patient called Frank Miller.[4] Yet Jung's work turns out also to represent a return to *Faust*, as is signalled in the first chapter, when he posits the view that 'there must be typical myths which are really instruments of a folk-psychological complex treatment', and cites Jacob Burckhardt in support of this insight. Burckhardt, Jung suggested, seemed to have 'suspected' or 'intuited' (*geahnt*) a similar view when he said 'that every Greek of the classical era carried in himself a fragment of Oedipus, just as every German carries a fragment of Faust'.[5] And, in the course of the work, Jung moves away from Oedipus and towards Faust; that is to say, away from the biological mother as the object of incestual desire and towards the Faustian Mothers as the symbol of a spiritual desire for rebirth. Despite the inaccuracies in her nevertheless serviceable translation, Beatrice Hinkle (1874–1953), a pioneering feminist, psychoanalyst and writer, seems to have understood what Jung was proposing when she wrote: 'That humanity is seeking a new message, a new light upon the meaning of life, and something tangible, as it were, with which it can work towards a larger understanding of itself and its relation to the universe, is a fact I think none will gainsay', and hence it seemed to her 'particularly timely' to introduce Jung's 'remarkable book' to 'the English-speaking world'.[6]

In *Symbols and Transformations of the Libido* Jung undertook an analysis of Miller's dreams, while in his Red Book he engaged with his own visionary experiences, elaborating and aestheticizing them into a 'cathedral for his soul'. Emerging towards the end of the decade from what *Memories, Dreams, Reflections* euphemistically refers to as his 'encounter with the unconscious' (or, in German, his *Auseinadersetzung mit dem Unbewussten*), Jung had now 'freed' himself from Freud and established a psychological system that, while having many points in common with Freudian psychoanalysis, was nevertheless distinctive in several respects, especially in its notions of the archetypes and the collective unconscious.

But first, a note on the term 'analytical psychology' that is associated with the psychological system he developed. As we have seen, initially Jung was happy to use Freud's term 'psychoanalysis', adopting its inventor's habit of referring to it by means of the Greek letters Ψ and A. But he came to prefer the term 'Zurich School' (as opposed to the 'Vienna School'), until in 1914 he used the phrase 'prospective psychology'; in the 1930s he renamed it 'complex psychology'.[7] The reasons for the term 'analytical psychology' are clear: rhetorically, it sounds similar to psychoanalysis, while yet being obviously distinct. But the emphasis on *analysis* obscures Jung's interest, first expressed in a letter to Freud of 2–12 April 1909, in the existence of what he termed 'some quite special complex, a universal one having to do with the prospective tendencies in humankind'. Drawing on ideas that have been shown to derive from the German Romantic novelist, E.T.A. Hoffmann (1776–1822), Jung went on to develop the notion of a psychology that does not just look back to the past, but also looks forward to the future. 'If there is a "psychoanalysis"', he argued, 'there must also be a "psychosynthesis" which creates future events according to the same laws'.[8]

This notion of a distinction between (psycho)analysis and (psycho)synthesis was to prove fundamental for Jung's views on dream interpretation (and, later, was to be developed by the Swiss psychotherapist Hans Trüb, 1889–1949, as well as the Italian psychiatrist Roberto Assagioli, 1888–1974).[9] Sonu Shamdasani has gone so far as to claim that, for Jung, 'psychology constituted the fundamental scientific discipline, upon which other disciplines should henceforth be based', because in his view it was 'the only discipline which could grasp the subjective factor that underlay other sciences'; hence, as Shamdasani sees it, 'the establishment of complex psychology was to enable the reformulation of the humanities and revitalize contemporary religions', with the result, however, that 'the history of Jungian psychology has in part consisted in a radical and unacknowledged diminution of Jung's goal'.[10]

A number of programmatic statements from Jung's later papers help clarify his early texts and later works alike. In 1927 Jung delivered a lecture in Karlsruhe that was subsequently published as 'Analytical Psychology and "Weltanschauung"'. Here he diagnosed modernity as an isolation (or sense of isolation) from nature, and presented analytical psychology as 'a reaction against an exaggerated rationalization of consciousness', and as a means of liberation from this alienation: 'Analytical psychology seeks to break through these walls, by digging up again the fantasy-images of the unconscious which the rational understanding has rejected'.[11] According to Jung, these images are 'part of the *nature in us*, which apparently lies buried in our past and against which we have barricaded ourselves behind the walls of *ratio*', and 'here arises the conflict with nature, which analytical psychology tries to resolve . . . by . . . enriching our consciousness with knowledge of the natural spirit'.[12]

In 1932, in a lecture to the Alsatian Pastoral Conference in Strasbourg, published as 'Psychotherapists or the Clergy', Jung spoke of 'the opening up of the unconscious' as 'the outbreak [*Ausbruch*] of great spiritual suffering', and related this experience to the First World War: 'Just such a breach [*Durchbruch*] was the World War, which showed as could nothing else how thin the separating wall is that keeps an ordered world apart from ever lurking chaos'.[13] His own therapy, Jung explains in this lecture, is intended to assist and accompany his patient through the experience when – 'it is like an inspired moment' – 'something Other rises up from the dark realm of the psyche [*Seele*] and confronts him'.[14] This moment, Jung assured his audience, marks 'the beginning of the cure', even though 'this spontaneous activity of the psyche often becomes intense to the point where an inner voice or visionary images are perceived': phenomena described as 'a true primordial experience of the spirit'.[15] Clearly the Red Book was just one such instance of the primordial experience of *Geist*, as well as an 'aesthetic elaboration' of that experience (and hence a work of art).

It is this essentially *cultural* dimension to Jung's project that emerges also from a famous dream, related in *Memories, Dreams, Reflections*, where it is dated to the time of Freud's and Jung's trip to the United States in 1909 and described as 'a kind of prelude' to

Transformations and Symbols of the Libido.[16] More specifically, it is said to have led Jung to the concept of the collective unconscious:

> I was in a house . . . in the upper storey . . . Descending the stairs, I reached the ground floor. There everything was much older . . . I discovered a stone doorway that led down to the cellar. Descending again, I found myself in a beautifully vaulted room which looked exceedingly ancient . . . the walls dated from Roman times . . . Again I saw a stairway of narrow stone steps leading down into the depths . . . Thick dust lay on the floor and . . . remains of a primitive culture [including] two human skulls, obviously very old.[17]

Recent commentators have traced the changes in Jung's account of this dream between 1925 and 1961, and uncovered its possible sources in texts written by Josef Breuer (1842–1925), an Austrian physician who was one of Freud's earliest collaborators, and by Edouard Claparède (1873–1940), a Swiss neurologist and child psychologist.[18] (In essence, Jung's dream is an example of cryptomnesia, much as an episode from Nietzsche's *Thus Spoke Zarathustra* had been, as Jung himself revealed.[19]) But Jung's dream also gives rise to a common topos in psychoanalytic literature, in which Freud himself, as late as 1930, was prepared to participate. In his *Civilization and its Discontents*, Freud discusses in considerable detail the various archaeological layers in a city like Rome: from Renaissance to early Christian, back to late Imperial, and beyond that to the earliest settlement on the Palatine. Freud proposes the following 'thought experiment': suppose Rome is 'not a human habitation' but 'a psychical entity' with 'a similarly long and copious past'; then we would be able to see all these different layers, not diachronically, but synchronically:

On the Piazza of the Pantheon we should find not only the Pantheon of today, as it was bequeathed to us by Hadrian, but, on the same site, the original edifice erected by Agrippa; indeed, the same piece of ground would be supporting the church of Santa Maria sopra Minerva and the ancient temple over which it was built.[20]

(A similar example that Freud could have mentioned, and that might have appealed to Jung, is the basilica of San Clemente in Rome, a site on which a medieval building stands on top of a fourth-century building, converted out of a nobleman's house whose basement had once served as a mithraeum.)

For Freud, this metaphor served to demonstrate how 'what is primitive is so commonly preserved alongside the transformed version which has arisen from it', or in other words that 'in mental life nothing which has been once formed can perish': for Freud as much a source of regret as a simple fact of life, but for Jung a cause for great rejoicing.[21] Yet in his foundational work, *The Interpretation of Dreams*, we find Freud investigating mythological motifs in dreams with exactly the same enthusiasm that is usually associated with Jung. In the case of 'a fourteen-year-old boy suffering from *tic convulsif*, hysterical vomiting, headaches, etc.', for instance, Freud invites the boy to close his eyes and tell him what pictures he sees. The boy replies:

[Before going to Freud] he had been playing at draughts with his uncle and saw the board in front of him. He thought of various positions, favourable or unfavourable, and of moves that one must not make. He then saw a dagger lying on the board – an object that belonged to his father but which his imagination placed on the board. Then there was a sickle lying on the board and next a scythe. And there now appeared a picture of an old peasant mowing the grass in front of the patient's distant home with a scythe.[22]

In the light of the boy's 'unhappy family situation', and in particular his father's divorce from his mother, 'a tender and affectionate woman', and her replacement by his father's new wife, 'a young woman . . . who was to be the boy's new mother', Freud interpreted what had been pictured in the boy's mind as 'a recollection from mythology'. Specifically, drawing on material from Homer and from Hesiod (in a way of which Jung himself would have been proud), Freud reads the dream as follows:

> The sickle was the one with which Zeus castrated his father; the scythe and the picture of the old peasant represented Kronos, the violent old man who devoured his children and on whom Zeus took such unfilial vengeance. His father's marriage gave the boy an opportunity of repaying the reproaches and threats which he had heard from his father long before because he had played with his genitals. (Cf. the playing at draughts; the forbidden moves; the dagger which could be used to kill.) In this case long-repressed memories and derivatives from them which had remained unconscious slipped into consciousness by a roundabout path in the form of apparently meaningless pictures.[23]

No wonder, then, that in 'The Question of Lay-Analysis' (1926), Freud was able to write (in connection with the same story of Kronos emasculating his father Uranus, and in turn being emasculated by his own son Zeus): 'And here again mythology may give you courage to believe psycho-analysis'.[24]

Jung would push this argument one stage further, declaring that analytical psychology was itself a new form of mythology, and that this was a good thing. For psychology, in his view, 'translates the archaic speech of myth into a modern mythologem – not yet, of course, recognized as such – which constitutes one element of the myth "science"'.[25] Because 'even the best attempts at explanation are only more or less successful translations into another metaphorical language' (and because, indeed, 'language itself is only an image'), all that we can do is 'to dream the myth onwards and give it a modern dress'.[26] This is why, in the language of *Memories, Dreams, Reflections*, 'myth is more individual and expresses life more precisely than does science', and so what matters is 'whether what I tell is *my* fable, *my* truth'.[27] In other words, analytical psychology is, *qua* myth, 'poetry', while it is also, *qua* science, 'truth'. 'Poetry' and 'truth': *Dichtung und Wahrheit*.

Psychological Types

'Plato and Aristotle! These are not merely two systems, they are types of two distinct human natures.' With this quotation from Heinrich Heine's *On the History of Religion and Philosophy in Germany* (1834–5) Jung opens his study of psychological types, published in 1921.[28] A glance at the table of contents confirms the considerable ambition and vast scope of Jung's work. From psychology in the classical age (the Gnostics, Tertullian, Origen) and the theological disputes of the early Church to the dispute over transubstantiation, nominalism and realism (or the problem of universals), and the controversy between Luther and Zwingli (chapter One); from Schiller's *On the Aesthetic Education of Humankind in a Series of Letters* (1795) and *On the Naïve and Sentimental in Literature* (1796) (chapter Two) to the Apollonian and the Dionysian in Nietzsche's *The Birth of Tragedy* (1872) (chapter Three); from the typology of John Furneaux Jordan (1830–1911) in his *Character as Seen in Body and Parentage* (1890; 3rd edn, 1896) (chapter Four) to the type problem in poetry (with reference to Carl Spitteler, Goethe, the Brahmanic conception of the uniting symbol, and to the relativity of the God-concept in the German medieval mystic Meister Eckhart) (chapter Five), from the type problem in psychopathology and in aesthetics (chapters

Six and Seven) to the type problem in modern philosophy (with reference to the American Pragmatic philosopher William James) and in biography (chapters Eight and Nine): all human life is here.

And that is precisely the point. These days typology has something of a bad reputation, thanks in part to the development of Jung's ideas to create the Myers-Briggs Type Indicator, a psychometric test devised by Isabel Briggs Myers (1897–1980) and used as a management tool in industrial, commercial and military contexts. Typology is seen as an approach that categorizes, delimits and depersonalizes, and is devoid of the aspirational, even transcendent, qualities that make other aspects of Jungian psychology so congenial to the mystical outlook or the New Age ethos. Yet, far from being a static system, Jung's typology is eminently *dynamic* in its conception of types.

In his introduction, Jung draws explicitly on Goethe's notions of systole and diastole, a view of the world as an interplay of polar forces. In psychological terms, the subject can demonstrate a movement of interest *away* from himself or herself and *toward* the object, an attitude that Jung terms 'extraversion'. Or the subject can demonstrate a movement of interest *away* from the object and *back toward* his or her own psychological processes, an attitude termed 'introversion'.[29] Correspondingly, we can understand human beings in terms of these mechanisms, 'a diastolic going out and seizing of the object' and 'a systolic concentration and detachment of energy from the object seized', whose 'rhythmic alternation' would correspond to 'the normal course of life'.[30] In reality, however, 'outer circumstances and inner disposition' tend to favour one mechanism, restricting or hindering the other, and thus giving rise to a *type*.[31]

On top of these basic attitudes or mechanisms, extraversion and introversion, Jung adds a distinction between four basic psychological functions: thinking, feeling, sensation, and intuition. The precise differences between these four functions can be hard to grasp, but Jung helps us by dividing them into two categories: rational and irrational. And he helps us even more by providing a chapter of definitions in *Psychological Types*, which serves as a basis for later dictionaries of Jungian terminology, such as *A Critical Dictionary of Jungian Analysis* (1986) or *The Handbook of Jungian Psychology: Theory, Practice and Applications* (2006). Here Jung tells us 'thinking' is the psychological function that 'brings the contents of ideation into conceptual connection with one another', distinguishing between active thinking (an act of the will) and passive thinking (a mere occurrence), equating to what, in *Transformations and Symbols of the Libido*, he had called 'directed thinking' and 'fantasy thinking' (or what he now also called 'intuitive thinking').[32] 'Feeling', by contrast, is a process that takes place between the ego and a given content, consisting essentially of a process of giving value, of accepting or rejecting ('liking' or 'disliking'). Again, Jung distinguishes between different kinds of feeling: 'concrete' or 'abstract', and although feeling as such is regarded by Jung as rational, strictly speaking only 'active, directed feeling' is rational, whereas 'passive feeling' is irrational.[33]

The irrational functions per se are sensation and intuition. According to Jung, 'sensation' is the function that 'mediates the perception of a physical stimulus' and hence is identical with perception. Unlike feeling, which assigns value, sensation – whether concrete or abstract – is not subject to rational laws, and Jung goes so far as to describe abstract sensation as 'aesthetic':

> The concrete sensation of a flower . . . conveys a perception not only of the flower as such, but also of the stem, leaves, habitat, and so on. It is also instantly mingled with feelings of pleasure or dislike which the sight of the flower evokes', or with simultaneous olfactory perceptions, or with thoughts about its botanical classication, etc. But abstract sensation immediately picks out the most salient sensuous attributes of the flower, its

brilliant redness, for instance, and makes this the sole or at least the principal content of consciousness, entirely detached from all other admixtures.[34]

For this reason, Jung notes, 'abstract sensation is found chiefly among artists'.

Finally, the trickiest function of all, 'intuition'. This function 'mediates perceptions in an *unconscious* way', constituting 'a kind of instinctive apprehension', and being either 'subjective' or 'objective', 'concrete' or 'abstract'; Jung even aligns intuition with what the Dutch Enlightenment philosopher Baruch de Spinoza (1632–1677), called *scientia intuitiva* and described as the highest form of knowledge, and with what the French vitalist philosopher Henri Bergson (1859–1941) also called 'intuition' and made his chief methodological tool of intellectual investigation.[35]

So far, so typological. But Jung makes his system dynamic by recognizing that, in practice, one function (or one set of functions) tends to dominate over the others, rendering those other functions (as he terms it) 'inferior', mixing these two basic attitudes with the four functions. As a consequence, thinking can be either extraverted or introverted, likewise feeling, and so on. (In *L'Âme et l'écriture* (1948), the Estonian-born graphologist and Jungian analyst, Ania Teillard (1889–1978), described Jung's psychological types in terms of the behaviour of guests at a dinner party: a perfect hostess (extraverted feeling), along with her husband (introverted sensation), receives a lawyer (extraverted sensation), a famous businessman (extraverted thinking) with his musician wife (introverted feeling), a distinguished scholar (introverted thinking) and his wife, a former cook (extraverted feeling). One guest – a poet (introverted intuition) – fails to arrive, because his typology has made him forget his invitation!)[36]

But this dynamic polarity is not merely internal to the individual, it applies on the intersubjective, interpersonal plane as well;

indeed, Jung places great emphasis on the significance of the *interaction* of the types. Because 'the world exists not merely in and for itself, but also as it appears to me', and because 'no two people see the same object in the same way', their interaction involves both objective and subjective factors.[37] Thus, on the intersubjective level, Jung develops a theory of gender relations based on the premise that one partner offers a form of unconscious compensation for the attitude of the consciousness of the other. For example, in the case of the male extraverted thinking type, 'the unconscious counterposition is embodied in a woman'; in the case of the male introverted thinking type, there can develop 'a vague fear of the feminine sex'; and, in the case of the female introverted feeling type, such a woman can acquire 'a mysterious power that may prove terribly fascinating to the extraverted man, for it touches his unconscious': 'this power comes from the deeply felt, unconscious images'.[38]

For those 'deeply felt, unconscious images' Jung had a particular name: the archetypes. Or rather he didn't, for in these early texts Jung did not yet speak about *der Archetyp*, but rather 'the primal image' (*das Urbild*) or 'primordial image' (*urtümliches Bild*), defining this concept in terms of both 'image' (*Bild*) and 'idea' (*Idee*).[39] In fact, as far as *Psychological Types* was concerned, the 'idea' is virtually synonymous with the 'image', so what did Jung understand by an image (*Bild*)? For Jung, an image was 'a condensed expression of the psychic situation as a whole', and it became 'primordial' (the *Bild* becomes an *Urbild*) when it possessed an 'archaic' character, that is, when it accorded with 'familiar mythological motifs'.[40] In other words, there is nothing mysterious or metaphysical about the *Urbild*, and in fact Jung was content to describe the *Urbild* 'from the scientific, causal standpoint' as 'a mnemic deposit, an imprint or *engram*' (using a term pioneered by the German zoologist and evolutionary biologist Richard Semon, 1859–1918).[41]

In his seminars we find some of Jung's clearest statements about the *Urbild* or (as he now called it) the archetype. In his *Visions* seminar (1930–34), for instance, Jung explained that 'mythological motifs contain many typically human situations', pointing as an example to 'the fairy-tale motif where a man is trapped somewhere or caught by dwarfs and put into a place where he cannot escape; then in the night a little mouse comes and tells him that if he does so-and-so, he can get out'; such animals in fairy tales, he suggested, are 'representations of lower instinctive forces in man'.[42] Accordingly, the archetype is 'absolutely indestructible' because it is 'the instinctive store of energy in man'.[43] For, as he further remarked, 'there are certain difficult situations in life when everything you have learned, everything you have slowly built up, crumbles away, nothing helps; and then you have a most foolish little idea or hunch and you go by that'.[44] Then again, in his seminar on Nietzsche's *Zarathustra* (1934–9), he told his audience that archetypes are 'images that represent typical situations of great vital and practical importance, which have repeated themselves in the course of history innumerable times'.[45] Hence there can, by definition, be no such thing as a 'new' archetype; rather, it 'comes into existence' because 'it is a customary or habitual way of dealing with critical situations', and so 'in any crisis in life, this archetype or another is constellated', since it is 'a sort of typical mechanism, or a typical attitude, by which one settles typical problems'.[46]

Within Jungian literature, it is true, a kind of canon of archetypes evolved: anima and animus, the mother and the wise old man, spirit and the trickster, and most problematically of all, the shadow and the self. Yet in his seminar Jung gave an example that is almost mundane, speaking of 'the archetype of the passage of the ford or the pass' and explaining that 'fording a river' is 'a typical situation expressing a sort of impasse, so just that archetype is formulated when one is in any dangerous predicament' and therefore 'many people become quite unnecessarily archetypally afraid' or 'caught by a most unreasonable fear'.[47] Elsewhere, Jung argued in 'The Concept of the Collective Unconscious' (1936) that 'there are as many archetypes as there are typical situations in life', while in 'Concerning the Archetypes, with Special Reference to the Anima Concept' (1936/1954) he noted that 'primordial images' (*Urbilder*) are never 'reflections of physical events', but rather 'autonomous products' of the psyche.[48] On one occasion (in 'Introduction to the Religious and Psychological Problems of Alchemy'), he made a link between *type* (in the sense of *Collected Works*, volume VI) and *archetype* (in the sense of volume IX/i) on etymological grounds, arguing that 'the word "type" [*Typus*] derives from τύπος = "blow" [*Schlag*], "imprint" [*Einprägung*]' and that 'the word archetype [*Archetypus*] presupposes something that imprints [*ein Prägendes*]', while yet insisting that 'psychology as a science of the soul has to confine itself to its subject and guard against overstepping its proper boundaries by metaphysical assertions'.[49]

On other occasions, however, Jung adopts a more nuanced position, as when (in 'Psychological Aspects of the Mother Archetype') he writes that 'it is Kant's doctrine of categories, more than anything else, that destroys in embryo every attempt to revive metaphysics in the old sense of the word', but adds that 'at the same time [it] paves the way for a rebirth of the Platonic spirit'.[50] After all, the notion of the 'interior man', so dear to Jung, is ultimately a Platonic concept, and the notion of *archetypon* features prominently in the thinking of Plotinus.[51] Indeed, as Hazel E. Barnes has argued, there are important affinities between Neoplatonism (the school of thought that developed in the third century CE in their teachings by Ammonius Saccas, Plotinus and Porphyry, and later by Iamblichus, Proclus and Damascius) and Jung's analytical psychology, and it is likely that these Neoplatonic aspects were enhanced by Jung's interest in such Romantic philosophers as F.W.J. von Schelling (1775–1854), whose thought in turn had been influenced by Neoplatonism.[52] But it should also be noted that, elsewhere, Jung defines the archetype as a linguistic metaphor and as an important aspect of what he terms 'psychic hygiene'.[53] Nevertheless, the tension between empiricism and Neoplatonism in Jung's thinking, as well as the notion of the archetype and the question of how to respond to it, in turn prompt the following question: what is the relation between the rational and the irrational in Jung's thought?

This question becomes pressing because, as we shall see, after *Psychological Types* Jung switches from a discourse about the 'soul' (*die Seele*) and instead uses a discourse about the psyche or *die Psyche*; instead of talking about the 'primordial image' (*urtümliches Bild* or *Urbild*), he now talks about the 'archetype' (*der Archetyp*); and the 'anima' (*die Anima*), while originally used as a synonym for the soul (more precisely, for the 'image of the soul' or *Seelenbild*), becomes a specific archetype of gender, to be distinguished from the 'animus' (*der Animus*) and, more broadly, such archetypes as the child or the self. The reasons for this terminological shift lie beyond the scope of this 'critical life'; but, taken together, it represents a move *away* from an emphasis on the visual or the pictorial or the imagistic – in short, anything related to *das Bild* – and *towards* a terminology that sounds more clinical, more technical or more scientific. Jung's work as the founder of a 'modern psychology' is, then, not simply 'the dream of a science' but a search for an appropriate discourse that combines his visionary and artistic inclinations (as expressed in the Red Book) with his aspirations to be a scientist, an empiricist or a phenomenologist, or in other words that unifies the 'rational' and the 'irrational' parts of his project.[54] For this reason let us examine two sections in the 'Definitions' section of *Psychological Types*, devoted to the rational and the irrational.

In his definition of what is rational, Jung identifies the rational with what is reasonable or 'corresponds to reason', reason in turn being defined as an 'attitude' (in the technical sense of *Einstellung*) whose principle is to 'shape' (*gestalten*) thinking, feeling and action according to 'objective values'.[55] In turn, the 'objectivity' of these values is determined by 'everyday experience' of two kinds of fact: external and inner (psychological) facts. The 'value' of these facts is established not by the individual subject alone, but by the collectivity of subjects: by 'human history'. Thus, for Jung, reason is not the Platonic *logos*, located outside space and time, nor is it the Kantian ideal that establishes knowledge and morality alike; rather it is 'a firmly established complex of ideas', 'handed down through the ages'. Ultimately, reason is a product of human adaptation, it is 'the adapted reaction of the living organism to average environmental influences' (an idea Jung attributes to Schopenhauer). Reason, then, is formed in very much the same way that archetypes are, being 'the expression of man's adaptability to average occurrences, *which have gradually become deposited in firmly established complexes of ideas* that constitute our objective values'.[56] In other words, Jung's definition of reason is essentially a pragmatic one. So how does he define the irrational?

Jung's definition of the irrational serves as an effective riposte to those many critics who accuse him of embracing irrationalism and basking in the irrational. Because, for Jung, the irrational is a term that denotes not what is '*contrary* to reason', but what is '*beyond* reason' or cannot be 'grounded' in reason.[57] As examples, Jung cites what he calls 'elementary facts', by which it turns out he means pure facticity (that the earth has a moon, that chlorine is an element, that water reaches its greatest density at 4°c, and so on). For Jung, this sheer facticity is what he calls 'a factor of being', which poses a challenge to the outlook of reason. Rational explanation may, he says, push what is irrational out of sight through a process he calls 'complication' (and which R.F.C. Hull translates as meaning 'an increasingly elaborate rational explanation'), yet this very process 'complicates' rational explanation to such an extent that it 'passes' or 'transcends' the 'powers of comprehension' of rational thought and reaches its limits before it has encompassed 'the entirety of the world' with the 'law of reason'.

Jung's definition here constellates the words *Grenze – Ganze – Gesetz* (limitation – entirety – law), the first two terms being logical opposites but phonetic relations, while the third is logically equivalent to the first yet implicit in the concept of the second. In two further sentences, Jung introduces a distinction between a fourth phonetically similar term, *gesetzt* or 'posited', and (true) being: 'A completely rational explanation of an object that actually exists (not one that is merely posited) is a utopian ideal. Only an object that is posited can be completely explained on rational grounds, since it does not contain anything beyond what has been posited by rational thinking.'[58] Jung's concern here is the incommensurability between being and thought (or between world and self), the sheer facticity of being exceeding the ability of rational thought to grasp it fully. Here is the basis of his critique of empirical science: the objects it posits are 'confined within rational bounds' and hence, 'by deliberately excluding the accidental', it cannot grasp the object in its entirety. In other words, 'it does not consider the actual object as a whole, but only that part of it which has been singled out for rational observation'.[59]

Here, too, is the basis of Jung's corrective thesis, that thinking and feeling alike should be directed to 'the perception of accidentals which the actual object never lacks', for therewith they (a) lose their attribute of directedness; (b) lose something of their rational character, 'for they then accept the accidental'; and so (c) they themselves 'begin to be irrational'.[60] The direction of thinking or feeling to the perception of accidentals (and hence the irrational) is itself the awakening of two very different functions, intuition or sensation. Unlike the 'rational functions' of thinking and feeling, which 'find fulfilment only when they are in complete harmony with the laws of reason', these 'irrational functions' instead 'react to every possible occurrence' and are 'attuned to the absolutely contingent', and hence 'find their fulfilment in the absolute perception of the flux of events'.[61] This attention to the contingent, to the accidental, to the 'chance' aspect of life, underpins Jung's interest in 'chance' as seen through the lens of his notion of synchronicity, which may be understood as an attempt to revive an understanding of the world 'as an aesthetic phenomenon' (to paraphrase Nietzsche).

Shortly after *Psychological Types*, as we have already mentioned, an important terminological shift takes place in Jung's writings. Because of the relative poverty of the English language (and its dependence on Latin) compared with the richness of German, it is hard to convey this shift in translation, yet it is a significant one. One of the original German words for psychology was *Seelenforschung*, literally 'research into the soul'. Even in the case of Freud, he talks far more frequently about *die Seele*, rather than *die Psyche*, although he is clearly using the word in a non-religious sense. (Bruno Bettelheim rightly recognizes the importance of recognizing the word *Seele* in his discussion of Freud in translation in *Freud and Man's Soul*, 1984.[62]) A glance through the index volume of Freud's *Gesammelte Werke* bears out this point. So, too, Jung in his early writings tends to talk about *die Seele*, distinguishing in *Psychological Types* the soul from the psyche (as 'the totality of all psychic processes, conscious as well as unconscious'), and relating it instead to the personality, to the 'persona' (or social mask, recalling the masks worn by actors in antiquity), and to the 'anima' (or 'soul-image').[63] In line with this shift, the anima acquires a more specific archetypal contour, becoming (instead of simply 'the inner attitude, the inward face') an archetype of gender, corresponding inversely to the sexual gender of the individual.[64]

Jung's teaching on the anima (the archetype of the female, or the archetype of femininity) and on the animus (the archetype of the male, or the archetype of masculinity) has earned him a bad reputation among feminists, largely for the crimes of gender-stereotyping, sexism and misogyny, but above all *essentialism*. (As a Neoplatonist of sorts, of course, Jung would have worn his 'essentialist' badge with pride.) And it is true that, in some of the cruder popularizing versions of Jungianism, this is how the ideas of anima and animus are used: to reinforce gender stereotypes and social inequalities. But Jung's theory of anima and animus is, like his typological system as a whole, far more sophisticated than that.

Not only is the anima the gendered unconscious 'other' for the heterosexual man, and the animus the gendered unconscious 'other' for the heterosexual woman, but this polarity does not simply exist internal to the man and the woman; rather, it informs their interaction and allows Jung to explain why interpersonal relations so often go awry. For when the heterosexual man looks at the woman, he engages with her on a conscious and on an unconscious level: consciously he sees a woman, but unconsciously he is becoming aware of another aspect of himself; his (gendered) (unconscious) 'other', his anima, and his own animus. And conversely, when the woman looks at the man, she engages on a conscious level with the man, but on an unconscious level with *her* (gendered) (unconscious) 'other', the animus, and her own anima. (Jung's theory does not limit itself to heterosexual relationships: in the case of homosexual men and women, the anima and the animus are at work as well.)[65] Although in Jung's own writings his theory of gender tends to conform to his own bourgeois ideals, it does not necessarily lead to these conclusions: and it would be no exaggeration to see, in Jung's theory of anima and animus, an important contribution to LGBT (lesbian, gay, bisexual and transgender) studies.

Ultimately, however, the notion of the archetype is trying to convey the notion that, as Bertrand Vergely has put it, 'not everything comes from Man, not everything comes from Nature', but 'there is something else':[66]

Here we touch on something which is exciting for our human condition: . . . the great problem for our age is the significance of the human condition, and in relation to the human condition there are two possibilities: one can think that everything comes from Nature or that everything comes from Man, one can be in a world that is self-sufficient or one can think that there is a world which is an open world, and it is here that wonder intervenes.

It is precisely this sense of wonder (or, as Vergely calls it, *émerveillement*) that Jung is seeking to capture with his notion of the archetype.

6

Back to the Future: Bollingen and Alchemy

Who – or perhaps what – are the Kabeiroi? Jung describes them in his Red Book as figures 'with delightful misshapen forms, young and yet old, dwarfish, shrivelled, unspectacular bearers of secret arts, possessors of ridiculous wisdom, first formations of the unformed gold, worms that crawl from the liberated egg of the Gods, incipient ones, unborn, still invisible'.[1] These mysterious figures appear toward the end of the *Liber secundus*, in a passage thought to have been written prior to the summer of 1915.[2] Within the narrative economy of the Red Book, the tower constructed for Jung by the Kabeiroi represents a turning point, a stage of consolidation and achievement.[3]

This tower is something literary, but soon it was to become something literal. In terms of Jung's intellectual development, the tower of the Red Book finds a counterpart in Jung's discussion in *Psychological Types* (1921) of the image of the tower in an early Christian work, *The Shepherd of Hermas*, a series of visions granted to a former slave called Hermas; in architectural terms it finds a counterpart from 1920 as Jung began work on his own 'tower' at Bollingen.[4] In the Red Book the tower is seen as something essentially symbolic: 'My tower grew for several thousand years, imperishable . . . Only he who finds the entrance hidden in the mountain and rises up through the labyrinths of the innards can reach the tower, and the happiness of him who surveys things from there and who lives from himself'.[5]

There is something equally symbolic about Jung's 'tower' at Bollingen, a project for which he began planning in 1920, with construction commencing in 1923, and to which various developments and additions were made in the 1950s.[6] In a letter of 2 January 1928 to Hermann Graf Keyserling (1880–1946), Jung explained how he had built 'a little house way out in the country near the mountains and carved an inscription on the wall': 'the Shrine of Philemon, the Repentance of Faust'.[7] The inscription was first placed above the gate of the Tower, and when the gate was walled up the inscription was then placed over the entrance to the second tower. The name 'Philemon' in this context recalls both the figures of Philemon and Baucis, the old couple whom Faust has to murder in order to pursue his project of land reclamation in Act Five of Part Two of Goethe's dramatic poem, and the figure

Jung's 'tower' at Bollingen, 1955.

A stone at Bollingen, on which a quotation from *Rosarium philosophorum* (16th century) is inscribed.

of Philemon from Jung's visionary experiences contained in the Red Book.

Jung's tower at Bollingen, currently not accessible for the general public to visit, remains a special place.[8] According to *Memories, Dreams, Reflections*, whenever Jung experienced a lack of creativity, he hewed stone or painted a picture. As early as 1920 Jung had carved two wooden figures, reminiscent of the Telesphorus-like manikin he had made as a child, later having one (a figure he called Atmavictu, 'the breath of life') reproduced in stone and placing it in the garden of his house in Küsnacht.[9] In his later years, working with stone proved to be what he called '*ein rite d'entrée*' for the thoughts and works that followed this activity. In fact, it has been claimed that everything Jung wrote in 1957 – that is, 'The

A stone at Bollingen with a Greek inscription showing
a Telesphorus.

A stone at Bollingen with a Latin inscription (including an allusion
to Horace).

Undiscovered Self (Present and Future)', 'Flying Saucers: A Modern Myth' and 'A Psychological View of Conscience' – 'grew out of' the stone sculptures that Jung made after the death of his wife Emma on 27 November 1955.[10] These sculptures and carvings included various reliefs, among them a bear rolling a ball and a woman milking a mare, a bull and a laughing trickster.[11]

At the end of the path near the boathouse there is a small pillar, carved in stone, dedicated to Attis, the beautiful shepherd of Phrygia who, unfaithful to the goddess Cybele, was driven by her into a state of madness and transformed into a fir-tree.[12] And there is the Bollingen Stone, which features various inscriptions: on one side, a Latin verse by a medieval alchemist, Arnaldus de Villa Nova (c. 1235–1311); facing the front, a little hooded figure carrying a lantern, a Telesphorus from the cult of Asclepius, and three Greek inscriptions from Heraclitus, the Mithras liturgy and Homer; on the third side, facing the lake, a selection of Latin inscriptions from various alchemical texts.[13] 'The stone', we read in *Memories, Dreams, Reflections*, 'stands outside the Tower', of which it constitutes 'the explanation'. It is, we are told, 'a manifestation of its occupant, which nevertheless remains incomprehensible for others'.[14]

In the pages of *Memories, Dreams, Reflections*, Jung's tower at Bollingen – or '*the* tower', as it is simply called – enjoys a status accorded to no other building or artefact. For at Bollingen, we are told, Jung is 'in the midst of [his] true life' and 'most deeply [him]self'.[15] At Bollingen, Jung becomes the alchemical 'age-old son of the mother', or 'the old man' or the 'ancient', his former Personality No. 2 who 'always has been and always will be'.[16] This second personality, who 'comes to life again at Bollingen', is here identified with Philemon from the fantasies of the Red Book.[17] (This is why there is an image of Philemon depicted as a massive icon-like mural in a room in Bollingen.) In terms that recall the passages from the Red Book quoted in chapter Four, Jung writes that he sometimes feels 'as if [he] is spread out over the landscape and inside things, and [is himself] living in every tree, in the plashing of the waves, in the clouds and the animals that come and go, in the procession of the seasons'.[18] And as if in answer to the question posed in the previous chapter about the status of *ratio* in Jung's system, we are told that he regarded analytical psychology, not as 'a product of rational(istic) thinking', but as 'a vision' (*eine Schau*) – a vision of almost Heideggerean proportions, produced by 'undertaking, with half-closed eyes and somewhat closed ears, to see and hear the form and voice of Being'.[19] Living in his tower, Jung was able to live 'as if one lived in many centuries simultaneously', a form

Jung at
Bollingen,
1958.

of being achieved by living in (or as) his 'second personality', which is another way of saying that one should 'see life in the round, as something forever coming into being and passing on'; or, as Nietzsche would put it, as 'a Dionysian world of the eternally self-creating, the eternally self-destroying'.[20]

Jung had a tower; Goethe had a garden-house. Was Bollingen based, at least in part, on the same need for seclusion (from others) and for escape (back to the self) that Goethe had when, in 1776, he purchased his house in an overgrown garden at the foot of the Rosenberg (in what is now the Park an der Ilm) Goethe decorated his garden with symbolic sculpture, too: in 1777 he erected his 'altar of good fortune', as he called it, or *Agathe Tyche* ('stone of good fortune').[21] This sculpture consists of a sphere, standing on a cube: a representation of the division in the human being between individuality (the cube) and the happiness of external circumstances (the sphere), or as an emblem of mobility (the sphere) supported by an emblem of stability (the cube).[22] So it was entirely in keeping with this spirit that in 1787 Martin Gottlieb Klauer erected on the left bank of the Ilm the 'serpent stone', depicting a large serpent coiled around a small classical column bearing the inscription *Genio huius loci* ('to the genius of this place').[23] It is very much a sculpture that would be at home at Jung's tower in Bollingen, with its own special sense of the *genius loci*.

Richard Wilhelm

In a handwritten (and unfinished) epilogue to the Red Book, dated to 1959, Jung wrote that he had been working on his book for sixteen years when he decided to discontinue the project.[24] One of the reasons for leaving the Red Book was his engagement with alchemy, so 'the beginning of the end' came in 1928 when Richard Wilhelm (1873–1930), a German sinologist and theologian who occupied the chair of Chinese history and philosophy at the University of Frankfurt am Main, sent Jung a copy of his new translation of an ancient Chinese alchemical text, *The Secret of the Golden Flower*. Jung had first met Wilhelm at one of the meetings of the so-called 'School of Wisdom' organized by Hermann Graf Keyserling in Darmstadt in the early 1920s, and in 1923 Wilhelm had, at the invitation of the Psychological Club, given a lecture in Zurich on the ancient Chinese oracle book, the *I Ching*. But it was not just the *I Ching*, of which Jung was an enthusiastic practitioner, for which both men shared a passion; Wilhelm was also fascinated by Goethe.

Just before he read *The Secret of the Golden Flower*, Jung had painted a mandala with a golden castle in the centre.[25] He considered the form and choice of colours to be Chinese, so when the text from Wilhelm arrived he sensed an affinity between Wilhelm's work and his own.[26] (Jung had learned to pay great attention to this sort of coincidence: or as he was later to call it, 'synchronicity'. But it is surely not a coincidence that a Viennese psychoanalyst, Herbert Silberer, 1882–1922, had already written about alchemy, publishing in 1914 a major study, *Problems of Mysticism and its Symbolism*, in which he discussed *Märchen*, alchemy, hermeticism, Rosicrucianism and Freemasonry, focusing on a hermetic-alchemical text, one of the 'Parabola' from the 'Golden Treatise of the Philosopher's Stone', 1625, contained in the collection *Secret Figures of the Rosicrucians*, 1785–8.[27]) Jung later referred to Silberer's interpretation of this text in 'Individual Dream Symbolism in Relation to Alchemy' (1936) and, later still, in the epilogue to *Mysterium coniunctionis* (1955–6), Jung paid tribute to Silberer as having been 'the first to discover the secret threads that lead from alchemy to the psychology of the unconscious'.[28]

Before either Silberer or Jung turned their attention to this arcane science, however, a revival of interest of sorts in alchemy had been taking place in the Anglo-American world.[29] In 1850

Konrad Gesner (1516–1565), *Alchymya*, 1599, woodcut.

Mary Anne Atwood (*née* South) (1817–1910) had published *A Suggestive Inquiry into the Hermetic Mystery*, a work that has been hailed by Manly Palmer Hall (1901–1990), the Canadian historian of occultism, as nothing less than a landmark of esoteric literature.[30] 'The pseudo Alchemists', Atwood wrote, 'dreamed of gold, and impossible transformations, and worked with sulphur, mercury, and the salt of mines, torturing all species, dead and living, in vain, without rightly divining the true Identity of nature', but it is 'Man', she argued, who is 'the true laboratory of the Hermetic art; his life the subject, the grand distillatory, the thing distilling and the thing distilled, and Self-knowledge . . . at the root of all Alchemical tradition'.[31]

Just seven years later, Ethan Allen Hitchcock (1798–1870) published a work entitled *Remarks on Alchemy and the Alchemists, Indicating a Method of Discovering the True Nature of Hermetic Philosophy*, a work that similarly argued that 'the whole subject of Alchemy is Man', that 'Man is the central figure in Alchemy and Hermetic Philosophy, and that the conscience is the starting-point of the Philosopher's Stone'.[32] (Hitchcock followed up this account with a study of Swedenborg as a hermetic philosopher, contrasting Spinoza and Swedenborg.[33]) Inspired by Wilhelm, as well as by Atwood and Silberer, Jung embarked on a massive reading programme, studying and excerpting the original alchemical texts, producing a series of eight copybooks, which he then carefully indexed: his approach was, without a doubt, exemplary in its scholarly thoroughness and rigour – truly *hoc opus, hic labor est* ('this is the task, this the toil'), in the words of Virgil's *Aeneid* placed as an epigram to one of his Eranos papers on alchemy.[34]

For the first time since his friendship with Freud, Jung had found in Wilhelm another person with whom he could 'establish ties', and in alchemy he detected 'the historical basis which [he] had hitherto lacked'.[35] Although between 1918 and 1926 Jung had, on his own account, been 'seriously' studying the Gnostic writers (largely through the accounts of their opponents, the Church Fathers, in whose texts brief extracts from Gnostic works survive), he had been unable to find a 'bridge' that led from Gnosticism or Neoplatonism – both traditions of thought that had much in common – to 'the contemporary world'.[36] But alchemy, as Jung saw it, represented at once 'the historical link with Gnosticism' and 'a continuity between past and present'.[37] In his *West-Östlicher Divan* Goethe had penned a famous quatrain: 'Those who cannot draw conclusions / From three thousand years of learning / Stay naïve in dark confusions, / Day to day live undiscerning'.[38] Jung took this message very much to heart and this is the real reason for his interest in alchemy: 'grounded in the natural philosophy of the Middle Ages', alchemy 'formed the bridge on the one hand into the past, to Gnosticism', and 'on the other into the future, to the modern psychology of the unconscious'.[39]

Some have regarded Jung's interest in alchemy as a strategic mistake. Like his interest in the occult and the paranormal, in telepathy and flying saucers, it places him on the fringe of academic interests, marginalizing his serious work and making him appear more 'New Age' than he is. Yet his writings on alchemy constitute a substantial part of his *Collected Works*, comprising volume xii, *Psychology and Alchemy*, which collects various papers on alchemy given by Jung at Eranos conferences in the late 1930s; volume xiii, *Alchemical Studies*, which collects a number of important papers (including his 'Commentary on "The Secret of the Golden Flower"', 1929); and volume xiv, *Mysterium coniunctionis*, subtitled *An Inquiry into the Separation and Synthesis of Psychic Opposites in Alchemy*, a massive study more than 500 pages long (published in the German edition in two volumes, to which a third is added, a commentary by one of Jung's followers, Marie-Louise von Franz, on the *Aurora consurgens*, 'the rising dawn', a fifteenth-century alchemical manuscript attributed, most now think falsely, to St Thomas Aquinas). To these one should add, hidden away in volume xvi with the apparently innocuous title *The Practice of Psychotherapy*, an essay entitled 'The Psychology of the Transference' (1946).

This essay of 1946 makes a good starting point for anyone intrigued by or even mildly curious about Jung's references to alchemy. It constitutes an examination of a sixteenth-century alchemical treatise, the *Rosarium philosophorum* ('Rose Garden of the Philosophers'), first published in 1550 as the second part of *De Alchimia Opuscula complura veterum philosophorum*. Reprinted in Basel in 1594 in the *Artis auriferae*, it consists of some twenty illustrations, reproduced as woodcuts, and it is the illustrations that form, so to speak, the rosary beads to which Jung attaches a series of meditations. Throughout the various stages of the alchemical transformation – the *nigredo* (or 'blackening'), the *albedo* (or 'whitening'), the *citrinitas* (or 'yellowing') and the *rubedo* (or 'reddening'), or the union (or *coniunctio*) of the alchemical king and queen, their death, ascent of the soul, purification, return of the soul, and rebirth – Jung discerns a series of images for what happens in the course of analytical psychological therapy.

For Jung, alchemy describes the same psychological phenomenology observed in the analysis of unconscious processes. These

Alchemical king and queen in the mercurial bath, from *Turba philosophorum; das ist, Das Buch von der güldenen Kunst* (1613).

unconscious processes begin when what Jung calls the 'specious unity' of the individual – '*I* want, *I* think' – breaks down under the impact of the unconscious. If we can blame someone else for our difficulties, then some semblance of unity can be saved; the function of blame, then, lies in its desperate attempt to shore up this sense of unity. But once we realize we have a shadow, and once we realize that our enemy is within our own heart, then the conflict begins: then 'one becomes two'.[40] In the 'obfuscation of the light', or the depotentiation of consciousness, the individual – in alchemy as in analysis – becomes at a loss to know where his or her personality begins or ends, and so, too (or so Jung tells us), does the analyst: 'Often the analyst is in much the same position as the alchemist who no longer knew whether he was melting the mysterious amalgam in the crucible or whether he was the salamander glowing in the fire.'[41] Hence the work of therapy affects analyst and client alike, inasmuch as 'psychological induction inevitably causes the two parties to get involved in the transformation of the third and to be themselves transformed in the process'.[42]

What is the difference between the consulting-room, where the analyst treats – or, rather, engages with – his clients and the alchemist's laboratory with its jars and retorts? In essence, Jung believed, there was none: 'Nothing gives a better picture of the psychological state of the alchemist', he wrote, 'than the division of his work-room into a "laboratory" . . . and an "oratory"': in the first, he 'bustles about with crucibles and alembics', but in the second he 'prays to God for the much needed illumination' in order (in the words of Notker Balbulus, cited in *Aurora consurgens*) to 'purge the horrible darknesses of our mind'.[43] Perhaps one could apply to the work of the alchemist what Aristotle said of the initiates of the ancient mystery cult celebrated at Eleusis: that they learned nothing, but that they 'experienced', that they 'suffered'.[44]

Over the years Jung began to like to lard his essays with alchemical quotations, some of his favourites being 'dissolve and coagulate' and 'transform yourselves into living philosophical stones!' In 'The Psychology of the Transference' he reminds us of Theobald de Hoghelande's adage in *De alchemiae difficultatibus liber*, 'the art requires the whole man'.[45] What Jung was trying to do – and, to a considerable extent, succeeding in doing – was to understand a lost rhetorical system and thereby recuperate an occluded tradition in Western thought.

'The people . . . found grace in the desert', thus the motto from the book of Jeremiah that Jung uses to introduce his analysis of the illustrations in the *Rosarium philosophorum*.[46] Jung's choice of text is strangely appropriate, for as well as harking back to his choice of the same biblical prophet to introduce the *Liber secundus* of his Red Book, its biblical context (a reminder of the desert as a scene of conversion as part of the promise of recovery to bring back Israel from exile in a second Exodus), like its context in the Red Book (in the desert Jung encounters an anchorite called Ammonius, a composite figure built out of Ammonius of Alexandria, a Christian philosopher, and Ammonius Saccas, the Neoplatonic teacher of Plotinus), announces what Jung does in 'The Psychology of the Transference' and in his other writings on alchemy: to make the apparently arid tracts of alchemical treatises yield vast quantities of psychological insight.[47]

Another important connection, too, emerges in the course of Jung's discussion. For Jung, 'the last and greatest work of alchemy' was not one of those by Arnaldus de Villa Nova, Johann Daniel Mylius (1583–1642) or Martin Ruland the Younger (1569–1611), not Gerhard Dorn (*c*. 1530–1584), Michael Maier (1568–1622) or Philipp Aureolus Theophrastus Bombastus von Hohenheim, otherwise known as Paracelsus (1493–1541), but none other than Goethe's great dramatic poem *Faust*. According to Jung, what Goethe is really doing in that work is describing 'the experience of the alchemist who discovers that what he has projected into the retort is his own darkness, his unredeemed state, his passion, his

Paracelsus, an anonymous copy of a lost original by Quentin Massys (1466–1529), 17th century, oil painting on wood.

struggles to reach the goal' or, in other words, 'to become what he really is': namely, 'to fulfil the purpose for which his mother bore him and, after the peregrinations of a long life full of confusion and error, to become the *filius regius*, son of the supreme mother'.[48]

Possibly for strategic reasons, *Memories, Dreams, Reflections* neglects to mention Goethe's interest in alchemy, particularly his early engagement, during his period of crisis in Frankfurt from 1768 to 1770, with works by such figures as Paracelsus, Basilius Valentinus (the pseudonym of a fifteenth-century Benedictine monk from Erfurt), Georg von Welling (1652–1727), Johann Baptist van Helmont (1577–1644) and George Starkey (1628–1665), whose teachings and precepts, Goethe wrote, were 'based more or less on nature and imagination'.[49] In *Dichtung und Wahrheit* Goethe specifically mentions the *Aurea catena Homeri*, the 'Golden Chain of Homer', describing it as representing nature 'in a beautiful, though perhaps fantastic, synthesis'.[50] *Memories, Dreams, Reflections* alludes to this text in its discussion of the significance of *Faust*, Part Two, but says no more.[51]

In his letter of 18 January 1941 to the Hungarian philologist and mythologist Karl Kerényi (1897–1973), Jung suggested that the influence of esoteric sources on Goethe's work had been an important, but also, at least in part, an unconscious one. Writing in response to Kerényi's commentary on the scene 'Rocky Inlets of the Aegean Sea', which brings the classical *Walpurgisnacht* in *Faust*, Part Two, to a close, Jung speculated that Goethe himself had not been aware of 'how profoundly' he had been influenced by alchemy.[52] What he had read at the instigation of Susanne von Klettenberg, Jung wrote, was not sufficient to explain the 'deep impulses' he had received from alchemy.[53] What Jung says here about the unconscious influence of alchemy on Goethe could also apply, *mutatis mutandis*, to the influence of Goethe on Jung himself.

After all, alchemy as 'the historical counterpart' of his psychology of the unconscious, and as evidence of 'the uninterrupted chain back to Gnosticism' that 'gave substance' to that psychology, also intersected with one of his greatest personal concerns.[54] In this sense, alchemy was 'a sign' of his 'inner relationship' to Goethe, since he, like Jung, had a 'secret', Goethe's being that he was 'in the grip of that process of archetypal transformation which has gone on through the ages': consequently, he regarded his *Faust* as a magnum opus or *divinum*, as his 'main business' (see Goethe's diary entry for 11 February 1826), his drama providing 'a framework' within which 'his whole life was enacted'. For Jung, what was 'alive and active' in Goethe was 'a living substance . . . a suprapersonal process, the great dream of the *unus mundus*', that is, the one archetypal world.[55] Here as elsewhere, Jung assimilates Dorn's specific notion to his own broader conception of alchemy, writing that 'the desperately evasive and universal Mercurius – that Proteus twinkling in a myriad shapes and colours – is none other than the '*unus mundus*', the original, non-differentiated unity of the world or of Being; the *agnosia* of the Gnostics, the primordial unconsciousness', but he also assimilates this vision to his understanding of *Faust*.[56]

What Micreris in his *Tractatus* (in volume v of *Theatrum chemicum*) calls the 'Nile of Egypt', 'the 'Sea of the Indians', or the 'Meridian Sea', and what Christian Rosencreutz in his *Chymical Wedding* describes as a sea journey, is identified by Jung as an alchemical motif in the second part of *Faust*, in the Aegean Festival scene as it had been analysed, in what Jung regarded as 'a brilliant amplificatory interpretation', by Kerényi. The astonishing scene conjured up by Goethe as the conclusion to the classical *Walpurgisnacht* reveals, for Kerényi and for Jung alike, the very same thing at which the bands of nereids on Roman sarcophagi also hint: the coincidence of 'the epithalamic and the sepulchral element', 'the identity of marriage and death on the one hand, and of birth and the eternal resurgence of life from death on the other' as 'basic to the antique Mysteries'[57] (or as Nietzsche had put it, the ancient Mysteries offered '*eternal* life, the eternal recurrence of life; the future promised and consecrated in the past; the triumphant Yes to life beyond death and change; *true* life as collective continuation of life through procreation, through the mysteries of sexuality'.)[58]

Moreover, at the very centre of *Memories, Dreams, Reflections*, Jung underscores, in the context of his project to understand alchemy, the peculiar significance of his relation to Goethe:

> I myself am haunted by the same dream, and from my eleventh year I have been launched upon a single enterprise which is *my* 'main business'. My life has been permeated and held together by one idea and one goal: namely, to penetrate into the secret of the personality [*in das Geheimnis der Persönlichkeit einzudringen*]. Everything can be explained from this central point, and all my works relate to this one theme.[59]

Jung's complicated relationship to Goethe also became involved, in quite a different way, with his controversial reaction to political developments in Europe in the 1930s and '40s.

Wotan

In his 'Introduction to the Religious and Psychological Problems of Alchemy', Jung admitted that 'the archetypal contents of the collective unconscious can often assume grotesque and horrible forms in dreams and fantasies, so that even the most hard-boiled rationalist is not immune from shattering nightmares and haunting fears'.[60] In German-speaking Europe (and then across Europe as a whole) in the 1930s and '40s, however, there were plenty of shattering nightmares and haunting fears outside the realm of dreams and fantasies.

There is an odd sense of dislocation between Jung's writings on alchemy and the drift in Europe towards fascism, and nowhere can one sense this dislocation more keenly than in Jung's seminars on Nietzsche's *Thus Spoke Zarathustra*, held in the rooms of the Psychological Club at Gemeindestrasse 25/27 in Zurich between May 1934 and February 1939. (These seminars followed earlier ones on analytical psychology, 1925, dream analysis, 1928–30, the visions of Christiana Morgan, 1930–34, and Kundalini Yoga, 1932, and were followed later by lectures series at the ETH in Zurich on modern psychology, 1938–40, and on the *Exercitia spiritualia* of St Ignatius Loyola, 1940.) In his first seminar on 2 May 1934, Jung stated his basic methodological proposition: '*Zarathustra* really led [Nietzsche] up to a full realization of the mysteries of the cult of Dionysos: he had already ideas about it, but *Zarathustra* was the experience which made the whole thing real'.[61] But what sort of reality was Jung talking about?

On one level Jung is offering a kind of psychobiography of Nietzsche, writing that 'the body is the alembic, the retort, in which materials are cooked, and out of that process develops the spirit, the effervescent thing that rises', and so 'Nietzsche returned to himself, isolated himself from the whole world, crept into his own retort and underwent this process . . . then suddenly he discovered that he was filled with a new orgiastic enthusiasm which he called his experience of Dionysos, the god of wine'.[62] Referring explicitly to a poem in Nietzsche's *Dithyrambs of Dionysos*, Jung remarks on how Nietzsche 'was digging down into himself, working into his own shaft', revealing 'how intensely he experienced the going-into-himself, till he suddenly produced the explosion of the most original form of spirit, the Dionysian'.[63] In making this comment, is Jung also echoing the words from Nietzsche's earlier essay on 'Schopenhauer as Educator' (1874), which observe that 'it is an agonizing, dangerous enterprise to dig down into yourself, to descend forcibly by the shortest route to the shaft of your being'?[64]

On another level, however, Jung saw Nietzsche's experience of the German version of Dionysos, Wotan, as presaging political developments. On the chapter of *Zarathustra* called 'The Prophet', Nietzsche commented that 'it is Wotan who gets [me], the old wind god breaking forth, the god of inspiration, of madness, of intoxication and wildness, the god of the Berserkers . . . the shrieking and whistling of the wind in a storm in the nocturnal wood, the unconscious', and as such 'a horrible foreboding of [his] insanity', but also a foreboding of the insanity of National Socialism in the political psyche of the German people. In 1936 Jung had observed that 'old Wotan has to a certain extent come to life again . . . the myth is *en marche*, old Wotan is going strong again; you might even include Alberich and those other demons', he added, for 'that thing lives'.[65] And in 1939, in what proved to be the penultimate seminar on Nietzsche, Jung declared that 'the old gods are coming to life again in a dark time when they should have been superseded long ago, and nobody can see it'.[66]

In 'Group Psychology and the Analysis of the Ego' (1921) Freud had offered a psychoanalytic explanation of totalitarianism, dividing society into its masses and its leaders. Using his theory of the primal horde expounded in 'Totem and Taboo', Freud argued that 'the father of the primal horde . . . at the very beginning of the history of mankind, was the "superman" whom Nietzsche only expected from the future', and that this *Urvater*'s legacy was still with us: 'The leader of the group is still the dreaded primal father; the group still wishes to be governed by unrestricted force; it has an extreme passion for authority; in [Gustav] Le Bon's phrase, it has a thirst for obedience'.[67] In Freud's view, it was possible for individuals to identify their super-ego with a single leader and their ego with each other, and the rise of Hitler and the National Socialists in the Weimar Republic seemed to bear out his point.

In turn, Jung offered an archetypal account of what had happened in the founding of the Third Reich and the events leading to the Second World War. In 'Wotan', an essay published in a Swiss cultural journal called the *Neue Schweizer Rundschau* in 1936, and in 'After the Catastrophe', published in the same journal in 1945, Jung explained what had happened in Germany – the rise of Hitler – in collective psychological terms: the return of the archetype.[68] Jung begins the second essay by admitting to a sense of complicity in the Second World War. This confession begins in the plural – 'we are, on the whole, much more deeply involved in the recent events in Germany than we like to admit' – but soon becomes more personal: 'I had not realized how much I myself was affected'.[69]

According to Jung, the rise of fascism and the Second World War revealed much about the German psyche, but no more than one could have discovered, it seems, from reading *Faust*. (In particular, Jung's attention was caught by the episode in Part Two, Act Five, in which Philemon and Baucis, an old couple named after characters in Ovid's *Metamorphoses*, are murdered on Faust's orders.) Playing on the Hölderlinian topos of the fragmentary German nature, Jung reflected on the 'inner contradictions, conflicts of conscience, disharmonies of character' that are said to be typical of the German psyche. In a passage alluding both to *Faust* and to the vitalist philosopher Ludwig Klages (1872–1956) – 'the longing of "hungering for the infinite" . . . that "Eros of distance", that eschatalogical expectation of great fulfilment' – Jung characterizes all these qualities as 'everything we see in Goethe's *Faust*'. Earlier, in 'Psychology and Literature' (1930), Jung had spoken of *Faust* as 'the expression of something profoundly alive in the soul of every German, which Goethe helped to bring to birth'; now he asked, 'could we conceive of anyone but a German writing *Faust* or *Thus Spoke Zarathustra*?'[70] Jung regards Faust as somehow a quintessentially German figure: 'Nobody but a German could ever have devised such a figure, it is so infinitely German'.[71]

Now, more than ever, Faust is presented in 'After the Catastrophe' as a highly specific symptom of the German psyche. 'Faust never attains the character of reality', Jung writes, 'he is not a real human being', he 'remains the German idea of a human being, and therefore an image – somewhat overdone and distorted – of the average German'.[72] In particular, Jung thought, the treatment of Philemon and Baucis in Part Two, Act Five, demonstrated the full extent of Faust's moral depravity:

> Faust, too, is split and sets up 'evil' outside himself in the shape of Mephistopheles, to serve as an alibi in case of need. He likewise 'knows nothing of what has happened', i.e., what the devil did to Philemon and Baucis. We never get the impression that he has real insight or suffers genuine remorse. His avowed and unavowed worship of success stands in the way of any moral reflection throughout, obscuring the ethical conflict, so that Faust's moral personality remains misty.[73]

These are strong words and are, perhaps, matched only by those spoken by Thomas Mann in 'Germany and the Germans', composed in the same year. In this speech, delivered in English on 29 May 1945 to the Library of Congress in Washington on the occasion of his 70th birthday, Mann spoke of 'a secret connection between the German mind and the daimonic', commenting that 'the devil, Luther's devil, Faust's devil, is, it seems to me, a very German figure'.[74]

Jung's use of the figure of Faust in his archetypal analysis of the politics of fascism in 'After the Catastrophe' not only stands in an important relationship to his discussion of Goethe's *Faust* in the 'Epilogue' to *Psychology and Alchemy*, but opens up an extremely personal dimension in Jung's reception of Goethe. In his letter of 5 January 1942 to the Swiss publisher and journalist Paul Schmitt (1900–1953), Jung related how, suddenly, he had understood the importance for him of Philemon and Baucis. 'I have taken over Faust as my heritage', he told Schmitt, 'as the advocate and avenger of Philemon and Baucis, who, unlike Faust's superhumanity [*Übermenschentum*], are the hosts of the gods in an age of ruthlessness and godforsakenness'.[75]

Jung insisted, as he had done in *Psychology and Alchemy*, that the drama of *Faust* posed a 'question' whose 'solution' would have important political consequences. 'It seems to me unavoidable to give an *answer* to Faust: we must continue to bear the terrible German problem that is devastating Europe', he wrote, although the nature of this solution itself is cast in this letter in terms derived from *Faust*, Part Two: 'we must pull down into our world some of the Faustian happenings in the Beyond, for instance, the benign activity of Pater Profundus'.[76] (In the 'Mountain Gorges' scene, the Pater Profundus is one of the anchorites who have settled among the clefts of the mountainside; he occupies, as his name suggests, a position in a lower region of the mountains.)

Like the Pater Ecstaticus and the Pater Seraphicus, the Pater Profundus speaks, in terms of voluptuous sensations, of the power of divine love.[77] It is not clear, however, that he is any more 'benign' than the two other figures. Even more mysteriously, Jung said that Faust had 'sinned from the beginning' against 'these primordial parents' (*diese Ureltern*), that is, against 'the kiss' (φίλημα) and against Baubo (the obscene female deity who, according to myth, made Demeter laugh after the abduction of Persephone by exposing herself indecently; hence her association with the female sexual organs). 'One must have nearly died, though', he added, 'before one understands this secret properly'.[78] The force of this remark appears to lie in a pun on Philemon/'philema' (the kiss) and Baucis/Baubo, but what does it mean exactly?

This is a difficult question to answer. In 'Psychological Aspects of the Mother Archetype' (1938/1954), Jung associates Baubo with the mind (*der Verstand*) in 'its original condition', that is 'as primitive, unrelated, and ruthless, but also as true and sometimes even as profound as nature'.[79] In 'The Psychological Aspects of the Kore' (1941) he contrasts the different manifestations of the Earth Mother, ranging 'from the Pietà type to the Baubo type', and in *Aion* (1951), Jung sets up an opposition between 'the heavenly goddess' and 'the chthonic Baubo'.[80] So in his letter to Schmitt Jung seems to be linking Faust's 'first sin' with the question of sexual pleasure (the kiss, the female genitalia) and with the chthonic Mothers, although the precise nature of the connection remains unclear. Or is there a link between Baubo exposing herself, those skirt-lifting rites during the festival in honour of Artemis at Boubastis observed by Herodotus, and the ancient rite of adoption described by Diodorus Siculus in his *Bibliotheca historica*, when 'the child to be adopted was hidden under the skirts of the adoptive mother and then drawn forth again'?[81] Or perhaps Jung was right after all, and one must have nearly died before one can understand this 'secret'.

The figures of Philemon and Baucis also crop up on two occasions in *Memories, Dreams, Reflections*. In the chapter on Jung's student years we find an expression of dissatisfaction with the final scene of *Faust* of the kind we have found in *Psychology and Alchemy*, accompanied by a reference to Faust's 'ruthless arrogance' and 'the murder of Philemon and Baucis'.[82] This passage is all the more significant for it follows a discussion of Jung's own identification with Faust: or, rather, of one of the two personalities inside himself with Faust. If the figure of Faust was 'the answer that Goethe had given to his times', then the drama of *Faust*, we are told, meant more to Jung than his 'beloved' Gospel according to St John.[83] On the second occasion, Philemon and Baucis are mentioned in the chapter called 'The Tower', which deals with the construction of the tower in Bollingen. Here their appearance in *Faust* is connected with Jung's sense of involvement with 'the fate of the Germans'. The 'heroic myth' of Faust is seen as 'prophetically anticipating' that fate, but it also signals Jung's sense of being 'personally implicated'. 'When Faust, as a consequence of his hubris and inflation, causes the murder of Philemon and Baucis', we read, 'I felt quite guilty'. Alarmed by this idea, Jung is said to have taken on 'the responsibility of atoning for this crime, or preventing its repetition'.[84]

As we have seen, Jung inscribed the phrase *Philemonis sacrum – Fausti poenitentia*, 'the Shrine of Philemon, the Repentance of Faust', on the wall of his tower at Bollingen, as he told Hermann Graf Keyserling in 1928. The inscription was first placed above the gate of the tower; when the gate was walled up, the inscription was then placed over the entrance to the second tower.[85] By making this inscription, Jung told Keyserling, he 'dis-identified' himself with God. Which God? one might ask, and the reference to Nietzsche's 'amor fati' in the same letter does not make matters any clearer.[86]

It is, however, worth noting that, across Jung's writings and *Memories, Dreams, Reflections*, a significant blurring of Jung's discussion about the First and Second World Wars can be observed. In *Memories, Dreams, Reflections* we read that Jung was 'unconsciously caught up' around 1890 in 'the spirit of the age' of the Wilhelmine era, the 'hubris' of which – like Faust's hubris? – is said to have 'prepared the way for the catastrophe of 1914'.[87] Already then, we read, 'the archetypes of Wagner' (*sic*) were knocking at the door, and with them 'the Dionysian experience of Nietzsche' or, more precisely, 'the god of ecstasy, Wotan'. In the 'Epilogue' to *Psychology and Alchemy*, Jung speaks of how 'an inflated consciousness is always egocentric and conscious only of its own present', of how it 'is doomed to catastrophes, that must strike it dead', and of how, when 'fate presented Europe for four years a way of grandiose awfulness, a war that nobody wanted', no one had asked 'who or what' had caused that war: presumably, he means here the First World War.[88]

Elsewhere, however, in the 'Epilogue' to *Psychology and Alchemy* he links Faust's 'superhumanity' (*Übermenschentum*) with the *Übermensch* in Nietzsche's *Zarathustra*, defining the superman as 'the hubris of the individual consciousness, which must come into immediate collision with the collective power of Christianity, and lead to the catastrophic destruction of the individual', and referring to such 'suffocation of personality' and 'impotence of Christianity' as 'the balance sheet of our time'.[89] When 'the fire chilled to air' and 'the air became the great wind of Zarathustra', the resulting 'inflation of consciousness' can be 'damped down' only by 'the most terrible catastrophe to civilization, another deluge let loose by the gods upon inhospitable humanity', he claims.[90] In 1936 Jung had ascribed the rise of National Socialism to the reawakening of Wotan, and in 1945, as we have seen, he spoke of the Second World War in just such terms of a 'catastrophe', making explicit the symbolic link between the murder of Philemon and Baucis at the behest of Faust and the rise of fascism that led to the Second World War.[91] So there seems to be a blurring here of Jung's reactions to these two World Wars, and of his explanations of the psychological mechanisms that lay behind them.

Moreover, in what sense can Jung be said to have atoned for Faust's murder of Philemon and Baucis? (How can one atone for the fate of fictional characters?) Or how did he prevent the repetition of this crime? How, in other words (that is, in the words of *Memories, Dreams, Reflections*), did Jung 'consciously' link his own work to what Faust had 'passed over': to 'everlasting human rights, to respect for the old, and the continuity of culture and intellectual history'?[92] It is important to answer this last question, for Jung places cultural activity at the very centre of the project of analytical psychology.

In the description given in *Memories, Dreams, Reflections* of Jung's life at Bollingen there is the suggestion that the entire building is nothing but a backdrop in front of which he could live out his own Faustian fantasies. 'At Bollingen', we read, 'I am in the midst of my true life'; in alchemical terms, 'the age-old son of the mother' (of Demeter? of Baubo?), in his own psychological terms, 'his personality no. 2', which in his youth he identified with Faust, and which now he identifies with Philemon.[93] Not Ovid's Philemon, nor Goethe's, but the pagan, Gnostic figure of an old man, with wings, the horns of a bull and a lame foot: Jung's Philemon, 'the spiritual aspect', the idea of 'meaning' (*Sinn*). In Jung's earlier fantasies this aspect of Jung 'took the form of Philemon'; now at Bollingen he 'comes to life' as Faust. In this sense Jung's (historical) Faust is his (Jungian) Philemon.

The tower itself is said to be 'a symbol of psychic totality'.[94] Here Jung can pursue his engagement with the past – 'thoughts surface, that reach back for centuries', we read – and here he can live in a Goethean state of 'anticipation' (*Antizipation*), 'anticipating distant futures'. In Bollingen, we are told, 'the torment of creation is lessened'; here, the creative and the ludic, *das Schöpferische und das Spielerische*, come close together, approaching a Schillerian synthesis.[95] Do Bollingen and Jung's experiences there represent what Schiller called the 'aesthetic state'? Jung's second personality, we have learned, was Faust, something 'in secret accord with the Middle Ages', something 'personified by Faust, the legacy of a past, by which Goethe was obviously deeply moved'.[96] In the tower at Bollingen, *Memories, Dreams, Reflections* tells us, Jung used to 'live as a "second personality"', seeing life 'in the whole'), as a ceaseless process of coming-into-being and dying-away-again.[97]

Nevertheless, Jung's reputation remains tarnished by allegations about his political stance: not so much his willingness for his name to go forward as a candidate to the Swiss parliament for the National Group of Independents (although this does not help), but rather the accusation that, in his presidency of the General Medical Society for Psychotherapy, later called the International General Medical Society for Psychotherapy from 1933 to 1940, and his editorship of the *Zentralblatt für Psychotherapie und ihre Grenzgebiete* (Journal for Psychotherapy and its Related Fields), as well as in various statements to journalists, Jung showed himself to be a supporter of National Socialism.[98] It is also true that some of Jung's pronouncements at the time seem to have been particularly open to misinterpretation. One thinks, for example, of his interview for Radio Berlin in 1933, when he was interviewed by his former pupil Adolf Weizsäcker (1896–1978), a member of the Deutsches Institut für psychologische Forschung und Psychotherapie (German Institute for Psychological Research and Psychotherapy) and of the National Socialist Party. In response to Weizsäcker's rather wordy questions, Jung congratulated 'German youth' on their 'assurance' in pursuit of 'their goal' and saluted 'a need for a common *Weltanschauung*'.[99] In 1938, in a lengthy interview given to H. R. Knickerbocker for *Cosmopolitan* magazine, Jung made a comparison between Hitler and Mussolini in which the Italian dictator came off quite well.[100] Nowhere, however, did he endorse the politics or policies of these leaders.

Over the years the charge has been repeatedly levelled at Jung that he held anti-Semitic views.[101] It is not hard to see why this charge has been made: for instance, in an essay published in 1918 in the cultural journal *Schweizerland: Monatshefte für Schweizer Art und Kunst*, under the title 'On the Unconscious', Jung drew a distinction between the psychology of Aryan Europeans and that of Jews.[102] He went on to locate the root of his theoretical differences with Freud's and Adler's psychoanalytical systems in race: 'These specifically Jewish doctrines', he wrote, 'are thoroughly unsatisfying to the Germanic mentality'.[103] Even more damagingly, however, Jung was still using this tone in a paper entitled 'The State of Psychotherapy Today', published in the *Zentralblatt für Psychotherapie und ihre Grenzgebiete* in 1934. Insisting on an essential difference between German and Jewish psychology, Jung attributed here a greater potential to the 'Aryan unconscious' and rejected the appropriateness of 'Jewish categories' to understand the German psyche.[104] Yet the matter is by no means as clear-cut or straightforward as it might at first appear to be.

First, neither Freudians nor Jungians come out with much credit from the episode with the General Medical Society for Psychotherapy (founded in 1933) and the Deutsches Institut für psychologische Forschung und Psychotherapie (founded in 1936), owing to the involvement in both of Matthias Heinrich Göring (1879–1945), a cousin of the notorious Nazi and chief of the Luftwaffe, Hermann Göring (1894–1946). Freud and the psychoanalysts Max Eitington (1881–1943) and Felix Boehm (1881–1958) were content for Wilhelm Reich (1897–1957), a Jewish psychoanalyst with Communist sympathies, to be excluded from the so-called Göring-Institut in 1933.[105] No such similar incidents are recorded, however, during Jung's tenure as President of the Allgemeine Ärztliche Gesellschaft für Psychotherapie. Indeed, it has been pointed out that, thanks to a charter for the International Allegemeine Ärztliche Gesellschaft für Psychotherapie (IAAGP) composed under Jung's direction and agreed at the Seventh Congress for Psychotherapy at Bad Nauheim in May 1934, it was possible for German Jewish psychiatrists and psychotherapists to apply for individual membership, and thus continue to practise in Germany, for longer than might otherwise have been possible.[106]

Second, as we have already noted, Freud entertained a kind of 'inverse anti-Semitism' with regard to Jung. Writing to Karl Abraham on 3 May 1908, he reassured his colleague that it was easier for him, as a Jew, to accept psychoanalysis than it was for Jung who, 'as a Christian and the son of a pastor', could only 'find his way' to Freud 'against great inner resistances', adding that this made Jung's adherence 'all the more valuable', inasmuch as 'his appearance saved psychoanalysis from the danger of becoming a Jewish national concern' or nearly did.[107] And in a letter of 13 August 1908 to Jung, Freud reassured Jung that his personality ('your strong and independent character') and his ethnic status ('your Germanic blood which enables you to command the sympathies of the public more readily than I') alike would enable him to act as an effective ambassador for psychoanalysis.[108]

It was not Jung's fault that he was not a Jew; but equally, when challenged by the (Jewish) analytical psychologist James Kirsch (1901–1989) about accusations of anti-Semitism in a letter of 7 May 1934, sent from Tel Aviv and written 'from the heart', did Jung have to reply as he did? Referring to these 'amusing rumours', he dismisses the charges against him, yet he does so in a way that suggests he did not really understand what was at stake. 'This sensitivity is simply pathological and makes every discussion almost impossible', he writes, going on to declare that 'with this readiness to sniff out anti-Semitism everywhere, the Jew directly evokes anti-Semitism'; whereas, he insists, 'in the great majority of cases, I've been getting along very well with my Jewish patients and colleagues'.[109] What Jung did not (or could not) understand, it seems, is that, while it was one thing for Jews to distinguish between 'Jewish' and 'German' culture or psychotherapy, it was another thing entirely for a non-Jew to do so, especially in the context of racial policies in Germany, which led in 1935 to the Nuremberg Laws (and, ultimately, to the Holocaust).[110] When, writing in the *Neue Zürcher Zeitung* in 1934, Jung confessed his 'total inability to understand why it should be a crime to speak of "Jewish" psychology', one can only squirm; Aniela Jaffé placed her finger on the problem when she wrote that the fact Jung 'dragged [the difference between Jewish and non-Jewish psychology] into the limelight at this particular moment, when being a Jew was enough to put one in danger of one's life . . . must be regarded as a grave human error'.[111]

Finally, it is important neither to misinterpret nor to misattribute motives. For instance, in his recent critique of Freud, Michel Onfray has drawn attention to Freud's decision, when the opportunity arose through a connection opened up by the father of one of his clients, to send Mussolini a copy of *Why War?*, a short tract he had co-authored with Albert Einstein, the Nobel Prize-winning physicist, and to inscribe it with a dedication. In this work, Freud spoke frankly about 'the innate and ineradicable inequality of men' and 'their tendency to fall into the two classes of leaders and followers'; in these and other lines, such as Freud's suggestion that 'more care should be taken than hitherto to educate an upper stratum of men with independent minds, not open to intimidation and eager in the pursuit of truth, whose business it would be to give direction to the dependent masses', Onfray detects a discreet reference to the struggle between Mussolini's National Fascist Party and the Roman Catholic Church, with a suggestion that Freud would have sided with the former against the latter.[112] But here Onfray shows himself insensitive to Freud's habit (shared with many German-speaking fellow intellectuals, including Goethe and Thomas Mann) of *irony*; a habit best displayed when, asked by the authorities for a statement to confirm he had not been ill-treated as a condition for being given permission to leave Austria for London, Freud wrote: 'I can most highly recommend the Gestapo to everyone'.[113]

All in all, it is not enough to accept Jung's remark to the rabbi and scholar Leo Baeck (1873–1956), made when they met in Zurich in 1946 – 'Well, I slipped up' (*Jawohl, ich bin ausgerutscht*) – as a sufficient explanation (even if, according to the account of the meeting given by Gershom Scholem, 1897–1982, Baeck was satisfied with this response and departed reconciled with Jung). He did not simply forget to water the plants or leave his umbrella on the train. It was more than a simple slip-of-the-tongue. Like Paul Celan visiting Martin Heidegger, in the spirit of 'a hope, today, / of a thinking man's / coming / word / in the heart', we can look through Jung's works for a single reference to the Holocaust; and we shall be as disappointed with Jung as Celan was with Heidegger.[114]

On the other hand, Jung (unlike Heidegger) was never a card-carrying member of the Nazi Party, and to reduce Jung's entire, vast output to this one point, with which he nevertheless (albeit indirectly) engages, would be to be unnecessarily restrictive in one's approach. Jung did not do apologies and this uncomfortable fact is one we shall have to live with. After admitting in 1934 that he had been 'so incautious as to do the very thing most open to misunderstanding at the present moment' and to have 'tabled the Jewish question', Jung's self-exculpatory attempts do little more than prove his maxim that 'one carries one's worst enemy within oneself'.[115] Nevertheless, his enunciation of precisely this insight gives one good reason, whatever his sins of commission or omission, to engage constructively (as well as critically) with Jung's work.

7

A Voyage of Discovery to the Other Pole of the World

After he had explored the inner world of his psyche in the Red Book, and at the same time as he was developing his mature psychological system and embarking on his investigations into alchemy, Jung began to undertake a number of journeys in the external world. His travels would literally take him halfway around the world, and illustrate his engagement with the 'real' world around him, and his encounter, not just with the unconscious, but with other cultures. These journeys are related in the chapter entitled 'Travels' in *Memories, Dreams, Reflections*; his 1925 visit to Africa has been discussed at length by Blake Burleson.[1]

Jung's Travels

In 1920 Jung undertook a journey to North Africa, visiting Algeria and Tunisia. In Sousse, a town located south of the capital, Tunis, Jung reflected that this land had already experienced three civilizations – Carthaginian, Roman and Christian – and was now Islamic. What, Jung wondered, will the technological age do with Islam? It was – and, from the 21st-century perspective of our post-9/11 world, it remains – a good question to ask.

Leaving Sousse and travelling further south to Sfax, and then into the Sahara, Jung was 'struck like a bolt of lightning' by thoughts that 'illuminated' his point of observation: he felt transported back many centuries to 'an infinitely more naïve world of adolescents who were beginning, with the aid of a slender knowledge of the Qu'ran, to emerge from their condition of twilight consciousness that had existed from time immemorial'.[2] In this part of the world, Jung encountered a different pace of life, free from the tyranny of the wristwatch and the alarm clock, and the further he 'penetrated' (*vordrang*) into the Sahara, the more he was impressed with the way the people of the desert lived their lives. 'These people', he reflected, 'live from their emotions, that is, they are lived out by their emotions', whereas 'what we lack is intensity of life'.[3] On the basis of his experience of the Sahara, Jung voices a Nietzschean critique of the West: in effect, like Walter Pater (1839–1894), he believed that 'to burn always with this hard, gem-like flame, to maintain this ecstasy, is success in life'.[4] In Africa, too, Jung came to acquire a keener appreciation of the famous lines by the German Romantic poet Friedrich Hölderlin (1770–1843): 'But where danger threatens / That which saves from it also grows'.[5] What, then, is it that saves us? For Jung, salvation lies in 'our ability to bring the unconscious urges to consciousness with the aid of warning dreams'.[6]

Jung's response to his journey into African and Islamic culture was thus a complex one. On the one hand, Jung experienced his encounter with Arabic culture as 'a primordial memory of an all-too-familiar prehistoric past which apparently we have entirely forgotten'.[7] On the other, this past can be made present, if we overcome our one-sided reliance on consciousness. 'In the living psychic structure', he wrote, 'nothing happens in a merely mechanical fashion, but within the economy of the whole, related to the whole: it is purposeful and has meaning'.[8] It should be noted: Jung is not arguing that we simply throw consciousness aside, for that would constitute 'a relapse into barbarism', but we should keep 'the life that we live' and 'the life we have forgotten' in a state of balance – or, rather, fruitful tension.

In December 1924 Jung made his third trip to the United States, going on in January 1925 to visit the Pueblo Indians in New Mexico, before returning to visit New Orleans and New York. In New Mexico the encounter with the Pueblo Indians (and, in particular, the chief of the Taos Pueblos, Ochwiay Biano or Chief Mountain Lake) stimulated and aroused in Jung 'something unknown and yet intimately familiar', that rose within him 'like a formless mist'.[9] In Joris-Karl Huysmans's great decadent novel *A rebours* (1884), the fictional figure of des Esseintes had been stimulated by a combination of a history of the councils of the Church, Father Philippe Labbe's multivolume *Sacrosancta concilia* (1671–83) and the paintings of the Symbolist painter Gustave Moreau to imagine – as had the English essayist Thomas De Quincey, when reading Roman history – great scenes from the past.[10] Similarly, in New Mexico Jung saw in his mind's eye, so to speak, historical images unravel themselves before him.[11]

Thomas De Quincy and Livy, Huysmans's des Esseintes and the Abbé Labbe, Jung and the Pueblo Indians: what the real and the fictional figures alike experience is the persistence of the past in the present. Indeed, in the mysterious rites of the Pueblo Indians, Jung felt he came to understand better the ancient cult at Eleusis and the reasons why such historians as Pausanias or Herodotus had written that it was not permitted to speak the name of the god.[12]

In the words of Mountain Lake (a figure who acquired for Jung an importance similar to the one that the Sioux Black Elk has more generally achieved), Jung realized that the 'dignity' or 'tranquil self-composure' of the individual Pueblo Indian was based on the fact that his life was 'cosmologically meaningful'.[13] Jung's visit to the Pueblos taught him that 'knowledge does not enrich us, but removes us ever further away from the mythical world in which we were once by right of birth at home'.[14] His outlook became an eminently intercultural, even transcultural one: 'The holiness of the mountains [of New Mexico], the revelation of Yahweh on Sinai, the inspiration granted to Nietzsche in the Engadine, all say the same thing'.[15]

Following a visit in 1925 to the British Empire Exhibition held in Wembley, Jung embarked in the autumn of that year on an expedition to Kenya and Uganda, culminating in a visit to the Elgonyi people (more correctly known as the Chepkitale people or the Ogiek) on Mount Elgon, located on the border between those two countries. Travelling out from Nairobi to visit the Athi plains (a giant game reserve, now the Nairobi National Park), Jung experienced, at the sight of the gigantic herds of animals grazing, set off against the horizon, what Roger Brook has called an 'ontological vision'.[16] And tellingly so, for Jung's encounter with something so quintessentially 'other' – 'the stillness of the eternal beginning, the world as it had always been, in the state of non-being' – found analogies from his own experience: the light of tropical Africa is reminiscent of the sunlight in the Engadine, he is reminded of an alchemical saying – 'what nature leaves imperfect, the art perfects' – and he speaks of humankind as a second creator of the world, giving the world its 'objective existence', much as Heidegger described humankind as *der Hüter des Seins*, a 'guardian' or 'shepherd' of Being.[17]

In Africa Jung was overwhelmed by its 'incredible beauty' and its 'incredible suffering', believing that he had never seen so clearly, in the words of Herodotus, 'man and other animals', and in our own age of mobile phones and text-messaging devices we can understand Jung's relief at being away from Europe and her daimons: 'no telegrams, no telephone calls, no letters, no visitors' (the equivalent for us of no emails, no text messages, no attachments, no tweets). Instead Jung's 'liberated psychic forces' (*befreite seelische Kräfte*) poured blissfully back into 'prehistoric expanses' (*vorweltliche Weiten*).[18] On Mount Elgon itself, at the rising of the sun, Jung admired the magnificent scene with 'insatiable delight', or even in 'timeless ecstasy'.[19]

Here we see Jung experiencing something akin to what Romain Rolland would have called the 'oceanic feeling'.[20] Whereas Freud always maintained a reductionist approach to religion, as did such followers as Karl Abraham (1877–1925), Ludwig Jekels (1867–1954) and Jacques Schnier (1898–1988), we can see that Jung was always open to living out the moment envisioned by Goethe at the beginning of *Faust*, Part Two, when Faust is rejuvenated by the sight of the rising sun, reflected in the waterfall.[21]

After a gap of some years in his travels (although he went on a cruise to Egypt and Palestine in 1933, and received an honorary doctoral degree from Harvard in 1936), in 1938 Jung accepted an invitation from the British government of India to take part in the celebrations on the 25th anniversary of the Indian Science Congress in Calcutta, a journey on which he also received honorary degrees from the universities of Calcutta, Benares and Allahabad. Jung's admiration for India, mixed with a sense of disquiet, emerges clearly from two essays arising from this visit, 'The Dreamlike World of India' (1939) and 'What India Can Teach Us' (1939).[22] As if to protect himself from the influence of India, Jung took with him, not a Baedeker or a *Rough Guide*, but the first volume of the *Theatrum chemicum* (1602), containing the principal writings of Gerhard Dorn (*c.* 1530–1584), an alchemist and pupil of Paracelsus.

In Konark, a small town on the Bay of Bengal, Jung visited the site of the thirteenth-century Sun Temple, famous – much like the group of temples at Khajuraho, south-east of Delhi – for its erotic sculptures. The pandit (or scholar) who was acting as Jung's tour guide emphasized the spiritual aspect of these sculptures, particularly two statues of dancing girls at the gate of the temples, and as he and Jung walked down a lane of lingams, he whispered to Jung: 'Do you what these mean? They are a man's private parts'.[23] Little can the pandit have known that his client for this visit knew all too well what they were, having had a vision of a giant subterranean phallus when he was still a very young child . . .

When visiting the famous Buddhist monuments in Sanchi, north-east of Bhopal, where Buddha is said to have delivered his Fire Sermon that teaches liberation from suffering through detachment from the mind and the five senses, Jung was a spectator to a rite being carried out by Japanese pilgrims. In this ceremony he grasped something important about Buddhism: that the Buddha himself was 'the reality of the self, which has broken into a personal life and laid claim to it'.[24] Moreover, this insight was, or so he believed, compatible with the understanding of Buddhism that had been developed by Schopenhauer.[25] In a dream that came to him towards the end of his stay in Calcutta, however, Jung imagined he saw the castle of the Grail, in front of which, among a black iron trellis in the shape of a grapevine, he saw a group of tiny houses and a tiny, iron, hooded gnome, a *cucullatus* or *kabir*, scurrying from one door to another. Out of his impressions of India, Jung understood this dream to be saying, an essentially European vision had emerged. What did it mean? First, that myth still lives: 'myths that the day has forgotten continue to be told by night'; and second, that 'the great ones of the past have not died . . . they have merely changed their names . . . "Small and slight, but great in might" [*Faust II*, lines 8174–5], the veiled *kabir* enters a new house'; and third, that Jung should concern himself less with India and more with 'what alchemy has to say about the *unum vas*, the *una medicina*, and the *unus lapis*'.[26] Back, in other words, to his alchemical books. On the way back, the ship docked at Bombay, but Jung decided not to go ashore. Instead, he buried himself in his Latin alchemical texts and the writings of Gerhard Dorn.[27]

Can one talk of Jung as a contributor to a discourse of postcolonialism? On the one hand, Jung's admiration for non-Western cultures is evident: and his quiet respect for, say, the customers of an Arab coffee-house, whose language he did not understand but whose gestures and expressions fascinated him, demonstrate his ability to watch, listen and learn. On the other hand, there is a tendency in the accounts of his travels given in *Memories, Dreams, Reflections* to understand the non-Western in terms of the Western (specifically, in terms of alchemy); in the end, Jung's appreciation of 'otherness' as a cultural phenomenon is always subordinated to the psychological 'other' of the collective unconscious. And his account of an evening episode in Sudan, where a tribal *ngoma* (or dance) threatens to get out of hand, until Jung, brandishing the rhinoceros whip he has been swinging while dancing along, shouts at them in Swiss German that it's time for everyone to go to bed, is decidedly colonial in outlook. But then, Jung was a child of his time; what is remarkable is how he was also able to sense, in foreign cultures and his own, the 'timeless' dimension of both.

Intimations of Mortality

In 1943 Jung had been appointed to the chair of Medical Psychology at Basel University, but in 1944 he was forced to resign on account of a critical illness. At the beginning of the year he had broken his foot and then suffered a heart attack. Drugged to the eyeballs with camphor injections, and barely clinging on to life, Jung experienced a series of deliriums and visions. In particular, he had what sounds very much like a near-death or out-of-body experience, in which he was high up in space, looking down on the globe beneath him. Turning around, he saw a tremendous dark block of stone, like a meteorite. It reminded him of stones he had seen in the Bay of Bengal, which had had been hollowed out into temples. Looking at this block, Jung saw that an entrance led into a small antechamber, to the right of which a Hindu sat in the lotus position, and Jung knew that this man was expecting him. (Inside the antechamber, the gate to the temple, with its innumerable tiny niches, reminded Jung of the temple of the sacred relic of the tooth, purportedly belonging to the Buddha, in the city of Kandy in Sri Lanka.)

As Jung approached the steps leading up to the entrance, he had the strange sensation that everything was being stripped away from him, and yet that something in him persisted: that his very identity was 'this bundle of what-has-been, and what-has-been-accomplished'.[28] Until this moment, his life as he had led it often seemed 'like a story that has no beginning and no end', but now he sensed he was going to receive an answer to why everything in his life had been as it had. Then, from below, an image floated up: the face of his doctor in the hospital, framed by a golden wreath, like the *basileus* (or king) of Kos, the Greek island on which the temple of Asklepios (Asclepius), the god of healing, is located. The image of the doctor told him that he was not going to die. And awaking from his vision, Jung began to recover.

Grimly, Jung knew that, instead of him, it was the doctor who was going to die (and in fact, a few weeks later, the doctor did). Further strange dreams followed, where Jung floated in blissful ecstasy; indeed, he speaks of being 'surrounded by images of all creation', like the realm of the Mothers in *Faust*, Part Two.[29] And in one particular trancelike vision, the nurse that brought him his food appeared to him like an old Jewish woman, with a blue halo round her head, bringing him a ritual kosher dish. It was as if, Jung writes, he was in a scene from *Pardes Rimonim* or 'The Pomegranate Orchard', a sixteenth-century Kabbalistic work by the Jewish mystic Moses ben Jacob Cordovero (1522–1570), where the wedding of Tifereth with Malkuth, the sixth and the tenth sephirot in the Tree of Life in Kabbalah, representing masculinity and femininity (or Shekhinah), takes place. Or else it was as if he were Shimon ben Yochai, a first-century rabbi to whom the authorship of the *Zohar*, the chief work of Kabbalah, is attributed, whose wedding in the afterlife was being celebrated.[30] This mystic marriage in the tradition of Kabbalah then merged into the Christian marriage of the Lamb, as the garden of pomegranates faded and was replaced by the city of Jerusalem, festively bedecked.

It was, Jung says, 'an ineffable state of joy'. There were angels, and there was light. Jung himself *was* the 'marriage of the Lamb'.[31] In turn, this image passed, to be replaced by a vision of a classical amphitheatre in a lush green landscape, as male and female dancers surrounded the *hieros gamos*, the holy marriage, consummated by Zeus and Hera on a flower-decked couch.[32]

What lay behind this triple vision, in turn Kabbalistic, Christian and classical (but in all three cases highly mystical), whose 'beauty and intensity of emotion' cannot, Jung emphasizes, be conveyed? To begin with, this was not the first time that Jung had entertained images of floating and of mystical union: in the Red Book he had imagined himself to be Christ/Odin hanging on the cross/tree of life, suspended above the earth for three days and three nights, and Elijah's offer of Salome to Jung in marriage reflects his realization that 'the two conflicting powers' of his own soul, or of the magician Philemon and his wife Baucis, must be kept together 'in a true marriage'.[33] But now, Jung insisted, these visions were no (mere) products of his imagination, but 'utterly real': they had the quality of 'objective experience'.[34]

In Jung's view, what these experiences revealed was something about the nature of objectivity itself; and about eternity. What does Jung mean by *the eternal*? We can understand Jung's notion of eternity better by considering it in the light of some of his intellectual predecessors. In a famous passage in his *Ethics* (published in 1677), Spinoza tells us that we know – indeed, that we *experience* – that we are 'eternal'.[35] In his *System of Transcendental Idealism* (1800), Schelling, in the context of a discussion of the categorical imperative (or the moral law), writes about what he calls 'the eternal in me'.[36] And in that same work, to which Eduard von Hartmann made reference in his *Philosophy of the Unconscious* (1869), Schelling proposed the notion of an 'eternal unconscious'.[37] In *Memories, Dreams, Reflections* Jung acknowledges that we tend to shy away from the word 'eternal' (*ewig*), but insists that what he experienced was 'the bliss of a non-temporal state . . . in which present, past, and future are one'.[38] As a consequence, the 'objectivity' experienced in these visions belongs to a 'completed individuation', something which enables a quasi-Nietzschean affirmation of all that is, or 'a "yes"-saying to being'.[39] In turn, this affirmation of being enables an affirmation of the self, or what Jung calls 'a "yes"-saying to one's destiny'. (Nietzsche's cry that one should love one's own fate, *amor fati*, is not far away here either.)

This medical crisis and the visions accompaying it raised the possibility of a life after death, a possibility explored in detail in *Memories, Dreams, Reflections*. Here Jung explicitly positions himself on 'the mythic side of Man'.[40] This side of humankind, he observes with regret, is given short shrift nowadays, and Jung would agree with Nietzsche's argument in *The Birth of Tragedy* (1872) that 'without myth every culture loses the healthy natural power of its creativity' and that 'only a horizon defined by myths completes and unifies a whole cultural movement'.[41] For Jung, because human beings can no longer 'create fables' (*fabulieren*, a good Goethean word), a good deal 'escapes' us, and we acquiesce in the fact that we are limited by our innate structure and therefore bound to this world: whereas 'mythic man' (*der mythische Mensch*) demands a 'going-beyond' (*Darüber-Hinausgehen*), 'the scientifically responsible man' (*der wissenschaftlich verantwortliche Mensch*) cannot permit this.[42] (Similarly, Nietzsche laments: 'The mythless man [*Der mythenlose Mensch*] stands eternally hungry, surrounded by all past ages, and digs and grubs for roots . . . what does all this point to, if not to the loss of myth, the loss of the mythical home, the mythical maternal womb?'[43])

According to Jung, it is 'important and salutary' to speak of 'unfathomable things', comparing such discourse to 'the telling of a good ghost story as we sit by the fireside and smoke a pipe' (and one can all too well imagine Jung doing this at home or at Bollingen).[44] For Jung, 'myths are the earliest forms of science', and myths and dreams about the afterlife are not merely 'compensating fantasies', because 'all life desires eternity'; rather, life does indeed desire eternity, and myth must be allowed to speak for itself.[45]

On the one hand, Jung's lucubrations about a life after death seem like a return to the parapsychological concerns of his earlier years, when he devoured spiritist literature and the works of Zöllner and Crookes, Carl du Prel and Swedenborg (as discussed in chapter Three). On the other, they are entirely in line with his pursuit of a Goethean programme, if we think of the stance on the afterlife attributed to Goethe. In a famous conversation that took place on the day of Wieland's funeral in 1813, as recorded by Johannes Daniel Falk (1768–1826), Goethe expounded his belief on the personal survival of our souls after death in considerable (and remarkable) detail.[46]

It is true that Falk's memoirs have been dismissed as untrustworthy, and their reliability was criticized in particular by Friedrich Wilhelm Riemer, who published his own memoirs of Goethe. Nevertheless, Goethe's views on personal survival are recorded by Friedrich von Müller, as are views on eternal survival, immortality and the future life by Eckermann. On the last of these occasions, however, Goethe also expressed a certain impatience with 'thoughts about immortality', describing a 'preoccupation' with them as 'a pastime for the aristocratic classes, and especially for women who have nothing better to do'. Instead, Goethe argued, 'an honest man who hopes to achieve something while he is still here on earth is working and striving and struggling every day to that end, will let the other world take care of itself and bestir himself usefully in this one'.[47] Similarly, for Jung – and this is the second implication of the visions experienced in 1944 – the notion that the present, the past and the future are really one gave him fresh insights into our life in the here-and-now.

In turn, this belief in what Jung, borrowing a phrase from the alchemist Gerhard Dorn, called the *unus mundus* informed two important collaborations that marked the final decade or so of Jung's intellectual activity: his work with the physicist Wolfgang Pauli and with the Dominican theologian Victor White.[48] From quantum mechanics to theological speculation about God, from the microcosm to the macrocosm, Jung's intellectual ambition in the final, intensely productive stage of his thought could not have been greater.

Wolfgang Pauli

Ever since Richard Wilhelm had given a lecture on the *I Ching*, the Chinese oracle text also known as *The Book of Changes*, to the Psychology Club in Zurich in 1923, Jung had been fascinated by this ancient divination system. In 1950 he wrote a foreword for the English translation of Wilhelm's edition of the *I Ching*, in which he hailed the significance of the oracle: it 'does not offer itself with proofs and results', it 'does not vaunt itself nor is it easy to approach' for, 'like a part of nature, it waits until it is discovered'. According to Jung, 'the *I Ching* offers neither facts nor power, but for lovers of self-knowledge, of wisdom – if there be such – it seems to be the right book'.[49] Jung spoke as a practitioner of the *I Ching*, as someone who had, as he had acknowledged, been interested in this oracle technique 'for more than thirty years'.[50]

As Jung explained in his appendix on Richard Wilhelm included in *Memories, Dreams, Reflections*, since 1920 he had been experimenting with the *I Ching* until, one summer in Bollingen, he decided to make 'an all-out attack on the riddle of this book', and he cut himself a bunch of reeds, in order to fashion for himself an equivalent of the traditional stalks of yarrow. On Jung's account, he would sit for hours on the ground beneath a hundred-year-old pear tree, with the *I Ching* beside him, 'practising the technique by referring the resultant oracles to one another in an interplay of questions and answers'.[51]

Jung was impressed with the results; and he became convinced that the oracle worked. He even recommended using the *I Ching* to his patients. (One such client, for instance, was a young man with a strong mother-complex. He was thinking of marrying a young woman who seemed suitable for him, but he was concerned that, under the influence of his complex, he would once again find himself in the power of an 'overwhelming mother'. Together with Jung, he consulted the *I Ching*. The resulting hexagram was number 44, *Kou* or *Coming to Meet*, the text of which reads: 'The maiden is powerful. One should not marry such a maiden.'[52] An unusually clear result for the *I Ching*. One assumes, although we are not told, that he did not marry the woman; nor are we told what *she* thought of the result of the consultation.)[53]

But how did – or does – the *I Ching* work? More precisely, how can there be a connection between psychic and physical events? (As Jung wrote in his foreword, 'the less one thinks about the theory of the *I Ching*, the more soundly one sleeps'.[54]) In answering this question, Jung came to develop the notion of an 'a-causal connection', which he was to call 'synchronicity': and this is where the Austrian theoretical physicist Wolfgang Pauli enters our story.[55]

Pauli had been born in Vienna in 1900 and, following study in Munich, he had worked as an assistant in Göttingen (to Max Born), in Copenhagen (to Neils Bohr) and in Hamburg (to Wilhelm Lenz). In 1928 Pauli took up a professorship in theoretical physics at the ETH in Zurich, and in 1930 he postulated the existence of a subatomic particle, the neutrino. (Pauli's scientific reputation today rests on his collaboration with Werner Heisenberg and Niels Bohr, as well as his discovery of the 'Pauli principle' or 'exclusion principle', according to which 'no two electrons can exist in an atom in the same state, that is, they cannot share the same set of quantum numbers'. At the time, however, he was also well known for the so-called 'Pauli effect', the propensity of scientific equipment to break down or fail when he was in the vicinity.[56]) Pauli's professional success, however, which was to lead in 1945 to his nomination by Albert Einstein for the Nobel Prize for physics, was not matched on the personal side: he divorced the wife to whom he had been married for less than a year and returned to the bon viveur lifestyle he had formerly developed in the bars and nightclubs of Hamburg's Sankt Pauli district, drinking and partying to the point of a breakdown.

It was fortunate, then, that one of the world's greatest analysts was his colleague at the ETH: Carl Jung. Pauli began analysis with Jung, seeking professional help for his drink problem, but the extent of Pauli's eventual 'cure' is reflected in an anecdote according to which Pauli drove from Lucerne to Zurich after a number of drinks, crying '*Ich fahre ziemlich gut!*' ('I'm driving rather well!') as the car swerved from side to side.[57] More important, the contact with Jung led to their collaboration around the notion of synchronicity, to which Jung attached the greatest significance.

In his foreword to Richard Wilhelm's translation of the *I Ching*, Jung suggested that the natural-scientific paradigm that had hitherto been generally accepted was gradually being eroded by recent discoveries. As he put it, 'what Kant's *Critique of Reason* failed to do is being accomplished by modern physics', inasmuch as 'the axioms of causality are being shaken to their foundations: we know now that what we term natural laws are merely statistical truths and thus must necessarily allow for exceptions'.[58] In fact, ever since *On the Distribution of Energy* (1900) by Max Planck (1858–1947), and the special (1905) and general (1915) theories of relativity of Albert Einstein (1879–1955), not to mention the work of Werner Heisenberg (1901–1976) and Niels Bohr (1885–1962), the assumptions of classical physics governing science since Francis Bacon had been constantly challenged and questioned. To use the expression coined by the American philosopher Thomas S. Kuhn (1922–1996), a 'paradigm shift' was taking place.[59]

The experiments of quantum mechanics suggested that reality, far from being the indivisible and mechanical whole of which, as

Descartes and Newton had believed, the particle was a mere aspect, was, particularly at the subatomic level, subject to unpredictable and apparently random changes. More specifically, discoveries such as X-rays and radioactivity, which had fascinated Jung as a student at university, indicated that matter, far from being something permanent, was subject to transformation and decay. As a result, the notion of causality was increasingly regarded as being too limited to explain the findings of particle physics. In other words, as Jung was well aware, what Kant had proclaimed to be an a priori constituent of human knowledge was gradually coming to be seen, at least by some, as merely statistical probability. That these developments represented a major challenge to the critical philosophy of Kant was clear to, among others, the theoretical physicist Heisenberg and the neo-Kantian philosopher Ernst Cassirer (1874–1945).

Jung sought to replace the principle of causality – or, more precisely, to supplement it – with another principle: with sychronicity. He suggested that it might supplement causality in a specific way, arguing that whereas causality governed the macrocosm (the external world), synchronicity governed the microcosm (the 'inner' world of the psyche). 'Unlike causality, which reigns without restraint over the whole picture of the macrophysical world and whose universal rule is shattered only in certain lower orders of magnitude', he argued, 'synchronicity is a phenomenon that seems to be primarily connected with psychic conditions, that is to say processes in the unconscious'.[60] Synchronicity itself was defined by Jung as an a-causal connection, as a *sinngemäße Koinzidenz*: a meaningful (or meaning-related) coincidence, an expression that is tantalizingly ambiguous.[61]

Furthermore, in the conclusion of his contribution to *The Interpretation of Nature and the Psyche*, a monograph he coauthored with Wolfgang Pauli, Jung supplemented the triad of classical physics – time, space, and causality – with synchronicity to produce a typically Jungian quaternity: space – causality – unconscious – time.

Over and beyond this quaternity, Jung and Pauli devised, on the model of Schopenhauer's four-fold root of the principle of sufficient reason, a four-fold root for modern physics, even if their quaternity of principles raises many difficulties.[62] This was not least because in the Jung–Pauli quaternity, consisting of (1) causality (constant causation through effect); (2) synchronicity (inconstant conjunction through contingency, equivalence or 'meaning'); (3) indestructible energy (what Jung elsewhere called libido?); and (4) the space–time continuum (even though this is said to be merely relative to the psyche), both the relationship between the individual elements of the Jung–Pauli quaternity and the relationship between that and Schopenhauer's 'quaternity' remain unclear.[63] As Arthur Koestler (1905–1983) once remarked, Jung 'offers no concrete explanations how the schema is meant to work, and his comments on it are so obscure that I must leave it to the interested reader to look them up in the library'.[64]

It should perhaps be noted that, throughout the development of his psychological system, Jung demonstrated a remarkable passion for the detection of opposites and their resolution through the constellation of quaternities.[65] Not only are there the four psychic functions of thinking, feeling, sensation and intuition, but he pointed to Empedocles' four elements, Hippocrates' four 'humours', the ascending quaternity of anima figures (Eve, Helen, Mary, Sophia), the four figures of the Trinity together with the Virgin Mary, and he frequently quoted the lines from the 'Kabeiroi Scene' of Goethe's *Faust II*: 'Three we took off beside us, / The fourth of them denied us'.[66] In this respect, Jung shares a passion with Jacques Lacan (1901–1981), who wrote in 'Kant avec Sade' (1963): 'A quadripartite structure has, since the introduction of the unconscious, always been required in the construction of a subjective ordering'.[67] (In addition to the quadripartite structure of the Oedipus Complex (mother, child, father, phallus), Lacan's 'schema L' has four nodes, there are four discourses (of the master, the university, the hysteric and the analyst), and there are four fundamental concepts of psychoanalysis.)[68]

In this period of Jung's life we see analytical psychology turning into a search for a unified theory of everything. For instance, in an Eranos lecture from 1946 later published as 'On the Nature of the Psyche', Jung argued that there was a reciprocal and complementary relationship between physics and psychology: 'Physics determines quantities and their relation to one another; psychology determines qualities without being able to measure quantities. Despite that, both sciences arrive at ideas which come significantly close to one another . . . Between physics and psychology there is in fact "a genuine and authentic relationship of complementarity"'.[69] In a letter written from the Eranos Conference of 1948 to the German theoretical physicist Pascual Jordan (1902–1980) on 1 April (despite the date, it is a serious letter), Jung mentioned his discussions with Pauli 'on the unexpected relations between psychology and physics', explaining that 'psychology as might be expected appears in the realm of physics in the field of theory-building' and that 'the outstanding question is a psychological critique of the space-time concept', a point of which he had just made 'a strange discovery' that he wanted to check out with Pauli 'from the physical side'.[70] (Jung's psychological critique of space and time is found in his writings on synchronicity, where he argues that they are purely 'relative'.)

Two years later, in a letter of 4 March 1950 to the analytical psychologist Edward Whitmont (1912–1998), Jung cited the notion of 'complementarity' (the notion that, under different experimental conditions, microparticles display different patterns of behaviour) as an example of the convergence of psychology and physics:

We can do no more than carefully tap out the phenomenology that gives us indirect news of the essence of the psyche. Similarly – from the other side – physics is tapping its way into irrepresentable territory which it can visualize only indirectly by means of models. Both sciences, the psychology of the unconscious and atomic physics, are arriving at concepts which show remarkable points of agreement.[71]

And six years later, in his letter to Fritz Lerch of 10 September 1956, Jung was yet more firmly convinced of the reciprocal relation between science and psychology, hinting at more important insights to come: 'I do not doubt that quite fundamental connections exist between physics and psychology, and that the objective psyche contains images that would elucidate the secret of matter. These connections are discernible in synchronistic phenomena and their acausality. Today these things are only pale phantoms and it remains for the future to collect, with much painstaking work, the experiences which could shed light on this darkness'.[72]

Why was so Jung concerned about synchronicity? Aside from his interest in cutting-edge discoveries in theoretical subatomic physics, there was a therapeutic aspect too. For instance, Jung related how a female client, whose 'animus' was 'steeped in Cartesian philosophy' (a code word for a logical or rational outlook), was making no progress in her therapy. One day she related to Jung a dream in which she was given a golden scarab. At this point in the consultation, they heard a gentle tapping at the window, and saw a common rose-chafer beetle (or *Cetonia aurata*) trying to fly into the room. Jung opened the window, and caught the insect in his hand as it flew in, handing the beetle to his client. 'Here is your scarab!' The experience, he added, 'punctured a hole' in her rationalism, shattering her 'intellectual resistance', so her therapeutic treatment could successfully continue.[73] Jung noted that in an ancient Egyptian funerary text, *The Book of the Netherworld*, the scarab is a classic symbol of rebirth.[74] He might also have noted, although he did not, that a scarab featured in his visions contained in the Red Book.[75]

Even in the case of synchronicity, Jung found a way to link his interests back to Goethe. He mentioned, for example, how Goethe once remarked to Eckermann that 'we all have some electrical and magnetic forces within us; and we put forth, like the magnet itself, an attractive or repulsive power, as we come in contact with something similar or dissimilar'.[76] But he could also have mentioned that, in *Dichtung und Wahrheit*, Goethe speaks precisely of 'the sensation of past and present being one' (*die Empfindung der Vergangenheit und Gegenwart in Eins*), describing it as 'a perception that introduces a spectral quality into the present'.[77] We do not have to look (as Freud did) to the great Romantic author E.T.A. Hoffmann (1776–1822) for examples of *the uncanny*, for precisely this quality, evident in what Jung called 'synchronicity', can be found in this, and other, examples from Goethe.

In the 1990s the Jungian analyst Carl Alfred Meier (1905–1995) edited and published the correspondence between C. G. Jung and Wolfgang Pauli.[78] In general, Jungian and post-Jungian work on synchronicity has appealed more to those who work in the humanities rather than to those who are empirical scientists. For example, the behavioural psychologist H. J. Eysenck (1916–1997) gave the Jung–Pauli correspondence a predictably unwelcome reception in his review published in one of the foremost international scientific journals, *Nature*.[79] Eysenck describes their published correspondence as 'a curious book', just as he finds that 'the association between an outstanding scientist such as Pauli and a mystic such as Jung is rather curious'. Arguing that the significance of the correspondence lies in its value as 'a clinical document', Eysenck suggests that 'it will not change Pauli's great scientific achievement, nor will it serve to shore up Jung's vanishing reputation'. Indeed, he concludes that 'its main effect will be to demonstrate to the reader the vagaries of a great mind', by which he presumably refers to Pauli, not to Jung. Nevertheless, there has been important work done on the Jung–Pauli collaboration by Suzanne Gieser, resulting in her groundbreaking study *The Innermost Kernel: Depth Psychology and Quantum Physics* (2005), and at the Max Planck Institute for Extraterrestrial Physics in Garching, Harald Atmanspacher has published a number of papers exploring and developing Jung's and Pauli's thinking.[80] Whatever its conceptual validity, the 'Quantum Jung' appears to be an area destined to expand in years ahead.

Victor White

According to the editors of Jung's published correspondence, Gerhard Adler and Aniela Jaffé, the 'strange discovery' that Jung related to Pascual Jordan in his letter of 1 April 1948 might have been the same quaternities or quaternios that are discussed in another letter Jung sent shortly afterwards to Father Victor White on 21 May 1948.[81] But how could Jung be writing to a scientist and to a theologian about the same thing? What could quantum mechanics and God have in common?

In his book *The Roots of Coincidence* (1972) Arthur Koestler recounts a social event that brought to a close the last evening of the 1932 Copenhagen conference on nuclear physics.[82] In a quantum mechanical parody of Goethe's *Faust* staged for this occasion, Wolfgang Pauli played the part of Mephistopheles, tempting Faust to discover the joys of Gretchen (or, in this case, the neutrino). In his Mephistophelian guise, Pauli warned:

> Beware, beware, of Reason and of Science
> Man's highest powers, unholy in alliance.
> You'll let yourself, through dazzling witchcraft yield
> To weird temptations of the quantum field.

Now Jung took the view that his investigations into synchronicity raised all sorts of first-order questions in the fields of philosophy and theology. So it was fortunate (or should one say synchronistic?) to say the least, that, in tandem with his collaboration with Wolfgang Pauli, Jung undertook a long correspondence with Victor White, a Dominican priest based at Blackfriars, the priory located on St Giles in Oxford.

Born in Croydon, Surrey, in 1902 as Gordon Henry White, he had converted from Anglicanism to Roman Catholicism and began training for ordination in 1920. On joining the Dominican Order in 1923, he took the name of Victor (or was assigned this name by the novice master). He entered Jungian analysis in Oxford during the Second World War. Impressed with Jung's writings, notably *Psychology of the Unconscious* (that is *Transformations and Symbols of the Libido*) and his commentary on *The Secret of the Golden Flower*, between 1942 and 1945 White wrote four essays on Jungian psychology and sent copies to Jung on 3 August 1945, along with a short accompanying letter.[83]

In one of two letters sent in reply, Jung drew White's attention to what he called his 'gnoseological standpoint' in *Transformations and Symbols of the Libido*, namely an important methodological statement buried away in a footnote in that work.[84] As we saw in chapter Five, *Transformations and Symbols of the Libido* was the first book in which Jung undertook to radicalize Freud's approach to myth. In a footnote in this work, Jung had proposed (in terms redolent of Goethe's remarks about religion and moral culture to Caroline Gräfin von Egloffstein in 1818) that 'the religious myth' was 'one of the greatest and most significant human institutions', while the symbol – which, considered 'from the standpoint of actual truth', is 'misleading', but is nevertheless *'psychologically true'* – was 'the bridge to all the greatest achievements of humanity'.[85] Further in this footnote, Jung explained that, in these remarks, he was only talking psychologically and not making any claims about the transcendent: 'We are moving entirely in the territory of psychology, which in no way is allied to transcendentalism, either in positive or negative relation', for 'it is a question here of a relentless fulfilment of the standpoint of the theory of cognition, established by Kant, not merely for the theory, but, what is more important, for the practice'.[86]

Adapting Kant's metaphysical dichotomy of the human being as the inhabitant of two different realms, the phenomenal and the noumenal, Jung added: 'Just as Man is a dual being, having an intellectual and an animal nature, so does he appear to need two forms of reality, the reality of culture, that is, symbolic transcendent theory, and the reality of nature which corresponds to our concept of the "true reality"'.[87] But although, only a page or so further, Jung had gone on to argue that '*belief should be replaced by understanding*', which would 'allow us to keep the beauty of the symbol, but still remain free from the depressing results of submission to belief', he nevertheless left the door open to believers, such as White, to enter his (psychological) system without having to jettison their (religious) convictions.[88] Not surprisingly, White sought clarification on this point and in the ensuing correspondence the extent to which White was worried by the critical philosophy's critique of religion became clear, as well as how he saw Jungian psychology as a possible route back to the transcendent. In April 1946 Jung took the unusual step of inviting White to visit him in Bollingen, and their subsequent correspondence bears witness to the depth and intensity of this dialogue between the theologian and the analyst. Some of their letters contain allusions to the strange episode of the *soror mystica*, the sobriquet for Barbara Robb, a friend of White's in London, who in a remarkable illustration of the principle of *actio in distans* began to have dreams about Jung. All of which demonstrates how, in philosophical (for Jung) and theological (for White) terms, both men were embarked on 'an adventurous and dangerous journey', as Jung called it.[89]

Sharing their dreams and ideas in equal measure, on 21 May 1948 Jung gave White a preview of his 'Moses-quaternio', a diagram of a double pyramid relating key figures in the mythical schema of the Naasenes (a Gnostic sect whose beliefs were recorded by Hippolytus of Rome, CE 170–235), a set of variants of which he discussed in *Aion*, 'a shocking and difficult book', as Jung warned White.[90] In that work, Jung explored the archetypal significance of the figure of Christ, whose birth coincides, in astrological terms, with the moment when the vernal equinox (the place on the ecliptic where the sun crosses the equator, round about March 21) comes into alignment with the first of the two fish that constitute the sign of Pisces (one fish, the northerly, standing vertical, and the other, the southerly, lying horizontally).[91] For Jung, the story of the star of Bethlehem and the three wise men indicates 'that Christ, possibly even at the time of the apostles, was viewed from the astrological standpoint'.[92] Naturally, the question arises: is this symbolic Christ the same Christ as the one preached by the Holy, Roman, Catholic and Apostolic Church?

On the one hand, the psychologist; on the other, the theologian: when they talked about God, were they really talking about the same thing? (This problem continues to bedevil attempts to use Jungian psychology in a theological context, however congenial its language may initially appear to be to those of a religious outlook.[93]) In his bull *Munificentissimus Deus*, announced in Rome on 15 August 1950, Pope Pius XII defined the doctrine of the Assumption of the Blessed Virgin Mary as an official dogma of the Catholic Church. In response, Jung was immediately able to assimilate the development to his (psychological) outlook. The pope's declaration, he wrote 'has stirred up something in the unconscious, viz. in the archetypal world', which seemed to mean that 'the *Hierosgamos*-motive: the cutdown tree' (of the Attis cult) 'has been brought into the cave of the mother' (the Great Mother, Cybele) so that, 'if the A[ssumption] means anything, it is a spiritual fact, which can be formulated as the integration of the female principle in the Christian conception of the Godhead'. The papal announcement was, Jung asserted, 'the most important religious development since 400 years'.[94]

But were Jung and Pius XII discussing the same Virgin Mary, the one whose rosary White would have been used to reciting, and in honour of whom, every evening after Vespers or Compline, he would have sung the *Salve regina*? Was, for Jung, the Blessed Virgin an historical and still existing personal being? Or was she a concept, an image, a *symbol*? As Jung told White early on in their dialogue, his lifework was 'essentially an attempt to understand what others apparently can believe', and their extended debate over the status of evil, in relation to the doctrine of the *privatio boni* – the view, attributed to St Augustine of Hippo and restated by St Thomas Aquinas, that evil is 'a privation of good' – alerted White to the possibility that they had reached 'a philosophical deadlock'.[95]

Perhaps such a deadlock was inevitable, inasmuch as the aspect of Christianity that most intrigued Jung, as it had Goethe, was its rich tradition of heretical thinkers. (In *Dichtung und Wahrheit*, Goethe recalls his delight as a student at discovering the *Impartial History of the Church and of Heresy*, published in two volumes in 1699–1700 by the Lutheran theologian and historian Gottfried Arnold, 1666–1714, from which Goethe received 'a more favourable impression of many heretics' who previously had been presented as 'mad or godless'.[96]) For Jung, one such fascinating figure was Origen (*c.* 185–*c.* 253).

In *The Psychology of the Transference* (1946), Jung attributed to this early Christian scholar and theologian the view that the psyche represents a microcosm within the individual. 'Understand that thou art a second little world and that the sun and the moon are within thee, and also the stars', said Origen, and this insight imposes the task on the individual of uniting the plurality within: 'Thou seest that he who seemeth to be is yet not one, but as many persons appear in him as he hath velleities'.[97] Jung's use of Origen poses the question: can theology really be read as psychology? (Here, too, the Goethean influence makes itself felt when Jung, in the next paragraph, alludes to the conclusion of *Faust*, Part Two, in his discussion of the alchemical Mercurius as *geeinte Zwienatur*, as 'united dual nature'.[98])

A breaking point in Jung's relations with White was reached with the publication in 1952 of *Answer to Job*, that late, great work by Jung: a veritable tour de force comprising an analysis of the biblical Book of Job in relation to the problem of evil, the Christian doctrine of the Incarnation, and the apocalyptic imagery of the Book of Revelation, via the Old Testament conception of wisdom in the Book of Proverbs, the prophetic writings of Ezekiel and Daniel, and the apocryphal Book of Enoch. The structure of this work is remarkably complex and the tone of writing is the most sophisticated ever achieved by Jung.[99] Here, yet again, we find a striking continuity within Jung's concerns: for the story of Job informed the framework to Goethe's dramatic poem *Faust*, and *Answer to Job*, which alludes to Mephisto's famous lines in Part One – 'Everything created / Is worth being liquidated' – and the reductionist words of the Proktophantasmist, is also a reckoning with the theme of 'evil and its universal power', and 'the mysterious role it played in delivering humanity from darkness and suffering', which Jung had long ago detected in *Faust* and had, in his eyes, lent Goethe the status of a 'prophet'.[100]

In 'Legendary Jung', Joyce Carol Oates rightly describes *Answer to Job* as Jung's 'masterpiece', while Jung is reported to have said of his *Answer to Job* to Anthony Storr: 'This is pure poison but I owe it to my people'.[101] Despite his initially positive response to the work, White found the book deeply problematic and in the March 1955 issue of *Blackfriars*, the Dominican review, he published a critical review of the work that took Jung to task on several accounts.[102] Understandably, Jung was upset by the difference in tone between their ongoing correspondence and White's published critique, and the frequency of their exchange of letters quickly fell. Nor were the circumstances propitious to their dialogue continuing: Jung, now in his eighties, was more often than not ill, and White was involved in an accident on his motor scooter in 1959; he died in May 1960.

In one of his first letters to White, sent in October 1945, Jung described White as a 'white raven', alluding to the biblical story in which Elijah, in the wilderness, is nourished by ravens sent by Yahweh (1 Kings 17:1–6): 'You are', he told him, 'the only theologian I know of who has really understood something of what the problem of psychology in our present world means . . . I cannot tell you how glad I am that I know a man, a theologian, who is conscientious enough to weigh my opinions on the basis of a careful study of my writings! This is a really rare occasion.'[103] But it turned out that Victor White did not 'really understand' Jung, or rather, that in the end he understood only too well what Jung was trying to do and found himself, as a believer, unable to accept it. No wonder Jung took such comfort as he did from a text in logion Ten of Oxyrhynchus Papyrus One, the 'Sayings of Jesus' (now thought to be part of the Gospel of Thomas), where Jesus declares, 'and when there is one alone I say I am with him', quoting the phrase in Greek and describing it as 'a consolation that has reached me across the gulf of an aeon'.[104]

The psychological system developed by Jung insists on the difference between the ego and the Self, but this could also be described as the difference between the one and the One. Yet where there is difference, there is also relation. In the magnificent concluding paragraph of *Answer to Job*, Jung – who had, in his 'Epilogue' to *Psychology and Alchemy*, accused Goethe, in *Faust*, of postponing the *coniunctio* and subsequent rebirth and transformation until the afterlife – himself apparently shifts the moment of total integration (or the transformation of the ego into the Self) from the here-and-now into the Gnostic-like wastes of infinite time.[105]

In a lecture of 1927, Jung had spoken of the fact that 'nowhere do we stand closer to the noblest secret of all origins than in the knowledge of our own selves, which we believe we always already know', for 'the immensities of space are better known to us than the depths of the self, where – even though we do not understand it – we can listen almost directly to the creativity of Being and Becoming'.[106] Half a century or so earlier, in *The Birth of Tragedy*, Nietzsche had trodden on similar terrain, asking (and citing Wagner's *Tristan*):

> Suppose a human being has thus put his ear, as it were, to the heart chamber of the world will and felt the roaring desire for existence pouring from there into all the veins of the world, as a thundering current or as the gentlest brook, dissolving into a mist – how could he fail to break suddenly? How could he endure to perceive the echo of innumerable shouts of pleasure and woe in the 'wide space of the world night', enclosed in the wretched glass capsule of the human individual, without inexorably fleeing toward his primordial home, as he hears this shepherd's dance of metaphysics?[107]

Once again we are reminded of the shared religious background between Nietzsche and Jung, as sons of pastors: 'and I know what that means', as Jung commented.

This metaphysical and ontological problematic has an existential solution that is also an aesthetic one. Those comments in *Memories, Dreams, Reflections* on the affirmation of one's destiny – in other words, the construction of 'an ego that does not fail when incomprehensible things happen', 'an ego that prevails, endures the truth, and is equal to the world and fate', so that 'to experience a defeat is also to experience victory' – find a counterpart in a letter from Jung to Victor White in 1954.[108] 'Doubt and insecurity are indispensable components of a complete life', he wrote, and 'only those who can lose this life *really*, can gain it really', because a 'complete' life does not consist in a theoretical completeness, but in the fact that one accepts the particular fatal tissue in which one finds oneself embedded without reservation, and that one tries to make sense of it or to create a kosmos from the chaotic mess into which one is born.[109]

Ultimately Jung's gospel was closer to Nietzsche's *amor fati* than to the *credo* taught by the Church in Rome. It has more in common with what Goethe called 'the gospel of beauty and, even more, of taste and agreeableness', or what Nietzsche described as an 'artists' gospel' (*Artisten-Evangelium*), a view of 'art as the real task of life, as life's *metaphysical* activity'.[110] Correspondingly, rather than seeing analytical psychology as a substitute for religion, let alone as a cult, should we see it as a form of *Philosophische Praxis* or philosophical consultancy? As Jung once observed, 'we psychotherapists ought really to be philosophers or philosophic doctors – or rather . . . we already are so, because of the glaring contrast between our work and what passes for philosophy in the universities'.[111]

In short: Jung, like Goethe, regards life as an 'art', which does not exclude the recognition that 'only a very few people' are 'artists in life', and 'the art of life' is 'the most distinguished and rarest of all the arts', for 'who ever succeeded in draining the whole cup *with grace* [literally, *with beauty*]?'[112] As Jung well understood, in this sense Goethe offers a model of what it means, in the precise sense of the word, to be a *Lebensphilosoph* (philosopher of life).[113]

Conclusion: Jung's Death and the Legacy of Analytical Psychology

Jung's Death

On 6 June 1961 C. G. Jung died in his house at Küsnacht, overlooking the Lake of Zurich, at the age of 86. When Elsbeth Stoiber, curator of the Medical History Museum of Zurich University, was commissioned to cast a death mask, she was struck by the sheer physical presence of Jung's corpse. 'His body, lying on his bed, was so impressive', she is recorded as recalling, and his face resembled 'something Asiatic, like Gengis Khan', while three lines on his forehead reminded her of the triton pattern she had seen in India on the faces of people worshipping Ra, the sun god.[1] (Her testimony recalls the remarkable account of Eckermann when he surveyed the dead body of Goethe: 'I wondered at the god-like magnificence of these limbs', for 'the chest was very powerful, broad and vaulted; the muscles of the arms and thighs were full and soft; the feet small and faultlessly shaped . . . a perfect man lay in great beauty before me . . . and I turned away to let my pent-up tears flow freely'.)[2]

It has become part of the legend which rapidly surrounded him that, shortly after Jung's death, a violent thunderstorm broke and a lightning bolt struck the poplar tree by the lake where he used to sit.[3] (According to Deirdre Bair, this tale is not quite true: there was a storm, but it occurred much later in the night, and the tree was struck, but nevertheless survived.[4]) And a second thunderstorm took place during the service when he was buried: 'That's Father

Jung's study in his house in Küsnacht, Switzerland.

grumbling', his daughter Agathe Niehus-Jung said (or so Bair
records her as saying).[5]

And it is appropriate that such electrical phenomena, a product
of the tension between the negative pole and the positive, should
apparently have been observed, for Jung's thinking was rooted, as

this critical account of his life has tried to suggest, in the polaristic thinking that he might have found in Goethe and in the Romantic German tradition of *Naturphilosophie*.[6] Moreover, precisely the ambition that characterizes the scientific work of Goethe and the Romantics is captured so well in the quotation from Coleridge that prefaces Jaffé's introduction to *Memories, Dreams, Reflections*: 'He looked into his own soul with a telescope. What seemed all irregular, he saw and shewed to be constellations: and he added to the consciousness hidden worlds within worlds'. Tellingly, Coleridge used this passage to describe an ambition to be 'a great metaphysician', and in *this* sense there was no greater metaphysician in the twentieth century than Jung.[7]

At the same time, this metaphysical impulse was underpinned in Jung's case with a pre-eminently *cultural* set of concerns, or as *Memories, Dreams, Reflections* admirably puts it: 'Attainment of consciousness is culture in the broadest sense, and self-knowledge is therefore the heart and essence of this process'.[8] In numerous ways, Jung – both explicitly and implicitly – inscribed himself into

The C. G. Jung Institut, Zurich.

Jung, *c.* 1950,
photograph
by Margareta
Fellerer.

the German conception and tradition of culture (*Kultur*). As well as
being a contributor to the fields of psychology, psychiatry and psychotherapy, it is in the light of the tradition of Goethe, Schiller and
Nietzsche that he may also, outside the analytic consulting-room,
be fruitfully – and 'critically' – read.[9]

Jung as the 'Other' of the Postmodern

Nowhere does the urgency of our need to appreciate Jung's
contribution come more clearly to the fore than in the arts and

humanities. Over recent years, a new canon of anti-canonical thinkers and an obscurantist style of writing have acquired an almost hegemonic position of dominance in academic discourse, one of the effects of which has been, as already mentioned, an attempt in many quarters to exclude Jung from the academy. But it is not simply Jung that such discourse seeks to exclude. For instance, a typical sentence from an introductory textbook on literary theory confidently asserts that 'humanist ideology depends upon a fundamental assumption about the primacy of the autonomous and unified individual'; yet at the same time it signally fails to interrogate the fundamental assumptions of its own anti-humanist view (or, if one will, ideology).[10] Such approaches frequently invoke the authority of the work – itself much more intellectually sophisticated, it should be acknowledged – of such thinkers as Jacques Derrida (1930–2004) and his notion of 'deconstruction'.

In 'Structure, Sign and Play in the Discourse of the Human Sciences' in *Writing and Difference* (1967), Derrida undertook a critique of the anthropological thought of Claude Lévi-Strauss (1908–2009) and outlined what he called a logic of the 'supplement'. In this work, as elsewhere, Derrida launched an attack on what he called the 'metaphysics of presence', an assumption that sets up a binary opposition, privileging one term, subordinating the second, and deriving the latter from the former.[11] Thus the term 'origin' becomes privileged over and against all that is said to derive from it, yet – paradoxically – it requires those secondary elements in order to establish and maintain its priority. To this 'difference' Derrida later opposed *différance*, an 'originality' without origin, inasmuch as *différance* is 'neither a word nor a concept', 'not only the play of differences within language but also the relation of speech to language, the detour through which I must pass in order to speak, the silent promise I must make', 'the play of the trace . . . which has no meaning and is not'.[12]

Now Jung's thought might in many ways appear ripe for a critique from a deconstructive perspective, given his notions of the archetype (= origin) and the self (= presence), his fascination with 'the primordial' and his commitment to 'depth'. Yet Jung can also be read, if we remove his texts from their anthropological or theological context and apply them to the same kind of philosophical issues that so vexed Derrida, as a formidable interlocutor for deconstruction. For Jung was greatly intrigued by the suggestion of the alchemical philosopher Gerhard Dorn (*c.* 1530–1584) that there is something 'diabolical' or problematic about binaries.

In two treatises, *De tenebris contra naturam et vita brevi* and *De duello animi cum corpore*, Dorn pointed out that, in the Biblical account of the Creation, God said on the evening of every day that what he had done was good: except for one, the evening of the second day, when he had separated the upper waters from the lower. The reason, Dorn argued, why God omitted to say on the evening of the second day that what He had done was 'good' was because, in so separating upper from lower, God had created the *binarius*, the cause of 'confusion, division, and strife'.[13] Even worse than the binary is the binary of the binary, that is to say, the quaternity, hence Dorn's description of the devil as the *quadricornutus binarius*, the 'four-horned devil'. Thus, in Dorn's account, from the *binarius* there is issued *sua proles quaternaria*, 'its quaternary offspring', and hence the number 2 is associated with Eve, number 3 with Adam, and number (2 × 2 =) 4 with the devil. Yet this argument should not be understood numerologically, but allegorically as resisting the logic that Four can attain Unity. But why is this important?

Dorn, and following him Jung, can be read as resisting the logic of assimilation, subsumption or identification, just as vigorously as did Theodor W. Adorno (1903–1969) when he propounded his notion of 'negative dialectics' as a resistance to 'identity thinking'.[14] In his Eranos lecture on 'A Psychological Approach to the Dogma of the Trinity', Jung provided a lengthy exposition of Dorn's thinking about the *binarius* in terms of the One and the Other: 'As soon as the number two appears, a unit is produced out of the original unity, and this unit is none other than that same unity split into two and turned into a "number"', but, so Jung continued, 'there is no opposition between one and two, for these are simple numbers which are distinguished only by their arithmetical value and by nothing else', whereas 'the "One" and the "Other" form an opposition'.[15]

The important point here is that this opposition between the One and the Other does not involve the privileging of – so to speak – the one over the other. Rather, as Jung explains, the relation between them is fluid and dynamic: 'The "One" . . . seeks to hold to its one-and-alone existence, while the "Other" ever strives to be another opposed to the One', and so 'the One will not let go of the Other because, if it did, it would lose its character; and the Other pushes itself away from the One in order to exist at all', and thus 'there arises a tension of opposites between the One and the Other'.[16] Indeed, a sustained meditation on the concept of the Other constitutes an important and often-overlooked element of Jung's later work as a whole.

It is true that Jung proposes a resolution of the tension between the One and the Other in the form of 'the third': 'Every tension of opposites culminates in a release, out of which comes the "third"'.[17] (Read in the light of Jung's earlier work *Psychological Types*, however, it is clear that Jung is restating in abstract or philosophical terms a dialectic he had originally understood in terms of the relation between consciousness and the unconscious.)[18] This 'third', identified in *Psychological Types* with the symbol, should not be over-hastily identified as a 'logocentric' master-category that binds together the material and the spiritual: rather, Jung's point is a cognitive one, akin to the 'transcendental unity of apperception' proposed by Kant in his first *Critique*: in other words, in order to see anything at all we must see it as a unity.[19]

Jung wearing a Gnostic ring while seated at his desk in his study, *c.* 1940s.

In the third, the tension is resolved and the lost unity is restored. Unity, the absolute One, cannot be numbered, it is indefinable and unknowable; only when it appears as a unity, the number one, is it knowable, for the "Other" which is required for this act of knowing is lacking in the condition of the One. Three is an unfolding of the One to a condition where it can be known – unity become recognizable; had it not been resolved into the polarity of the One and the Other, it would have remained fixed in a condition devoid of every quality.[20]

Although Jung writes here about the One with a passion and an intensity usually found only in the metaphysics of such Neo-platonists as Plotinus, Proclus or Porphyry, his point is essentially a psychological and philosophical one.

Similarly, Jung's embrace of the principle, attributed to the pre-Socratic philosopher Heraclitus, of *enantiodromia* – 'the emergence of the unconscious opposite in the course of time', or the mechanism according to which the libido streams back to the source of life, that is, when the libido introverts and returns to the unconscious – underscores the processual, dynamic character of his approach. Drawing on Derrida's critique of the origin, Gilles Deleuze and Félix Guattari (1930–1992) substituted for the logocentric notion of the 'root' the term 'rhizome', opposing the horizontality of their postmodern approach to the supposed verticality of classical metaphysics.[21] Intriguingly, however, the concept of the 'rhizome' is found (as we saw) not just in Deleuze, but also in Jung; not surprisingly, given Deleuze's early fascination with Jung's *Symbols and Transformations of Libido*. Oddly, however, Jung is rarely thought of as a postmodern thinker, despite the multiple, non-hierarchical and pluralist assumptions of his theory of the archetypes.[22]

Indeed, what marks out the postmodern character of Jung's thought, as well as its *post*-postmodern character, is its embrace of ambiguity, ambivalence, playfulness and paradox. In the context of a discussion of Gnostic writings, Jung observes that paradox 'does more justice to the *unknowable* than clarity can do, for uniformity of meaning robs the mystery of its darkness and sets it up as something that is known'.[23] Rightly Jung warns against the rush in identity thinking – and, by extension, in all reductionist approaches to life (be they scientistic, bureaucratic or managerial) – to assume that we know anything at all. In fact, Jung describes the violent subsumption of the unknown to the known as 'a usurpation', adding that 'it leads the human intellect into hybris by pretending that it, the intellect, has got hold of the transcendent mystery by a cognitive act and has "grasped" it'.[24] (In so writing, Jung aligns himself with Goethe's rejection of Baconian empiricism as a kind of torture of the phenomenon, and with the Goethean embrace of a 'tender empiricism'.)[25]

Instead, Jung urges us here – as he did throughout his life and work – not simply to accept paradox but wholeheartedly to embrace it, for paradox alone reflects 'a higher level of intellect'.[26] As he puts it, paradox, by 'not forcibly representing the unknowable as known', gives 'a more faithful picture of the real state of affairs'.[27] And this, after all, is precisely the message of *Faust*: that one replaces the violent striving, indexed to the masculine or patriarchal, to attain something essentially unknowable – to 'perceive the inmost force / That bonds the very universe' – by an acceptance of a gentler, almost imperceptible dynamic (indexed to the feminine) of being-pulled-along, 'the Eternal Feminine / Draws us on high'.[28] (Thus the Eternal Feminine is an expression of alchemical Wisdom or *Sapientia*.)[29] In other words, ultimately Jung subscribed to a position one might well call Goethean vitalism: he believed that 'the point of life is life'.[30]

References

Introduction

1 *MDR*, p. 134.

2 *MDR*, p. 17.

3 *Xenien aus dem Nachlaß*, no. 209, 'Das Motto'; Goethe, *Werke* [*WA*], I.5/i, p. 235.

4 *MDR*, p. 18.

5 Ibid.

6 Ibid.

7 Goethe, *Werke* [*HA*], XII, p. 512; *Maxims and Reflections*, ed. Hecker, no. 155.

8 Goethe, *Werke* [*WA*], I.3, p. 235.

9 Goethe, *GE*, XII, p. 57.

10 Ibid., p. 63.

11 *MDR*, p. 17.

12 Whereas the word 'personality' has become debased in English through its association with celebrity culture and the cult of the superficial (as in, for example, the phrase 'TV personality'), in the sense that Jung uses the word *Persönlichkeit* it implies a totality of different functions, conscious and unconscious (see 'The Development of the Personality' in *CW*, XVII, §284-§323); *MDR*, p. 17.

13 *MDR*, p. 17.

14 *Ethics*, part 5, propositions 29 and 30, in *Spinoza: Selections*, ed. John Wild (London, 1928), pp. 387–8. For Freud's sarcastic use of this expression in his 'On the History of the Psycho-Analytic Movement' (1914), see *SE*, XIV, p. 58; *Ethics*, part 5, proposition 25; *Selections*, p. 386.

15 *MDR*, p. 356; *Ethics*, part 5, proposition 23, scholium; *Selections*, p. 385.

16 *MDR*, p. 17.

17 See Gilles Deleuze and Félix Guattari, *Milles Plateaux* (Paris, 1980); *A Thousand Plateaus*, trans. Brian Massumi (New York and London, 2004).

18 Christian Kerslake, *Deleuze and the Unconscious* (London and New York, 2007). And see Christian Kerslake, 'Rebirth through Incest: On Deleuze's Early Jungianism', *Angelaki*, IX/1 (2004), pp. 135–57.

19 Psalms 102 (103):15 (*DRV*); Isaiah 40:6.

20 *MDR*, p. 18.

21 Ibid.

22 See Jung's essay 'Archaic Man' (1931); *CW*, X, §104–§147. For further discussion, see the essays collected in Paul Bishop, ed., *The Archaic: The Past in the Present* (London and New York, 2012).

23 Wilhelm Dilthey, *Selected Works*, III: *The Formation of the Historical World in the Human Sciences*, ed. Rudolf A. Makkreel and Frithjof Rodi (Princeton, NJ, 2002), p. 216.

24 Jung, *CW*, XI, §37.

25 Jung, *CW*, V, p. xxiv; *CW*, V, p. xxiv; cf. Lao Tzu, *Tao Te Ching*, chap. 1, 25, 52.

26 *MDR*, p. 43.

27 Jung, 'Analytical Psychology and "Weltanschauung"' (1928/1931) in *CW*, VIII, §739.

28 Ibid.

29 Jung, 'Psychotherapists or the Clergy'; *CW*, XI, §534.

30 Ibid., §535.

31 Jung, 'Freud and Jung: Contrasts' (1929); *CW*, IV, §776. (First published in the *Kölner Zeitung* on 7 May 1929.) Compare with Jung's reference above to 'natural spirit' (*natürlicher Geist*) in 'Analytical Psychology and "Weltanschauung"' (*CW*, VIII, §739).

32 Jung, 'Freud and Jung'; *CW*, IV, §780.

33 Ibid.

34 *Dichtung und Wahrheit*, part 3, book 14; Goethe, *GE*, IV, p. 457.

35 Goethe, *GE*, IV, p. 457.

36 Sonu Shamdasani, *Jung Stripped Bare by His Biographers, Even* (London and New York, 2005).

37 Ibid., pp. 66 and 68.

38 For further discussion, see F. X. Charet, 'Understanding Jung: Recent Biographies and Scholarship', *Journal of Analytical Psychology*, XLV (2000), pp. 195–216.

39 C. G. Jung, *The Red Book: Liber Novus*, ed. Sonu Shamdasani, trans. Mark Kyburz, John Peck and Sonu Shamdasani (New York and London, 2009).

40 See *C. G. Jung-Bibliothek: Katalog* (Küsnacht-Zürich, 1967).

41 *MDR*, p. 228.

42 Sonu Shamdasani, *C. G. Jung: A Biography in Books* (New York and London, 2012), p. 49.

43 Ibid., pp. 83 and 90.

44 Ibid., pp. 107 and 127.

45 Ibid., p. 193.

46 Goethe, *GE*, IV, pp. 255–6.

47 Jung, *CW*, XI, §903.

1 A Child of Goethe

1 *Campaign in France 1792. Siege of Mainz*, night of 19 September (Goethe, *GE*, V, p. 652). For further discussion of Jung's life and thought in relation to Goethe, see Paul Bishop, *Analytical Psychology and German Classical Aesthetics: Goethe, Schiller, and Jung*, vol. I: *The Development of the Personality*, and vol. II: *The Constellation of the Self* (London and New York, 2008–9).

2 *MDR*, p. 52. For an insightful discussion of parallels between Jung and his grandfather, written by Jung's grandson, see Andreas Jung, 'The Grandfather', *Journal of Analytical Psychology*, LVI (2011), pp. 653–73.

3 Exodus 33:18–23; compare with Guillaume de Digueville's vision of heaven, described in *SNZ*, II, p. 1081.

4 Job 9:30–31 (*DRV*); cf. *MDR*, p. 59. The Latin Vulgate *sordibus* is variously translated as 'pit', 'ditch', 'dung', or 'mire'; Jung, *CW*, XI, §561.

5 *MDR*, pp. 78–9.

6 Jung's vision of God defecating onto the roof of Basel Cathedral hugely radicalizes the use of a defecating jibe at Napoleon in Goethe's *Zahme Xenien* that Freud placed as an epigraph at the opening of the third section of 'On the History of the Psycho-Analytic Movement'

(1914): 'Cut it short! / On the Day of Judgement it is no more than a fart!' (*Mach es kurz! / Am Jüngsten Tag ist's nur ein Furz!*) (Freud, *SE*, XIV, p. 42; Goethe, *Werke* [*WA*], vol. 1.5/i, p. 141).

7 For an emotionally charged account, see Linda Donn, *Freud and Jung: Years of Friendship, Years of Loss* (New York, 1988); and for an analytical account, see George B. Hogensen, *Jung's Struggle with Freud: A Metabiological Study* (Brooklyn, NY, 1994).

8 See Jung's letter to Freud of 20 February 1908, Moses and Joshua (see Freud's letter to Jung of 17 January 1909), and analyst and analysand (see their letters of 29 November and 3 December 1912); *F/J*, pp. 122, 196–7, 524 and 525–6.

9 Goethe, *Faust I*, lines 2585–6; Freud, letter to Jung of 9 March 1909; *F/J*, p. 211.

10 Jung, letter to Freud of 18 January 1911; *F/J*, pp. 384–5.

11 See Jung's letter to Freud of 3 March 1912 (*F/J*, p. 491); cf. 'On the Bestowing Virtue', §3; Friedrich Nietzsche, *Thus Spoke Zarathustra*, trans. Graham Parkes (New York, 2005), p. 68.

12 See Freud, 'Leonardo da Vinci and a Memory of his Childhood' [1910] (*SE*, XI, pp. 63–137); Freud, *SE*, XI, p. 113.

13 See Jung's letter to Freud of 17 June 1910; *F/J*, p. 329; Jung, *PU*, §5 (the name that Jung would give to this technique is 'amplification').

14 Jung, *CW*, IX/i, §93–§94.

15 *MDR*, pp. 79 and 107.

16 Harold Bloom, *The Western Canon: The Books and School of the Ages* (New York, 1994), pp. 203–35.

17 Ibid., p. 210.

18 Ibid., pp. 204 and 203.

19 John Kerr, *A Most Dangerous Method: The Story of Jung, Freud, and Sabina Spielrein* (London, 1994), p. 327.

20 *MDR*, pp. 21–2.

21 Ibid., p. 22.

22 Ibid., pp. 30–31.

23 Ibid., p. 23.

24 Ibid., pp. 23–4. The girl in question was Bertha Schenk; see Deirdre Bair, *Jung: A Biography* (Boston, MA, 2003), p. 72.

25 Ibid., pp. 98–9.

26 Ibid., p. 23.

27 Ibid., p. 99.

28 Ibid., p. 24.

29 Jung, *The Psychology of Dementia Praecox* (1907); *CW*, III, §131.

30 From a discussion of 'active imagination' in his *Tavistock Lectures* of 1935; Jung, *CW*, XVIII, §397. See also C. G. Jung, *Visions: Notes of the Seminar Given in 1930–1934*, ed. Claire Douglas, 2 vols (Princeton, NJ, 1997), I, pp. 122–3.

31 'My Jesus, stay Thou by me, / And let no foe come nigh me, / Safe, sheltered by the wing; / But would the foe alarm me, / O let him never harm me, / But still Thine angels round me sing!' (*Breit aus die Flügel beide, O Jesu meine Freude / Und nimm dein Küchlein ein. / Will Satan es verschlingen, / So laß die Englein singen: / Dies Kind soll unverletzet sein*) (trans. Catherine Winkworth, 1855).

32 *MDR*, pp. 28 and 30.

33 Deuteronomy 4:39 (*DRV*); *MDR*, p. 58.

34 See the episode of the puppet-play of David and Goliath in the novel *Wilhelm Meister's Apprenticeship*, book 1, chap. 2 (Goethe, *GE*, IX, pp. 3–4).

35 *MDR*, p. 31.

36 Ibid., p. 33; cf. *Dichtung und Wahrheit*, part 1, book 1 (Goethe, *GE*, IV, p. 38).

37 *MDR*, p. 23.

38 Ibid., p. 33.

39 Alfred Baeumler, *Das mythische Weltalter: Bachofens romantischer Deutung des Altertums* (Munich, 1965), pp. 204 and 59; cited in Peter Murphy and David Roberts, *Dialectic of Romanticism: A Critique of Modernism* (London and New York, 2004), p. 39.

40 *MDR*, p. 33.

41 Ibid.; see Freud, 'The "Uncanny"' (1919), in *SE*, XVII, pp. 217–55.

42 *MDR*, p. 69.

43 Goethe, *Maxims and Reflections*, ed. Hecker, §441.

44 *MDR*, p. 69. See Heinrich Zschokke, *Eine Selbstschau* (Aarau, 1842), part 1, *Das Schicksal und der Mensch*, 'Des Mannes Jahre', chap. 11, 'Die Blumenhalde', pp. 271–6. What Zschokke called his *inneres Gesicht* ('inner vision') apparently allowed him to know a person's past history within a second of meeting him or her. The incident recounted by Zschokke to which Jung refers is said to have taken

place in a tavern called Zum Rebstock in Waldshut (see pp. 275–6). See also Willy Schröder, *Okkulte Historietten* (St. Goar, 2003), pp. 331–2.

45 As the punctuation suggests, this phrase is a quotation: it is, in fact, a quotation from *Memories, Dreams, Reflections* itself (cf. *MDR*, p. 21); *MDR*, p. 35.

46 *MDR*, p. 36. Compare with Spinoza's idea of seeing things *sub specie aeternitatis* and that 'we feel and know by experience that we are eternal' (*Ethics*, part 5, propositions 23, 29 and 30; in *Spinoza: Selections*, ed. John Wild (London, 1928), pp. 384–5 and 387–8).

47 C. G. Jung, *Analytical Psychology: Notes of the Seminar Given in 1925*, ed. William McGuire (Princeton, NJ, 1989), pp. 132–3; see Richard Noll, *The Jung Cult: Origins of a Charismatic Movement* (Princeton, NJ, 1994), pp. 99–102.

48 Jung, *CW*, VII, §403.

49 Ibid.

50 *MDR*, p. 95.

51 Ibid., p. 96. *Die Jobsiade* was a satirical epic written in 1783–4 by a doctor, Carl Arnold Kortum (1745–1824); it was published in 1784 and in a revised form in 1799, inspiring Wilhelm Busch (1832–1908) to illustrate the work in an edition published in 1872; cf. Genesis 1:26–30; *MDR*, p. 96; cf. *The Birth of Tragedy*, §1; Friedrich Nietzsche, *Basic Writings*, ed. and trans. Walter Kaufmann (New York, 1968), p. 37.

52 *MDR*, p. 97.

53 *Faust I*, line 940.

54 Nietzsche, 'The Homecoming' in *Thus Spoke Zarathustra*, p. 161.

2 Secrets – Manikins and Pencil-Cases in the Loft

1 Adage II.iii.32, in *Collected Works of Erasmus*, vol. 33, *Adages, II.i.1. to II.vi.100*, trans. and annotated R.A.B. Mynors (Toronto; Buffalo, NY; and London, 1991), p. 146; 1 Corinthians 15:47 (*DRV*).

2 T.G.H. Strehlow, *Aranda Traditions* (Melbourne, 1947), pp. 85–6. See Jung's comments in passing in *CW*, VI, §325 and §496, and his *Visions* Seminar in C. G. Jung, *Visions: Notes of the Seminar Given in 1930–1934*, ed. Claire Douglas, 2 vols (London, 1998), I, p. 66.

3 *MDR*, p. 38.

4 Telesphorus was, in fact, the son of Asclepius and is typically depicted as a dwarf wearing a hooded cape or cloak, sometimes accompanied by his sister, the goddess Hygieia. The Kabeiroi were deities worshipped at various mystery sanctuaries, including Thebes in Boeotia, Lemnos and Samothrace.

5 *MDR*, p. 27.

6 Cf. Bertrand Vergely, 'La dialectique du secret', seminar held at IDÉE PSY (Institut pour le Développement, l'Éducation et l'Enseignement en PSYchothérapie), Paris, 5 September 2012.

7 *MDR*, p. 37.

8 Ibid., p. 58.

9 Jung, *CW*, IX/i, §124.

10 *MDR*, pp. 59–60.

11 Ibid., p. 64.

12 Ibid., p. 65.

13 Ibid., pp. 74 and 73.

14 In *Dichtung und Wahrheit*, part 2, book 8, Goethe relates how, as a young man, he drew on Neoplatonism, Hermeticism, mysticism and Kabbalism to develop his own conception of God and 'a very strange-looking world' (*GE*, IV, pp. 261–3).

15 *MDR*, p. 50.

16 Ibid.

17 Ibid., pp. 61–2.

18 Ibid., p. 51. This early nineteenth-century statuette is based on a painting (1826) by Hieronymus Hess recording a celebrated incident: one day Dr Johann Jakob Stückelberger (1758–1838) was crossing the Rhine Bridge when he encountered one of his patients, the old widow Frau Ochs-Fuss, known as the 'Oggsefuessene'. On her querulous and hypochondriac demand that he examine her on the spot, the doctor told her to stick out her tongue and close her eyes – and then slipped away. See Eugen A. Meier, *Aus dem alten Basel* (Basel, 1970), pp. 52–3. On Jung's identification with Goethe, see Henri F. Ellenberger, *The Discovery of the Unconscious: The History and Evolution of Dynamic Psychiatry* (New York, 1970), pp. 664 and 738.

19 Walter Kaufmann, *Discovering the Mind*, I: *Goethe, Kant, and Hegel* (New York, 1980), pp. 46–9. For further discussion, see Rudolf Steiner,

'Goethe and Mathematics' [1883], in *Goethean Science*, trans. William Lindemann (Chestnut Ridge, NY, 1988), pp. 114–16.

20 *MDR*, p. 42.

21 Did, however, being forced to copy prints of Greek deities or, on one occasion, a goat's head later influence the aesthetic of the Red Book? *MDR*, pp. 45–6.

22 Ibid.

23 Ibid., p. 47.

24 Ibid., p. 47.

25 See Goethe's poem 'Primal Words. Orphic' (*Urworte. Orphisch*), stanza 1; Goethe, *GE*, I, p. 231. For further discussion of this text from a Jungian perspective, see Paul Bishop, *Reading Goethe at Midlife: Ancient Wisdom, German Classicism, and Jung* (New Orleans, LA, 2011).

26 *MDR*, p. 47. It seems there was an analogous moment in Freud's life: 'When I was seven or eight years old . . . one evening before going to sleep I disregarded the rules which modesty lays down and obeyed the calls of nature in my parents' bedroom while they were present. In the course of his reprimand, my father let fall the words: "The boy will come to nothing." This must have been a frightful blow to my ambition, for references to this scene are still constantly recurring in my dreams and are always linked with an enumeration of my achievements and successes, as though I wanted to say: "You see, I *have* come to something"' (Freud, *SE*, IV, p. 216). On Jung and neurosis, see *MDR*, pp. 47–8.

27 According to the psychoanalysts Jean Laplanche (1924–2012) and Jean-Bertrand Pontalis (*b.* 1924), a neurosis is 'a psychogenic affection in which the symptoms are the symbolic expression of a psychical conflict whose origins lie in the subject's childhood history' and 'constitute compromises between wish and defence' ; see *The Language of Psycho-Analysis*, trans. Donald Nicholson-Smith (London, 1973), p. 266.

28 *MDR*, p. 47.

29 Ibid., pp. 49–50.

30 Ibid., p. 61.

31 Ibid., p. 84.

32 See Tacitus, *Annals* 1.1.

33 Spinoza, *Ethics*, part 5, proposition 30, in *Spinoza: Selections*, ed. John
Wild (London, 1928), pp. 387–8; compare with the quatrain from
Goethe's *West-Östlicher Divan*, 'Those who cannot draw conclusions /
From three thousand years of learning / Stay naïve in dark confu-
sions, / Day to day live undiscerning' (*Wer nicht von dreitausend Jahren
/ Sich weiss Rechenschaft zu geben, / Bleib im Dunkeln unerfahren, / Mag
von Tag zu Tage leben*) (Goethe, *Poems of the West and East:
West-Eastern Divan – West-Östlicher Divan: Bi-Lingual Edition of the
Complete Poems*, trans. John Whaley [Bern, 1998], p. 189); *MDR*, p. 84.

34 *MDR*, p. 49.

35 Ibid.

36 For the term *hapax existentiel*, see Michel Onfray, *L'art de jouir* (Paris,
1991), p. 27; *Le désir d'être un volcan: Journal hédoniste I* (Paris, 1996),
pp. 320–47 (esp. p. 324); and *La puissance d'exister: Manifeste hédoniste*
(Paris, 2006), pp. 81–5.

37 *MDR*, p. 49.

38 Wilhelm Traugott Krug, *Allgemeines Handwörterbuch der philosophischen
Wissenschaften*, 4 vols, then 5 vols (Leipzig, 1827–8; 1829–34; 2nd edn,
5 vols, Leipzig, 1832–8).

39 Alois Emanuel Biedermann, *Christliche Dogmatik* (Zurich, 1869).

40 *MDR*, p. 89.

41 Raphaël Enthoven and Michaël Foessel, *Kant* (Paris, 2009), p. 13.

42 B xvi, in Immanuel Kant, *Critique of Pure Reason*, ed. and trans. Paul
Guyer and Allen W. Wood (Cambridge, 1997), p. 110.

43 Jung, letter to Josef Goldbrunner, 8 February 1941; L, I, p. 294.

44 Jung, letter to August Vetter, 8 April 1932; L, I, p. 91.

45 Jung, letter to Walter Robert Corti, 2 May 1955; L, II, p. 249.

46 B xxx, in Kant, *Critique of Pure Reason*, p. 117.

47 William McGuire and R.F.C. Hull, eds, *C. G. Jung Speaking: Interviews
and Encounters* (Princeton, NJ, 1977), p. 428.

48 For discussion of Schelling's relevance to psychoanalysis and
analytical psychology, see Matt FFytche, *The Foundation of the
Unconscious: Schelling, Freud and the Birth of the Modern Psyche*
(Cambridge, 2012); and S. J. McGrath, *The Dark Ground of the Spirit:
Schelling and the Unconscious* (London and New York, 2012). Jacobi
says on the subject of history as the self-expression of 'spirit': '*Without*
this presupposition [of the "thing in itself"] I was unable to enter into

[Kant's] system, but *with* it I was unable to stay within it' (Friedrich Heinrich Jacobi, *David Hume über den Glauben oder Idealismus und Realismus*, 1787, in Jacobi, *Werke*, II [1815], Darmstadt, 1976, pp. 301–2.

49 Arthur Schopenhauer, *The World as Will and Representation*, trans. E.F.J. Payne, 2 vols (New York, 1966), I, §29 p. 162.

50 *MDR*, p. 88. For further discussion, see James L. Jarrett, 'Schopenhauer and Jung' [1981], in Paul Bishop, ed., *Jung in Contexts: A Reader* (London and New York, 1999), pp. 193–203.

51 *MDR*, p. 88.

52 Schopenhauer, *The World as Will and Representation*, I, §68, p. 390.

53 *MDR*, p. 89.

54 Jung, *CW*, VIII, §328–§396.

55 Ibid., §387.

56 Jung, 'Archetypes of the Collective Unconscious' (1934; 1954); *CW*, IX/i, §50.

57 Jung, *CW*, IX/i, §259.

58 Ibid., IX/ii, §11.

59 Ibid., *CW*, XI, §375.

60 Ibid., *CW*, VIII, §358.

61 Ibid.

62 *MDR*, p. 122.

63 Jung, 'The Hypothesis of the Collective Unconscious' (*CW*, XVIII, §1223) and 'Depth Psychology' (*CW*, XVIII, §1143); F.W.J. Schelling, *System of Transcendental Idealism*, trans. Peter L. Heath (Charlottesville, VA, 1978), pp. 208–9; see Eduard von Hartmann, *Philosophie des Unbewussten*, 2 vols, 10th edn (Leipzig, 1893), vol. I, *Phänomenologie des Unbewussten*, p. 22, where Hartmann cites this passage from Schelling; cf. vol. II, *Metaphysik des Unbewussten*, pp. 120 and 170.

64 Friedrich Nietzsche, 'Why I am So Wise', in *Ecce Homo*, trans. R. J. Hollingdale (Harmondsworth, 1992), §1 p. 8.

65 *MDR*, p. 78.

66 Ibid.

67 Ibid.

68 *Faust I*, lines 1338 and 1343–4; Johann Wolfgang von Goethe, *Faust: A Tragedy*, ed. Cyrus Hamlin, trans. Walter Arndt, 2nd edn (New York and London, 2001), p. 37.

69 See John Milton, *Paradise Lost*, ed. Alastair Fowler, 2nd edn (Harlow, 1998), book 1, lines 217–18; *Faust I*, lines 1335–6; *Faust*, trans. Arndt, p. 36.

70 *MDR*, p. 78. By using the term the 'great mysteries', Jung assimilates the conclusion of *Faust*, part 2, and Faust's vision of the *Mater Gloriosa* to the *Magnum Mysterium* of pagan times – to the Eleusinian and other Mysteries of the ancient cults. For Jung, the essence of those cults lay in the message: 'If we do not submit to the pains of the task, we shall not reap our reward when the time of harvest is come' (Jung, *Visions: Notes of the Seminar Given in 1930–1934*, I, p. 64).

71 *MDR*, p. 79.

72 Ibid.

73 Ibid., p. 72.

74 Ibid., p. 77.

75 *Faust I*, line 409; cf. *Faust*, trans. Arndt, p. 13 [trans. modified].

3 Science or Spiritism?

1 *MDR*, p. 107.

2 Ibid., pp. 78–9 and 107.

3 In his *Visions* seminar (1930–34), Jung describes 'the idea of the living shadow behind one' as 'a precious idea', adding that 'the Greeks have a beautiful word for it: *synopadós*, meaning the one that comes with me and is behind me' and explaining 'but that is by no means what we would call shadow, a lack of light, but a living thing of great mana, great power' (C. G. Jung, *Visions: Notes of the Seminar Given in 1930–1934*, ed. Claire Douglas, 2 vols (London, 1998), I, p. 18).

4 *MDR*, p. 111.

5 Thomas Mann, *The Story of a Novel: The Genesis of 'Doctor Faustus'* (New York, 1961), p. 143; *Die Entstehung des Doktor Faustus: Roman eines Romans* (Amsterdam, 1949), pp. 126–7. Mann adds that such an individual 'lack[s] clear knowledge of his organic function and therefore [is] quite capable of wrong judgments also'!

6 Augustine, *Liber de vera religione*, chap.39, §72, in *Patrologiæ cursus completus*, vol. 34, *Augustini Opera Omnia*, III (Paris 1841), col. 154; Augustine, *Earlier Writings*, ed. and trans. John H. S. Burleigh

(Philadelphia, PA, 1953), p. 262. See *MDR*, p. 111; and a prooemium in 'A Psychological Approach to the Dogma of the Trinity' (1942/1948) (*CW*, XI, p. 107).

7 *MDR*, p. 117.

8 See C. G. Jung, *The Zofingia Lectures*, trans. Jan van Heurck (London, Melbourne and Henley, 1983).

9 Albert Oeri, 'Some Youthful Memories', in William McGuire and R.F.C. Hull, eds, *C. G. Jung Speaking: Interviews and Encounters* (Princeton, NJ, 1977), pp. 3–10 (p. 7).

10 *Erinnerungen, Träume, Gedanken von C. G. Jung: Aufgezeichnet und herausgegeben von Aniela Jaffé* (Olten and Freiburg im Breisgau, 1990), p. 103. This passage is omitted in *MDR*.

11 McGuire and Hull, eds, *C. G. Jung Speaking*, p. 9.

12 Lionel Gossman, *Basel in the Age of Burckhardt: A Study in Unseasonable Ideas* (Chicago, IL, and London, 2000), p. 8.

13 Ibid.

14 *MDR*, p. 133.

15 Jung, *SNZ*, II, p. 862; I, p. 635; II, p. 1301.

16 Ibid., I, p. 162.

17 Ibid., I, pp. 29 and 274.

18 *MDR*, p. 122.

19 Jung, *SNZ*, II, p. 1095.

20 *MDR*, p. 122; ibid., p. 109.

21 Ibid., p. 124.

22 Ibid., p. 117.

23 In the view of Michel Onfray, the impact on Nietzsche of the death of his father – after suffering 'terrible pains' ('Aus meinem Leben', in Nietzsche, *Werke in drei Bänden*, ed. Karl Schlechta [Munich, 1966], p. 16) – is a key to grasping Nietzsche's own self-understanding, his portrait in *Ecce Homo* of his father (Nietzsche, *Ecce Homo*, trans. R. J. Hollingdale, Harmondsworth, 1992, pp. 8–15) being essentially a self-portrait in disguise (Michel Onfray, *La Construction du surhomme* [Paris, 2011], pp. 202–3).

24 *MDR*, p. 128.

25 Ibid., p. 121.

26 Adolf Portmann, 'Jung's Biology Professor: Some Recollections', *Spring: A Journal of Archetype and Culture* (1976), pp. 148–54.

27 See the work collected in C. G. Jung, *Psychology and the Occult*, trans. R.F.C. Hull (Princeton, NJ, 1978); Roderick Main, ed., *Jung on Synchronicity and the Paranormal* (London, 1997); and F. X. Charet, *Spiritualism and the Foundations of C. G. Jung's Psychology* (Albany, NY, 1993).

28 For further discussion, see Stefanie Zumstein-Preiswerk, *C. G. Jungs Medium: Die Geschichte der Helly Preiswerk* (Munich, 1975); William B. Goodheart, 'C. G. Jung's First Patient: On the Seminal Emergence of Jung's Thought', *Journal of Analytical Psychology*, XXIX (1984), pp. 1–34; and Henri F. Ellenberger, 'The Story of Helene Preiswerk: A Critical Study with New Documents', *History of Psychiatry*, II (1991), pp. 41–52.

29 Jung, 'Flying Saucers: A Modern Myth of Things Seen in the Sky' (1958); *CW*, X, §700.

30 Ibid.

31 On Mann and occulistic phenomena, see 'Fragment on Religion' (1931), in Thomas Mann, *Gesammelte Werke*, 13 vols (Frankfurt am Main, 1960–74), XI, pp. 423–5, and the essays 'Three Reports on Occult Séances' (1924), in XIII, pp. 33–48, and 'Occult Experiences' (1924), in X, pp. 135–71, as well as the seance scene in *The Magic Mountain* (1924). On Rilke and spiritualism, see Rainer Maria Rilke, *Gesammelte Briefe*, ed. by Ruth Sieber-Rilke and Carl Sieber, 6 vols (Leipzig, 1936–9), I, p. 32. For further discussion, see Paul Bishop, 'Rilke: Thought and Mysticism', in *The Cambridge Companion to Rilke*, ed. Karen Leeder and Robert Vilain (Cambridge, 2010), pp. 159–73. Nietzsche refers to his seance visit in a letter to Heinrich Köselitz of 2 October 1882; cited in Raymond J. Benders and Stephan Oettermann, *Friedrich Nietzsche: Chronik in Bildern und Texten* (Munich and Vienna, 2000), pp. 534–5.

32 See Alfred J. Gaby, *The Covert Enlightenment: Eighteenth-century Culture and its Aftermath* (West Chester, PA, 2005).

33 *MDR*, p. 126.

34 Ibid., p. 181.

35 See Jung's letter of 27 November 1934 to J. B. Rhine, in L, I, pp. 180–82. A photograph of the shattered knife is included: surely proof to convince even the most hardened sceptic. Moreover, the knife and the walnut dining table still exist: owned, according to Deirdre Bair, by descendants of Jung (Sibylle Willi-Niehus, in the case of the table, and

the occupants of Jung's house at Seestrasse 228, in the case of the knife); see Deirdre Bair, *Jung: A Biography* (Boston, MA, 2003), pp. 664–5.

36 *MDR*, pp. 119–20. Jung's library contains works by nearly all these writers.

37 Ibid., p. 120.

38 Ibid., p. 119.

39 Ibid., p. 120.

40 Krafft-Ebing also published studies on sensory delirium (*Die Sinnesdelirien: Ein Versuch ihrer physiopsychologischen Begründung*, 1864) and on melancholy (*Die Melancholie: Eine klinische Studie*, 1874).

41 Richard von Krafft-Ebing, *Lehrbuch der Psychiatrie auf klinischer Grundlage für praktische Ärzte und Studirende*, 4th edn (Stuttgart, 1890), p. v; cf. *MDR*, p. 129.

42 *MDR*, p. 130.

43 Ibid., p. 131. The allusion is to *Faust II*, line 11962; see Goethe, *Faust: A Tragedy*, ed. Cyrus Hamlin, trans. Walter Arndt, 2nd edn (New York and London, 2001), p. 340.

44 *MDR*, p. 131.

45 Ibid. Compare with Gernot Böhme's remarks about Goethe's ability to discern the meaning of human events: 'It is an important aspect of his greatness that he recognizes the principle in the detail, in other words the *significant* in the factual' (Gernot Böhme, *Goethes Faust als philosophischer Text* [Zug, 2005], p. 197).

46 Richard Noll, *The Aryan Christ: The Secret Life of Carl Jung* (New York, 1997), p. 42.

47 *MDR*, p. 132.

48 Noll, *The Aryan Christ*, p. 43.

49 Ibid., pp. 43–4.

50 See Jung, *PU*, §9; cf. *PU*, §196, n. 80. For a discussion of the likely impact of Stuck's work on Jung, see Noll, *The Aryan Christ*, pp. 44–5.

51 Noll, *The Aryan Christ*, p. 45.

52 *MDR*, p. 118; Jung, L, II, p. 528; see Hermann Reimer, *Georg Andreas Reimer: Erinnerungen aus seinem Leben, insbesondere aus der Zeit der Demagogen-Verfolgung* (Berlin, 1900).

53 See G. Palmai and B. Blackwell, 'The Burghölzli Centenary', *Medical History*, X/3 (July 1966), pp. 257–65.

54 *MDR*, p. 133.

55 Ibid., p. 134.

56 In a protocol of a conversation with Aniela Jaffé, Jung recalled that his colleagues at the Burghölzli wondered whether Jung was psychically abnormal, since during his first six months at the clinic, he never went out once (cited in Sonu Shamdasani, *Jung and the Making of Modern Psychology: The Dream of a Science* [Cambridge, 2003], p. 46).

57 Anthony Storr, *Jung* (London, 1983), p. 16. Another anecdote tells how Jung once responded to the question why he did not deal with children by replying that they didn't have much symbolic material. To which his wife, Emma Jung, responded: 'Oh, Carl, no one interests you who doesn't have much symbolical material!' (Maggy Anthony, *The Valkryies: The Women around Jung* [Longmead, 1990], p. 17).

58 See 'The Psychology of Dementia Praecox' (1907) and 'The Content of the Psychoses' (1908/1914); Jung, *CW*, III, §198–§202 and §363–§384.

59 *MDR*, p. 147–8.

60 Jung, *CW*, III, §383.

61 See 'The Content of the Psychoses'; ibid., §358.

62 *MDR*, p. 146.

63 See the entry on 'word association test' in Andrew Samuels, Bani Shorter and Fred Plaut, *A Critical Dictionary of Jungian Analysis* (London and New York, 1986), pp. 161–2. See also Edmund D. Cohen, *C. G. Jung and the Scientific Attitude* (New York, 1975).

64 William McGuire, 'Jung's Complex Reactions (1907): Word Association Experiments Performed by Binswanger', *Spring* (1984), pp. 1–34.

65 Protocols of interview with Aniela Jaffé, in Shamdasani, *Jung and the Making of Modern Psychology*, pp. 45–6.

66 *MDR*, p. 137.

67 Ibid., p. 138.

68 Jung, *CW*, I, §1–§150.

69 Ibid., §38.

70 Théodore Flournoy, *Des Indes à la planète Mars: Étude sur un cas de somnambulisme avec glossolalie* (1900); *From India to the Planet Mars: A Case of Multiple Personality with Imaginary Languages*, trans. Daniel B. Vermilye [1901], ed. Sonu Shamdasani (Princeton, NJ, 1994).

71 Jung, *CW*, I, §28.

72 Ibid.

73 Goethe, *Werke* [*WA*], II.11, pp. 269–84 (p. 282); trans. in Jeremy Naydler, ed., *Goethe on Science: An Anthology of Goethe's Scientific Writings* (Edinburgh, 1996), p. 119; cf. Jung, *CW*, I, §28, n. 16.

74 Jung, *CW*, I, §140; cf. 'Cryptomnesia', in Jung, *CW*, I, §181.

75 Michel Onfray, *Apostille au Crépuscule: Pour une psychanalyse non freu-dienne* (Paris, 2010), pp. 44–51.

76 Freud, letter to Martha Bernays of 7 December 1889; Freud, *Briefe 1873–1939*, ed. Ernst and Lucie Freud (Frankfurt am Main, 1960), p. 189.

77 For a presentation of this view, see especially the section 'Jung without Freud' in Shamdasani, *Jung and the Making of Modern Psychology*, pp. 11–13.

78 See Emma Jung and Marie-Louise von Franz, *The Grail Legend* [1970], trans. Andrea Dykes, 2nd edn (Boston, MA, and London, 1986).

79 For an illustrated history of the construction of the house and a pres-entation of its recent renovation, see Andreas Jung et al., *Haus C. G. Jung: Entstehung und Erneuerung des Wohnhauses von Emma und Carl Gustav Jung-Rauschenbach* (Küsnacht-Zürich, 2009).

4 Occultism, Psychoanalysis and Beyond

1 Jung, letter to Freud, 28 October 1907; *F/J*, p. 95.

2 Jung, 'Psychoanalysis and Association Experiments'; *CW*, II, §660.

3 'Our Aryan comrades are really quite indispensable to us, otherwise psychoanalysis would fall victim to anti-Semitism' (*The Complete Correspondence of Sigmund Freud and Karl Abraham, 1907–1925*, ed. Ernst Falzeder, trans. Caroline Schwarzacher (London, 2002), p. 72.

4 See Jung's letter to Freud of 20 February 1908), Moses and Joshua (see Freud's letter to Jung of 17 January 1909), and analyst and analysand (see their letters of 29 November and 3 December 1912); *F/J*, pp. 122, 196–7, 524 and 525–6.

5 *F/J*, p. 115; ibid., p. 122.

6 Ibid., pp. 27–8, 168, 218–19.

7 Ibid., p. 248; Beatrice interview, Richard Noll interviewed by Ron Hogan; available at www.beatrice.com. Accessed 15 September 2013.

8 Jung, *The Psychology of Dementia Praecox*; *CW*, II, §123.

9 Ibid., §124–§133.

10 Ibid., §132.

11 *F/J*, p. 14.

12 See Herbert Lehmann, 'Jung contra Freud/Nietzsche contra Wagner', *International Review of Psycho-Analysis*, XIII (1986), pp. 201–9.

13 *F/J*, p. 17.

14 Ibid., p. 7.

15 See Aldo Carotenuto, *A Secret Symmetry: Sabina Spielrein between Jung and Freud*, trans. Arno Pomerans, John Shepley and Krishna Winston (New York, 1982). For further discussion, see John Kerr, *A Most Dangerous Method: The Story of Jung, Freud, and Sabina Spielrein* (London, 1994).

16 *F/J*, pp. 230–31. Freud uses these expressions in English.

17 Carotenuto, *A Secret Symmetry*, p. 93.

18 Ibid., p. 94.

19 Kerr, *A Most Dangerous Method*, p. 207.

20 Carotenuto, *A Secret Symmetry*, p. 86.

21 Ibid., p. 12; Richard Noll, *The Jung Cult: Origins of a Charismatic Movement* (Princeton, NJ, 1994), p. 74.

22 Goethe, *GE*, IV, p. 344.

23 Ibid., pp. 344–5.

24 See Sabina Spielrein, *Sämtliche Schriften*, ed. Erika Kittler (Freiburg im Breisgau, 1987); and *Sämtliche Schriften* (Giessen, 2002); see *Prokolle der Wiener Psychoanalytischen Vereinigung*, ed. Herman Nunberg and Ernst Federn (Frankfurt am Main, 1976–81), III, pp. 314–20; see Sabina Spielrein, 'Destruction as the Cause of Coming into Being', *Journal of Analytical Psychology*, XXXIX/2 (April 1994), pp. 155–86; Bettelheim, in *A Secret Symmetry*, p. xxxix.

25 *MDR*, p. 173.

26 Michel Onfray, *Le crépuscule d'une idole: L'affabulation freudienne* (Paris, 2010), pp. 349–86. See also the excursus 'Freud's Interest in the Occult', in Paul Bishop, *Synchronicity and Intellectual Intuition in Kant, Swedenborg, and Jung* (Lewiston, NY, 2000), pp. 102–29.

27 Freud, *SE*, XVIII, p. 177.

28 Ibid., p. 178. That said, as far as cooperative work between occultists and analysts was concerned, Freud saw various dangers, and he

concluded this part of his paper (in a passage not quoted by Onfray): 'My personal attitude to the material remains unenthusiastic and ambivalent' (Ibid., p. 181).

29 Freud/Abraham, *Correspondence*, p. 550.

30 Eduardo Weiss, *Sigmund Freud as a Consultant: Recollections of a Pioneer in Psychoanalysis* (New Brunswick, NJ, 1991), p. 69.

31 Ibid., p. 70.

32 Freud, *SE*, VI, p. 261.

33 Ibid. Nevertheless, and unacknowledged by Onfray, Freud does have an explanation (of sorts) for what he also calls *superstition*: 'Superstition is in large part the expectation of trouble; and a person who has harboured frequent evil wishes against others, but has been brought up to be good and has therefore repressed such wishes into the unconscious, will be especially ready to expect punishment for his unconscious wickedness in the form of trouble threatening him from without' (Freud, *SE*, VI, p. 260).

34 Freud, *New Introductory Lectures on Psycho-Analysis*, Lecture 30; *SE*, XXII, p. 43.

35 *The Complete Letters of Sigmund Freud to Wilhelm Fliess, 1887–1904*, ed. and trans. Jeffrey Moussaieff Masson (Cambridge, MA, and London, 1985), pp. 175–6; ibid., p. 85.

36 *F/J*, pp. 219–20.

37 Freud, *SE*, VI, pp. 242–3.

38 See Arthur I. Miller, *Deciphering the Cosmic Number: The Strange Friendship of Wolfgang Pauli and Carl Jung* (New York and London, 2009).

39 *MDR*, p. 179.

40 *F/J*, p. 216.

41 Ibid., p. 218. Cf. the lines by Schiller: 'E'en unmindful of her Maker's praise — / Like the dead beat of the swinging hour, / Nature, of her Gods bereft, obeys, / Slave-like, mere mechanic power' (*Fühllos selbst für ihres Künstlers Ehre, / Gleich dem todten Schlag der Pendeluhr, / Dient sie knechtisch dem Gesetz der Schwere / Die entgötterte Natur!*) in Friedrich Schiller, *Minor Poems*, trans. John Herman Merivale (London, 1844), p. 21; *Sämtliche Gedichte und Balladen*, ed. Georg Kurscheidt (Frankfurt am Main and Leipzig, 2004), p. 224.

42 Freud, *SE*, XI, pp. 82–101; *F/J*, p. 329.

43 Freud, *SE*, XII, p. 82.

44 Ibid., XIV, p. 286.

45 Ibid., V, p. 549; ibid; cf. Nietzsche, *Human, All Too Human: A Book for Free Spirits*, trans. A. J. Hollingdale (Cambridge, 1986), p. 18; cf. Jung, *PU*, §37.

46 Freud, *SE*, XIX, pp. 36–8; ibid, XXIII, p. 167; ibid.

47 Cf. Hans Vaihinger (1852–1933), *Philosophie des Als Ob* (Leipzig, 1911); repr. and ed. Esther von Krosigk (Saarbrücken, 2007); *The Philosophy of "As If": A System of the Theoretical, Practical and Religious Fictions of Mankind*, trans. C. K. Ogden (London, 1924), repr. 2000. Subsequently, the analyst James Hillman has developed the idea of 'seeing through our meanings', rather than being literal in our approach: see *Healing Fiction* [1983] (Woodstock, CT, 1994), p. 110.

48 Freud, *SE*, V, pp. 360–61.

49 Ibid., p. 361.

50 Ibid., XIII, p. 85; ibid, p. 89.

51 Ibid., p. 83.

52 Ibid., p. 79; cf. ibid., p. 83.

53 See Jung, 'Archaic Man' (1931); *CW*, X, §104–§147.

54 *F/J*, p. 258.

55 *The Landmark Herodotus: The Histories*, ed. Robert B. Strassler, trans. Andrea L. Purvis (London, 2008), p. 144.

56 Ibid., p. 145.

57 Ibid.

58 Jung, *PU*, §397–§398. See also Jung's letter to Freud of 15 November 1909 (*F/J*, p. 263).

59 *F/J*, p. 258. In his *Histories*, Herodotus' discretion is an important topos (see, for example, 2.61.2, 2.65.2 and 2.171–172), and at one point (perhaps the passage Jung was thinking of?), he comments that he would 'rather not mention' why Pan is depicted as goatlike (2.46.2).

60 *The Landmark Herodotus*, p. 139.

61 *F/J*, p. 263.

62 Ibid., p. 279.

63 Ibid.

64 Ibid., p. 280.

65 Ibid., p. 294.

66 Ibid., p. 295.

67 Ibid., p. 421; *Faust II*, lines 6287–90; Goethe, *Faust: A Tragedy*, ed. Cyrus Hamlin, trans. Walter Arndt, 2nd edn (New York and London, 2001), p. 178.

68 Jung, letter to Freud of 23 June 1911; *F/J*, p. 431.

69 *F/J*, p. 487.

70 See Richard M. Capobianco, 'In the Beginning: Jung and Freud on Introversion', *Psychological Perspectives: A Quarterly Journal of Jungian Thought*, XIX/2 (1988), pp. 244–55.

71 *F/J*, p. 334; ibid., p. 335.

72 On the cult of Mithras, see Manfred Clauss, *The Roman Cult of Mithras: The God and his Mysteries* [1990], trans. Richard Gordon (Edinburgh, 2000); and Reinhold Merkelbach, *Mithras: Ein persisch-römischer Mysterienkult* (Königstein/Taunus, 1984).

73 *F/J*, p. 334; ibid., p. 336; ibid.

74 Ibid., p. 336.

75 *On the Genealogy of Morals*, part 3, §13; Friedrich Nietzsche, *Basic Writings*, ed. and trans. Walter Kaufmann (New York, 1968), p. 556.

76 See 'On Self-Overcoming', in Friedrich Nietzsche, *Thus Spoke Zarathustra*, trans. Graham Parkes (New York, 2005), p. 99.

77 *F/J*, p. 336.

78 Jung, *PU*, §398; cf. *PU*, §249 and §457.

79 *F/J*, p. 336.

80 Ibid.; ibid.; ibid., p. 337.

81 Ibid., p. 337.

82 Ibid., p. 336.

83 For the significance of this journey, see Saul Rosenzweig, *Freud, Jung, and Hall the King-Maker: The Historic Expedition to America (1909) with G. Stanley Hall as Host and William James as Guest* (St Louis, MO, and Seattle, WA, 1992). It was on this voyage across the Atlantic that Freud came across his cabin steward reading *The Psychology of Everyday Life* and realized he was now someone famous (Peter Gay, *Freud: A Life For Our Time* [New York and London, 1988], p. 209).

84 *MDR*, p. 180.

85 Ibid.; Ernest Jones, *The Life and Work of Sigmund Freud*, I: *The Formative Years and the Great Discoveries, 1856–1900* (New York, 1953), p. 317. (In this episode we see Jung, for once, arguing as an advocate of monotheism rather than polytheism; no wonder Freud fainted!)

86 *F/J*, p. 487. The *katabasis* or the heroic descent to the underworld is a
    major motif of world mythology in general and classical literature in
    particular: see, for instance, *Odyssey* 21.295–306; 11.631; Apollodorus,
    Bibliotheke, 2.5.11–12; Virgil, *Aeneid* 6.393; Ovid, *Metamorphoses* 12.218.
    For Jung's citation of Nietzsche see *F/J*, p. 491. Cf. *Zarathustra*, part 1,
    'Of the Bestowing Virtue', §3, p. 68.

87 *F/J*, p. 511.

88 Freud, *SE*, XIV, p. 62.

89 Ibid., p. 64.

90 Ibid., p. 62.

91 Ibid.

92 Sonu Shamdasani in his 'Introduction' to C. G. Jung, *The Red Book:
    Liber Novus*, ed. Sonu Shamdasani, trans. Mark Kyburz, John Peck
    and Sonu Shamdasani (New York and London, 2009), p. 196.

93 Jung, L, II, p. 359. For the suggestion that this comment may have
    been written by Aniela Jaffé, albeit with Jung's approval, see
    Shamdasani, 'Memories, Dreams, Omissions' [1995], in *Jung in
    Contexts: A Reader*, ed. Paul Bishop (London and New York, 1999),
    pp. 33–50 (p. 38).

94 *MDR*, p. 194.

95 Ibid.

96 Ibid., p. 195.

97 Ibid., pp. 196–9.

98 *The Black Books*, II, pp. 24–5, cited in Jung, *RB*, p. 198.

99 E. A. Bennet, *Meeting with Jung: Conversations Recorded by E. A. Bennet
    during the Years 1946–1961* (London, 1982), p. 93.

100 Ibid., p. 75.

101 *MDR*, p. 196.

102 C. G. Jung, *Analytical Psychology: Notes of the Seminar Given in 1925*,
     ed. William McGuire (Princeton, NJ, 1989), p. 39.

103 Of the numerous places where Freud discusses the unconscious as
     'archaic vestiges', see for example 'Creative Writers and Day-
     Dreaming' [1907] (1908): 'Myths . . . are distorted vestiges of the
     wishful phantasies of whole nations, the *secular dreams* of youthful
     humanity' (*SE*, IX, p. 152). In 'An Outline of Psycho-Analysis' [1938]
     (1940) Freud is still speaking of 'the *archaic heritage* which a child
     brings with him into the world' (*SE*, XXIII, p. 167).

104 *MDR*, p. 197.

105 Ibid., p. 196.

106 Ibid., p. 198.

107 Goethe, *Dichtung und Wahrheit*, part 1, book 1; *GE*, IV, p. 44.

108 *MDR*, pp. 197–8.

109 Ibid., p. 198.

110 Ibid., pp. 197–8.

111 'The inner non-material world can be transposed by sandplay into a concrete outer picture of psyche. This transposition symbolically objectifies the inner archetypal content through allowing it to have an outer material form': from Joel Ryce-Menuhin, *Jungian Sandplay: The Wonderful Therapy* (London, 1992), p. 28.

112 Letter 15, §9; Friedrich Schiller, *On the Aesthetic Education of Man in a Series of Letters*, ed. and trans. Elizabeth M. Wilkinson and L. A. Willoughby (Oxford, 1982), p. 107.

113 *MDR*, p. 199.

114 William McGuire and R. F. Hull, eds, *C. G. Jung Speaking: Interviews and Encounters* (Princeton, NJ, 1977), p. 232.

115 *MDR*, p. 199.

116 Ibid., p. 200.

117 Ibid.; cf. Peter Homans, *Jung in Context: Modernity and the Making of a Psychology* (Chicago, IL, and London, 1979), p. 79.

118 *F/J*, p. 324.

119 McGuire and Hull, eds, *C. G. Jung Speaking*, p. 233.

120 Ibid., p. 234.

121 See Thomas Anz, 'Kafka, der Krieg und das grösste Theater der Welt', in *'Krieg der Geister': Erster Weltkrieg und literarische Moderne*, ed. Uwe Schneider and Andreas Schumann (Würzburg, 2000), pp. 247–62; see Jürgen Eder, 'Die Geburt des "Zauberbergs" aus dem Geiste der Verwirrung: Thomas Mann und der erste Weltkrieg', in *'Krieg der Geister'*, pp. 171–87.

122 See Hans-Ulrich Wehler, *Deutsche Gesellschaftsgeschichte, 1914–1949*, IV (Munich, 2003), pp. 14–15.

123 McGuire and Hull, eds, *C. G. Jung Speaking*, p. 234.

124 *MDR*, p. 201.

125 Ibid., p. 202.

126 Ibid., p. 213.

127 For further analysis and discussion, see Sandford L. Drob, *Reading the Red Book: An Interpretive Guide to C. G. Jung's 'Liber Novus'* (New Orleans, LA, 2012); and Thomas Kirsch and George Hogenson, eds, *The Red Book: Reflections on C. G. Jung's 'Liber Novus'* (London and New York, 2013).

128 G.W.F. Hegel, 'Jenaer Realphilosophie', in *Jenaer Systementwürfe III* (Hamburg, 1987), p. 172; trans. in Donald Phillip Verene, *Hegel's Recollection: A Study of Images in the 'Phenomenology of Spirit'* (Albany, NY, 1985), pp. 7–8 [trans. modified].

129 *MDR*, p. 207.

130 Ibid.

131 Ibid.; ibid., p. 208; cf. the title of a collection of Jung's papers, *Die Wirklichkeit der Seele*; ibid.

132 Jung, letter to Victor White of 30 January 1948; *The Jung-White Letters*, ed. Ann Conrad Lammers and Adrian Cunningham (London and New York, 2007), p. 116; on the importance of the guru in the transmission of transcendental knowledge, see the *Bhagavad Gita*, chap. 4, §34: 'Just try to learn the truth by approaching a spiritual master. Inquire from him submissively and render service unto him. The self-realized souls can impart knowledge unto you because they have seen the truth': in *Bhagavad-Gītā As It Is* (Abridged Edition), ed. A. C. Bhaktivedanta Swami Prabhupāda (New York, 1975), p. 87.

133 Goethe, *Dichtung und Wahrheit*, part 3, book 13; *GE*, IV, p. 424.

134 Ibid.

135 According to an account by Stephan Schütze, cited in *Goethe: Conversations and Encounters*, ed. and trans. David Luke and Robert Pick (London, 1966), p. 92; based on *Werke* [Artemis edn], XXII, p. 691.

136 Goethe, *Dichtung und Wahrheit*, part 3, book 15; *GE*, IV, pp. 468–9. For further discussion of this passage, see Peter J. Burgard, *Idioms of Uncertainty: Goethe and the Essay* (University Park, PA, 1992), pp. 147–8.

137 Goethe, *GE*, IV, p. 469.

138 Ibid.

139 For further discussion of 'active imagination', see *The Tavistock Lectures* (1935), Lecture 5 (*CW*, XVIII, §390–§406); and Joy Schavarian, 'Art within Analysis: Scapegoat, Transference and Transformation', *Journal of Analytical Psychology*, XLIV (1999), pp. 479–510.

140 Jung, *SNZ*, I, p. 259.

141 Ibid., p. 391. Jung then goes on to make the following extraordinary claim: 'One misses in *Zarathustra* the concept of the unconscious; there is only the conscious.'

142 See Gerhard Schmitt, 'Vom Übermensch und Übersinn: Nietzsches Metaphorik im *Roten Buch*', in *Recherches germaniques*, special edn, VIII (2011), pp. 117–33.

143 For further discussion, see Paul Bishop, 'Jung's *Red Book* and its Relation to Aspects of German Idealism', *Journal of Analytical Psychology*, LVII/3 (June 2012), pp. 335–63; *MDR*, p. 203.

144 *MDR*, p. 203.

145 Ibid.

5 Out with New, in with the (Very) Old: From Psychoanalysis to Analytical Psychology

1 *F/J*, p. 263.

2 Ibid., p. 280.

3 Jung, *PU*, §1.

4 Théodore Flournoy, 'Quelques faits d'imagination créatrice subconsciente', *Archives de psychologie*, V (1906), pp. 36–51. For further information on this case, see Sonu Shamdasani's seminal essay, 'A Woman called Frank', *Spring*, L (1990), pp. 26–56.

5 Jung, *PU*, §56.

6 See her *The Re-Creating of the Individual: A Study of Psychological Types and their Relation to Psychoanalysis* (London, 1923); an autobiographical essay by Hinkle, 'Why Feminism?', is published in *These Modern Women: Autobiographical Essays from the Twenties*, ed. Elaine Showalter (New York, 1989), pp. 137–40; Jung, *PU*, p. xxxiii.

7 William McGuire, 'Firm Affinities: Jung's Relations with Britain and the United States', *Journal of Analytical Psychology*, XL (1995), pp. 301–26; Sonu Shamdasani, *Jung and the Making of Modern Psychology: The Dream of a Science* (Cambridge, 2003), p. 13.

8 See Jung's letter to Freud of 11 March 1909 (*F/J*, p. 212); and John Kerr, '*The Devil's Elixirs*, Jung's "Theology" and the Dissolution of Freud's "Poisoning Complex"' [1988], in *Jung in Contexts: A Reader*, ed. Paul

Bishop (London and New York, 1999), pp. 125–53; Jung, *L*, I, p. 10; *F/J*, p. 216.

9 The Italian psychologist Roberto Assagioli (1888–1974) founded his own school of therapy on a similar concept of 'psychosynthesis'.

10 Shamdasani, *Jung and the Making of Modern Psychology*, p. 15.

11 Jung, 'Analytical Psychology and "Weltanschauung"' (1928/1931); *CW*, VIII, §739; ibid.

12 Ibid. Cf. Jung's claim in his paper 'Psychological Types' (1923) that 'the unconscious is the residue of unconquered nature in us, just as it is also the matrix of our unborn future' (*das Unbewusste ist der Rest unbezwungener Urnatur in uns, so wie es auch der Mutterboden ungeschaffener Zukunft in uns ist*) (*CW*, VI, §907). Subsequently this idea can also be found in Freud in 'Civilization and its Discontents' (1930) (*SE*, XXI, p. 86), and later in the Frankfurt School (Max Horkheimer, Theodor W. Adorno and Jürgen Habermas).

13 Jung, 'Psychotherapists or the Clergy' (1932); *CW*, XI, §531.

14 Ibid., §534.

15 Ibid., §535.

16 *MDR*, p. 182.

17 Ibid., pp. 182–3. Compare with Jung's remarks in his *Visions* seminar (1930–34), where he argues that it is 'practical and permissible to assume that the mind is built in sorts of strata; the top layer would be the actual consciousness, and below would be the historical layers . . . All original revelation takes place on that level where the mind is objectified, where it seems not to belong to the person itself, but to be definitely a strange factor': Jung, *Visions: Notes of the Seminar Given in 1930–1934*, ed. Claire Douglas, 2 vols (London, 1998), I, p. 94.

18 Raya Jones, 'A Discovery of Meaning: The Case of C. G. Jung's House Dream', *Culture & Psychology*, XIII (2007), pp. 203–30; Steve Myers, 'The Cryptomnesic Origins of Jung's Dream of the Multi-Storeyed House', *Journal of Analytical Psychology*, LIV (2009), pp. 513–31.

19 See Jung, 'On the Psychology and Pathology of so-called Occult Phenomena' (1902); *CW*, I, §140–§142.

20 Freud, *SE*, XXI, p. 17.

21 Ibid., p. 15; ibid., p. 16.

22 Ibid., V, pp. 618–19.

23 Ibid., p. 619.

24 Ibid., xx, p. 211.

25 Jung, 'The Psychology of the Child Archetype' (1940); *CW*, IX/i, §302. This is so because psychology, 'as one of the many expressions of psychic life, operates with ideas which in their turn are derived from archetypal structures and thus generate a somewhat more abstract kind of myth' (ibid.). The structure of Jung's argument here conforms to an argumentational logic that has been called 'binary synthesis'.

26 Ibid., §271.

27 *MDR*, p. 17.

28 Jung, *CW*, VI, p. 2. Cf. Heinrich Heine, *The Romantic School and Other Essays*, ed. Jost Hermand and Robert C. Holub (New York, 1997), p. 172. In so writing, Heine in his turn is drawing on a topos that opposes Plato and Aristotle; see, for example, Proclus' remark in his commentary on the *Timaeus* that Aristotle seemed to have 'arranged his whole treatment of nature, as far as possible, in rivalry with that of Plato': in John P. Dillon and Lloyd P. Gerson, eds, *Neoplatonic Philosophy: Introductory Readings* (Indianapolis, IN, 2004), p. 337.

29 Jung, *CW*, VI, §4.

30 Ibid., §6.

31 Ibid.

32 Ibid., §830.

33 Ibid., §723–§729.

34 Ibid., §794.

35 Spinoza, *Ethics*, part 1, proposition 40, scholium 2; in *Spinoza: Selections*, ed. John Wild (London, 1928), p. 186. This 'intuitive science' proceeds, according to Spinoza's mysterious formulation, 'from an adequate idea of certain attributes of God to the adequate knowledge of the essence of things' (part 5, proposition 25, demonstration; in *Selections*, p. 386). On Bergson and intuition, see Henri Bergson, *The Creative Mind: An Introduction to Metaphysics* [trans. 1946 of *La Pensée et le mouvant*, 1934], trans. Mabelle L. Andison (New York, 2007), chap. 4, 'Philosophical Intuition', pp. 87–105.

36 See Vincent Brome, *Jung: Man and Myth* (London, 1978), p. 174.

37 Jung, *CW*, VI, §621.

38 Ibid., §591, §637, §642.

39 Ibid., §743, §754, §732–§737.

40 Ibid., §745, §746.

41 Ibid., §748. For further discussion of Jung's use of Semon's theory of mnemes and his later abandonment of it, see Walter A. Shelburne, *Mythos and Logos in the Thought of Carl Jung: The Theory of the Collective Unconscious in Scientific Perspective* (Albany, NY, 1988).

42 Jung, *Visions*, I, p. 9.

43 Ibid., p. 65.

44 Ibid., p. 133.

45 Jung, *SNZ*, I, p. 21.

46 Ibid., p. 22.

47 Ibid., pp. 22–3.

48 Jung, *CW*, IX/i, §99; ibid., §117.

49 Ibid., XII, §15.

50 Jung, *CW*, IX/i, §150.

51 See Plato, *Republic* 9.589a; Plato, *The Collected Dialogues*, ed. Edith Hamilton and Huntington Cairns (Princeton, NJ, 1989), p. 817: 'All our actions and words should tend to give the man within us complete domination over the entire man'; cf. Plotinus, *Enneads*, 1.1.10 or 5.1.10; *The Enneads*, trans. Stephen MacKenna, revised B. S. Page (London, 1956), pp. 28 and 378; see, for example, Plotinus' *Enneads* 1.2.2, 5.1.4, or 5.7.1; ibid., pp. 31–2, 371–2, 419–20.

52 Hazel E. Barnes, 'Neo-Platonism and Analytical Psychology', *Philosophical Review*, LIV (1945), pp. 558–77; see C. Bigg, *Neoplatonism* (London, 1895); and Manly P. Hall, *Neoplatonism: Theology for Wanderers in the New Millennium*, ed. Richard G. Geldard (Los Angeles, CA, 1983; 2nd edn 2010); see Werner Beierwaltes, 'The Legacy of Neoplatonism in F.W.J. Schelling's Thought', *International Journal of Philosophical Studies*, X (2002), pp. 393–428.

53 'An archetypal content expresses itself, first and foremost, in metaphors' (Jung, 'The Psychology of the Child Archetype'; *CW*, IX/i, §267); Jung, 'Psychological Aspects of the Mother Archetype'; *CW*, IX/i, §173. Tellingly, in a way that reveals how Jung really regarded the ontological status of archetypes, he added: 'Even if all proofs of the existence of archetypes were lacking, and all the clever people in the world succeeded in convincing us that such a thing could not possibly exist, we would have to invent them forthwith in order to keep our highest and our most important values from disappearing into the unconscious' (*CW*, IX/i, §173).

54 See the title of Sonu Shamdasani's book, *Jung and the Making of a Modern Psychology: The Dream of a Science*, written as a defence against the charges that Jung is an occultist, a prophet, or even a charlatan.

55 In his definition of *Einstellung*, Jung says the term is derived from the work of G. E. Müller and F. Schumann, and he distinguishes between its use by Oswald Külpe and by Hermann Ebbinghaus (*cw*, VI, §687); Jung, *cw*, VI, §785.

56 Jung, *cw*, VI, §786, my italics. Compare with Jung's remarks in 'The Psychology of the Unconscious' (1917/1926/1943): 'I have often been asked where the archetype or primordial images come from. It seems to me that their origin can only be explained by assuming them to be deposits of the constantly repeated experiences of humanity' (*cw*, VII, §109). Yet Jung emphasizes that the archetypes are not passive, but *active*: 'Not only are the archetypes . . . impressions of ever-repeated typical experiences, but . . . they behave empirically like agents that tend towards the repetition of these same experiences. For when an archetype appears in a dream, in a fantasy, or in life, it always brings with it a certain influence or power by virtue of which it either exercises a numinous or a fascinating effect, or impels to action' (ibid.).

57 Jung, *cw*, VI, §774.

58 Ibid., §775.

59 Ibid., §836.

60 Ibid., §776.

61 Ibid.

62 Bruno Bettelheim, *Freud and Man's Soul* (New York, 1984). For further discussion, see the papers collected in Darius Gray Ornston, ed., *Translating Freud* (New Haven, CT, and London, 1992).

63 Jung, *cw*, VI, §797; ibid., §798–799, §800–802, §803–806; cf. ibid., §808–812.

64 Ibid., §803.

65 For further discussion, see Robert Hopcke, *Jung, Jungians, and Homosexuality* (Boston, MA, and London, 1989).

66 Bertrand Vergely, 'Sur l'émerveillement', given at the Institut Saint-Serge, Paris, 4 June 2011. For further discussion of the Vergelyesque notion of wonder, see *Retour à l'émerveillement* (Paris, 2010).

6 Back to the Future: Bollingen and Alchemy

1 Jung, *RB*, p. 320.

2 See Sonu Shamdasani's editorial note in ibid., n. 310.

3 Ibid., p. 321.

4 See Jung, *CW*, VI, §381–§391. For Jung, the text is characteristic of a transition from 'the worship of the woman' to 'the worship of the soul' (ibid., §381), *The Shepherd of Hermas* revealing how the elimination of 'earth-bound desire, sensuality in all its forms, attachment to the lures of this world, and the incessant dissipation of psychic energy in the world's prodigal variety' as 'the main obstacle to the development of a coherent and purposive attitude' had been 'one of the most important tasks of the time [the second century CE]' (ibid., §391).

5 Jung, *RB*, p. 321.

6 For a recent discussion of Jung's tower, see Theodor Ziolkowski, *The View from the Tower: Origins of an Antimodernist Image* (Princeton, NJ, 1999), pp. 133–48.

7 Jung, *L*, I, p. 49.

8 I remain grateful that I was given permission by Jung's son, Franz Jung, to visit the tower at Bollingen on a hot afternoon in 1992.

9 *MDR*, pp. 38–9.

10 Ibid., pp. 198–9.

11 Pictures of these sculpted figures can be found in David Rosen, *The Tao of Jung: The Way of Integrity* (New York, 1996), pp. 129, 130, 142, 144, 145, 149 and 154.

12 See *Meetings with Jung: Conversations Recorded by E. A. Bennet during the Years 1946–1961* (London, 1982), p. 107.

13 *MDR*, pp. 253–4.

14 Ibid., p. 255.

15 Ibid., p. 252.

16 Or 'the first son of the mother' (see Jung, 'Archetypes of the Collective Unconscious' (1934/1954), *CW*, IX/i §74); or 'the *filius regius*, son of the supreme mother' (see Jung, 'The Psychology of the Transference' (1946), *CW*, XVI §407). For discussion of how, in alchemy, 'in order to enter into God's Kingdom the king must transform himself into the prima materia in the body of this mother, and return to the dark initial state which the alchemists called "chaos"' or the *massa confusa*,

see *Mysterium coniunctionis* (*CW*, XIV §381-§385); on Jung's second personality see *MDR*, p. 252.

17 *MDR*, p. 252.

18 Ibid.

19 Ibid., p. 264. Such an enterprise is related to the experience that Jung talks about in a lecture of 1927 (Jung, 'Analytical Psychology and "Weltanschauung"' (1928/1931); *CW*, VIII, §737).

20 *MDR*, pp. 264–5; trans. modified; Friedrich Nietzsche, *The Will to Power*, ed. Walter Kaufmann, trans. Walter Kaufmann and R. J. Hollingdale (New York, 1968), §1067 (p. 550).

21 See Goethe's letter to Lavater of 3–5 December 1779 (*Briefe* [*HA*], I, pp. 287–9).

22 *Baedeker Allianz Reiseführer: Weimar*, 2nd edn (Ostfildern, 1997), p. 81; Nicholas Boyle, *Goethe: The Poet and the Age*, I: *The Poetry of Desire (1749–1790)* (Oxford and New York, 1991), p. 286.

23 For an illustration and commentary of Klauer's 'serpent stone', see Gerhard Schuster and Caroline Gille, eds, *Wiederholte Spiegelungen: Weimarer Klassik 1759–1832: Ständige Ausstellung des Goethe-Nationalmuseums*, 2 vols (Munich and Vienna, 1999), I, pp. 282–3.

24 Jung, *RB*, p. 360.

25 See ibid., p. 163.

26 *MDR*, p. 223.

27 Herbert Silberer, *Probleme der Mystik und ihrer Symbolik* (Vienna and Leipzig, 1914); *Problems of Mysticism and its Symbolism*, trans. S. E. Jelliffe (New York, 1917).

28 Jung, *CW*, XII, §89; ibid., XIV, §792.

29 See Sonu Shamdasani, *C. G. Jung: A Biography in Books* (New York and London, 2012), pp. 164–202.

30 M. A. Atwood, *A Suggestive Inquiry into the Hermetic Mystery: With a Dissertation on the more celebrated of the Alchemical Philosophers: Being an Attempt towards the Recovery of the Ancient Experiment of Nature* (London, 1850). Jung owned the revised 1920 edition of this work.

31 Ibid., pp. 136 and 153.

32 Ethan Allen Hitchcock, *Remarks upon Alchemy and the Alchemists* (Boston, MA, 1857), pp. 43 and 57.

33 Ethan Allen Hitchcock, *Swedenborg, A Hermetic Philosopher: Being a Sequel to Remarks upon Alchemy and the Alchemists* (New York, 1858).

34 Jung, 'Individual Dream Symbolism in Relation to Alchemy: A Study of the Unconscious Processes at Work in Dreams', *cw*, XII, p. 39; cf. Virgil, *Aeneid* 6.129. As Shamdasani has remarked, this use of Virgil is also a gentle swipe at Freud, who prefaced *The Interpretation of Dreams* with a citation from the same part of the same work: 'If I cannot bend the higher powers, I will move the Acheron!'

35 *MDR*, pp. 223 and 226.

36 Ibid., p. 226. For Jung, 'the central ideas of Christianity are rooted in Gnostic philosophy, which, in accordance with psychological laws, simply *had* to grow up at a time when the classical religions had become obsolete' ('Introduction to the Religious and Psychological Problems of Alchemy'; *cw*, XII, §41), and given the new obsolescence of the symbolism of Christianity, analytical psychology is in its turn a reaction and a response to this situation: 'Since the stars have fallen from heaven and our highest symbols have paled, a secret life holds sway in the unconscious', and 'that is why we have a psychology today, and why we speak of the unconscious' ('Archetypes of the Collective Unconscious'; *cw*, IX/i, §50).

37 *MDR*, p. 227.

38 Goethe, *Poems of the West and East: West-Eastern Divan – West-Östlicher Divan: Bi-Lingual Edition of the Complete Poems*, trans. John Whaley (Bern, 1998), p. 189; Goethe, *Werke* [*HA*], II, p. 49.

39 *MDR*, p. 227.

40 Jung, 'The Psychology of the Transference', *cw*, XVI, §399.

41 Ibid.

42 Ibid.

43 Ibid. See *Aurora consurgens*, I, chap. 9, §4, citing a sequence of Notker Balbulus (or 'the Stammerer') for the feast of Pentecost (Migne, *Patrologiae cursus completus: Series Latina*, CXXXI (Paris, 1884), cols 1012–13), and drawing on the Collect in the Breviary for the Third Sunday of Advent, 'and by the grace of your coming enlighten the darkness of our souls' (*et mentis nostræ tenebras gratia tuæ visitationis illustra*). For other instances of where Jung cites the *Aurora*/Notker, see *cw*, XII, §41 and §438.

44 See Synesius, *Dio* 10.48a, citing Aristotle: 'As Aristotle claims that those who are being initiated into the mysteries are to be expected not to learn anything but to suffer some change, to be put into a

certain condition, i.e., to be fitted for some purpose': David Ross, ed.,
The Works of Aristotle, XII: *Select Fragments* (Oxford, 1952), 'Fragments
on Philosophy', no. 15, p. 87; cf. Synesius of Cyrene, *The Essays and
Hymns*, trans. Augustine Fitzgerald, 2 vols (Oxford and London,
1930), I, p. 163.

45 Jung, *Aion* (1951), *CW*, IX/ii, §410; *Mysterium coniunctionis*, *CW*, XIV,
p. v; Jung, 'Religious Ideas in Alchemy: An Historical Survey of
Alchemical Ideas' (1937), *CW*, XII, §378; cited from Dorn's *Speculativae
philosophiae*, in *Theatrum chemicum* [1602], 3rd edn, vol. I,
(Argentorati [Strasbourg], 1659), pp. 228–76 (p. 239); Jung, *CW*, XVI,
§400; see *Theatrum chemicum*, 3rd edn, I, pp. 109–91 (p. 126).

46 Jeremiah 31:2 (*DRV*).

47 Jung, *RB*, p. 259.

48 Jung, *CW*, XVI, §407. Cf. 'Introduction to the Religious and
Psychological Problems of Alchemy': '*Faust* is, consciously or
unconsciously, an *opus alchymicum* . . . So long as the alchemist
was working in his laboratory he was in a favourable position,
psychologically speaking, for he had no opportunity to identify
himself with the archetypes as they appeared . . . The disadvantage
of this situation was that the alchemist was forced to represent the
incorruptible substance as a chemical product . . . which led to the
downfall of alchemy . . . But the psychic part of the work did not
disappear. It captured new interpreters, as we can see from the
example of *Faust*' (*CW*, XII, §42 and §43).

49 Goethe, *Dichtung und Wahrheit*, part 2, book 8; *GE*, IV, p. 256.

50 Ibid.

51 *MDR*, p. 213.

52 *Faust* II, lines 8034–87; for further discussion, see Karl Kerényi, *Das
Aegäische Fest: Die Meergötterszene in Goethes 'Faust II'* (Amsterdam,
1941).

53 Jung, *L*, I, p. 291.

54 *MDR*, p. 231.

55 An allusion to the expression *leben und weben*, found in Goethe who,
in turn, borrowed it from Luther's translation of the Bible; the *unus
mundus* is a phrase used by Gerhard Dorn, as Jung repeatedly reminds
his readers. In *Mysterium coniunctionis* (*CW*, XIV, §659, n. 39) for
instance, Jung cites two passages from Dorn's *De medio spagirico*

dispositionis, ad adepte philosophiae veram cognitionem, et lucii naturae purum conspectum (or *Physica Trismegisti*) (*Theatrum chemicum*, 3rd edn, I, pp. 362–3 and 368).

56 See the passages from Dorn's *Speculativae philosophiae* cited in Jung's *Aion* (*CW*, IX/ii, §250) (quoted from *Theatrum chemicum*, 3rd edn, I, pp. 247 and 274); Jung, *CW*, XIV, §660.

57 Jung, *CW*, XIV, §658, citing Kerényi, *Das Aegäische Fest*, p. 55.

58 Friedrich Nietzsche, 'What I Owe to the Ancients', *Twilight of the Idols/The Anti-Christ*, trans. R. J. Hollingdale (Harmondsworth, 1968), §4, p. 109.

59 *MDR*, p. 232.

60 Jung, *CW*, XII, §38.

61 Jung, *SNZ*, I, p. 10.

62 Ibid., pp. 368–9.

63 Jung could be thinking of the poem in 'The Sorcerer' (otherwise known as 'Ariadne's Complaint') (cf. Jung, *PU*, §454–§455), 'Amid Birds of Prey' – 'Why did you trap / yourself in your wisdom? / Why did you lure yourself / into the old serpent's garden? / Why did you creep / into *yourself*?' (cf. *PU*, §456–§457), or the poem in 'The Song of Melancholy' (otherwise known as 'Only a Fool! Only a Poet!') – 'so I myself sank once / from my delusion of truth, / from my daytime longings, / weary of day, sick with light / – sank downwards, down to evening, down to shadows': Friedrich Nietzsche, *Dithyrambs of Dionysus*, trans. R. J. Hollingdale (London, 1984), pp. 43 and 27; Jung, *SNZ*, I, p. 369.

64 'Schopenhauer as Educator', §1, in Friedrich Nietzsche, *Unmodern Observations*, ed. William Arrowsmith (New Haven, CT, and London, 1990), pp. 165–6.

65 Jung, *SNZ*, II, p. 1227; ibid., p. 868.

66 Ibid., p. 1518. For further discussion, see Nicholas Lewin, *Jung on War, Politics and Nazi Germany: Exploring the Theory of Archetypes and the Collective Unconscious* (London, 2009).

67 Freud, 'Group Psychology and the Analysis of the Ego', §10; *SE*, XVIII, p. 123; ibid, p. 127.

68 For a recent discussion of the first of these essays, see Carrie B. Dohe, 'Wotan and the "archetypal Ergriffenheit": Mystical Union, National Spiritual Rebirth and Culture-Creating Capacity in C. G. Jung's

"Wotan" Essay', *History of European Ideas*, xxxvii/3 (2011), pp. 344–56.

69 Jung, *CW*, x, §402.

70 The Nereids and Tritons speak of the Kabeiroi as 'suffering from desire and hunger / For what is out of reach' (*Sehnsuchtsvolle Hungerleider / Nach dem Unerreichlichen*) (*Faust II*, lines 8204–5). Ludwig Klages speaks of the 'Eros of distance' (Klages, *Vom kosmogonischen Eros* [1922], 2nd edn (Jena, 1926), p. 99). On Jung on Goethe, see Jung, *CW*, xv, §159.

71 Jung, *CW*, x, §423.

72 Ibid.

73 Ibid.

74 Thomas Mann, *Werke*, 2nd edn, 13 vols (Frankfurt am Main, 1974), xi, pp. 1126–48 (p. 1131).

75 Jung, *L*, i, pp. 309–10.

76 Ibid., p. 310.

77 *Faust II*, lines 11866–89.

78 Jung, *L*, i, p. 310.

79 Jung, *CW*, ix/i, §167. Compare with the definition of 'natural mind' as found in *Memories, Dreams, Reflections* (*MDR*, pp. 67–88).

80 Jung, *CW*, ix/ii, §24.

81 Herodotus, *Histories*, 2.58.60; *The Landmark Herodotus: The Histories*, ed. Robert B. Strassler, trans. Andrea L. Purvis (London, 2008), p. 144; Jung, *CW*, xiv, §383.

82 This passage is omitted from MDR. See *Erinnerungen, Träume, Gedanken von C. G Jung*, ed. Aniela Jaffé (Olten, 1990), p. 92.

83 *MDR*, p. 107.

84 Ibid., p. 261.

85 According to the note by Aniela Jaffé (*MDR*, pp. 262–3).

86 Jung, *L*, l, p. 29.

87 *MDR*, p. 262.

88 Jung, *CW*, xii, §563.

89 Ibid., §559.

90 Jung, *CW*, xii, §562.

91 Ibid., §423.

92 *MDR*, p. 262.

93 Ibid., p. 252.

94 Ibid.

95 Ibid., p. 253.

96 Ibid., p. 107.

97 Ibid., p. 265.

98 Jung has been accused of an inclination toward 'ultra-conservativism', see Frank McLynn, *Carl Gustav Jung: A Biography* (London, 1996), pp. 347–54; for further discussion on Jung as a supporter of National Socialism, see 'Appendix D: A Brief History of the aagp/iaagp', in *The Jung-Kirsch Letters: The Correspondence of C. G. Jung and James Kirsch*, ed. Ann Conrad Lammers, trans. Ursula Egli and Ann Conrad Lammers (London and New York, 2011), pp. 306–14.

99 William McGuire and R.F.C. Hull, eds, *C. G. Jung Speaking: Interviews and Encounters* (Princeton, nj, 1977), pp. 62–3.

100 Ibid., pp. 126–8.

101 For a summary of the arguments against and for Jung, see Aryeh Maidenbaum and Stephen A. Martin, *Lingering Shadows: Jungians, Freudians, and Anti-Semitism* (Boston, ma, and London, 1991).

102 Jung, *cw*, x, §18.

103 Ibid., §19.

104 Ibid., §353–§354.

105 See Freud's letter to Max Eitington of 17 April 1933; Sigmund Freud and Max Eitington, *Briefwechsel 1906–1939*, ed. Michael Schröter, 2 vols (Tübingen, 2004), ii, p. 854.

106 *The Jung-Kirsch Letters*, Appendix D, 'A Brief History of the aagp/iaagp', p. 310.

107 Sigmund Freud and Karl Abraham, *Briefe 1907–1926*, ed. Hilda C. Abraham and Ernst L. Freud (Frankfurt am Main, 1965), p. 47.

108 *f/j*, p. 168.

109 *The Jung-Kirsch Letters*, p. 46.

110 See Tilman Evers, *Mythos und Emanzipation: Eine kritische Annäherung an C. G. Jung* (Hamburg, 1987), p. 141.

111 Jung, 'A Rejoinder to Dr. Bally' (*Zeitgenössisches*), published in the *nzz* (*Neue Zürcher Zeitung*), 13 and 14 March 1934; *cw*, x, §1027; Aniela Jaffé, *From the Life and Work of C. G. Jung*, trans. R.F.C. Hull (London, 1972), pp. 84–5.

112 Freud, *se*, xxii, p. 212; ibid.; Michel Onfray, *Le crépuscule d'une idole: L'affabulation freudienne* (Paris, 2010), pp. 531–2.

113 Martin Freud, *Sigmund Freud: Man and Father* (New York, 1958), p. 217; cited in Peter Gay, *Freud: A Life for our Time* (New York and London, 1988), p. 628.

114 Aniela Jaffé, *From the Life and Work of Jung*, p. 98; thus the famous lines (here translated by Michael Hamburger) in Paul Celan's poem, 'Todtnauberg', alluding to his entry in the visitor's book in Heidegger's hut when he visited on 25 July 1967.

115 Jung, *CW*, X, §1024; Jung, *Symbols of Transformation*; *CW*, V, §553.

7 A Voyage of Discovery to the Other Pole of the World

1 Blake W. Burleson, *Jung in Africa* (New York, 2005). See also Graham Saayman, ed., *Modern South Africa in Search of a Soul: Jungian Perspectives on the Wilderness Within* (Boston, MA, 1990).

2 *MDR*, p. 267.

3 Ibid., p. 270.

4 Walter Pater, *The Renaissance: Studies in Art and Poetry* [1873] (Oxford and New York, 1986), 'Conclusion', p. 152.

5 Friedrich Hölderlin, *Poems & Fragments*, trans. Michael Hamburger (London, 1994), pp. 482–3.

6 *MDR*, p. 273.

7 Ibid., p. 274.

8 Ibid.

9 Ibid., p. 276.

10 J.-K. Huysmans, *Against Nature*, trans. Robert Baldick (Harmondsworth, 1959), pp. 90–91. See Thomas De Quincey, *Confessions of an English Opium-Eater* (London, 1821).

11 *MDR*, pp. 276–7.

12 Ibid., p. 278. Cf. Pausanias, *Description of Greece* 1.14.3, 1.38.7 and 8.25.7; and Herodotus, *Histories* 8.65.4–5.

13 *MDR*, p. 280.

14 Ibid., p. 281.

15 On the revelation of Yahweh on Sinai, see Exodus 19:16–25; Deuteronomy 4:9–20; on the inspiration granted to Nietzsche in the Engadine, see Friedrich Nietzsche, 'Thus Spoke Zarathustra', *Ecce Homo*, trans. R. J. Hollingdale (Harmondsworth, 1992), §3, pp. 72–3; *MDR*, p. 281.

16 Roger Brooke, *Jung and Phenomenology* (London and New York, 1991), pp. 52–62.

17 *MDR*, p. 284; associated by Jung with Paracelsus in *CW*, XIII, §195; and alluded to in connection with the alchemical *opus* in *CW*, XI, §310. The exact reference is not given by Jung, but the saying may have its source in Roger Bacon's *Opus minus* (in turn citing Avicenna, *On the Soul*) or Aristotle's *Physics* 2.8.199a ('art partly completes what nature cannot bring to a finish, and partly imitates her'). For further discussion of the Baconian context, see William R. Newman, *Promethean Ambitions: Alchemy and the Quest to Perfect Nature* (Chicago, IL, and London, 2004), p. 88; on Heidegger and humankind, see Martin Heidegger, 'Letter on Humanism' [1947], in *Basic Writings*, ed. David Farrell Krell, revised edn (London, 1993), p. 234.

18 *MDR*, p. 293.

19 Ibid., pp. 297–8.

20 See Romain Rolland's letter to Freud of 5 December 1927, referred to by Freud in *Civilization and its Discontents* (1930), §1; Freud, *SE*, XXI, pp. 66–8.

21 *Faust II*, lines 4679–85, 4715–40, 4725–8; Johann Wolfgang von Goethe, *Faust: A Tragedy*, ed. Cyrus Hamlin, trans. Walter Arndt, 2nd edn (New York and London, 2001), pp. 137–8. Cf. Robert Schumann, *Scenes from Goethe's 'Faust'* (1842–53).

22 Jung, *CW*, X, §981–§1001 and §1002–§1015.

23 *MDR*, pp. 307–8.

24 Ibid., p. 309.

25 Ibid. For further discussion, see Bryan Magee, 'A Note on Schopenhauer and Buddhism', *The Philosophy of Schopenhauer* (Oxford, 1983), pp. 316–21; and Peter Abelson, 'Schopenhauer and Buddhism', *Philosophy East and West*, XLIII/2 (April 1993), pp. 255–78.

26 *MDR*, p. 312.

27 Ibid., p. 314.

28 Ibid., p. 321.

29 Ibid., pp. 325–6; cf. *Faust II*, line 6289; *Faust*, p. 178.

30 As Jung explains later in *Memories, Dreams, Reflections*, when the Kabbalist Shimon ben Yochai came to die, his friends said he was celebrating his wedding (*MDR*, p. 346).

31 See Revelation 19:1–10.

32 See *Iliad* 14.292–351; *The Iliad of Homer*, trans. Richmond Lattimore
    (Chicago, IL, and London, 1951), pp. 302–3. Compare with Jung's
    remarks in *PU*, §368–§369, esp. n. 66.

33 Jung, *RB*, p. 326; ibid., pp. 323 and 314.

34 *MDR*, pp. 326–7.

35 Spinoza, *Ethics*, part 5, proposition 22, scholium; in *Spinoza:
    Selections*, ed. John Wild (London, 1928), p. 385.

36 F.W.J. Schelling, *System of Transcendental Idealism*, trans. Peter L.
    Heath (Charlottesville, VA, 1978), p. 188; Schelling, *System des
    tranzendentalen Idealismus*, in *Sämmtliche Werke*, 14 vols (Stuttgart
    and Augsburg, 1856–61), I/3, pp. 327–634 (p. 574).

37 See Schelling, *System of Transcendental Idealism*, trans. Heath,
    pp. 208–9; Schelling, *System des tranzendentalen Idealismus*, in
    Sämmtliche Werke, I/3, p. 644. See Eduard von Hartmann, *Philosophie
    des Unbewussten*, I: *Phänomenologie des Unbewussten*, 10th edn (Leipzig,
    1893), p. 22, where Hartmann cites this passage from Schelling;
    cf. vol. II, *Metaphysik des Unbewussten*, pp. 120 and 170.

38 *MDR*, p. 327.

39 Ibid., p. 328.

40 Ibid., p. 331.

41 Nietzsche, *The Birth of Tragedy*, §23; Friedrich Nietzsche, *Basic
    Writings*, ed. and trans. Walter Kaufmann (New York, 1968), p. 135.

42 See Goethe's lines: 'My build from Father I inherit, / His neat and
    serious ways; / Combined with Mother's cheerful spirit, / Her love
    of telling stories' (*Vom Vater hab' ich die Statur, / Des Lebens ernstes
    Führen, / Von Mütterchen die Frohnatur / Und Lust zu fabulieren*) (*GE*, I,
    p. 197); *MDR*, p. 331.

43 Nietzsche, *The Birth of Tragedy*, §23; *Basic Writings*, p. 136.

44 *MDR*, p. 331.

45 Ibid., p. 335. Compare Jung's words on myths with Zarathustra's cry,
    'For all joy wants Eternity', *denn alle Lust will Ewigkeit* (Friedrich
    Nietzsche, *Thus Spoke Zarathustra*, trans. Graham Parkes (New York,
    2005), pp. 199–200 and 284.

46 *Goethe: Conversation and Encounters*, ed. and trans. David Luke and
    Robert Pick (London, 1966), pp. 86–7. The question must remain
    open here whether Goethe is expressing his own views or synthesizing
    those of Wieland.

47 Ibid., p. 129.

48 See Thomas Arzt, 'Unus mundus: Die *Eine Welt*', *Philosophia naturalis*, XXXI (1994), pp. 250–62; Thomas Arzt, Maria Hippius-Gräfin Dürckheim and Roland Dollinger, eds, *Unus Mundus: Kosmos und Sympathie: Beiträge zum Gedanken der Einheit von Mensch und Kosmos* (Frankfurt am Main, 1992); and Gotthilf Isler, 'Einige Überlegungen zum unus mundus: Die Ganzheit der Welt als Erkenntnisproblem', in *Jungiana: Beiträge zur Psychologie von C. G. Jung*, Reihe A, vol. XVI (Zurich, 2010), pp. 87–135.

49 Jung, *CW*, XI, §1018.

50 Ibid., §966.

51 *MDR*, p. 405.

52 *The I Ching or Book of Changes*, trans. Richard Wilhelm [into German] and Cary F. Baynes [into English] (London, 1965), p. 171.

53 *MDR*, p. 406.

54 Jung, *CW*, XI, §1017.

55 For further discussion, see Arthur I. Miller, *Deciphering the Cosmic Number: The Strange Friendship of Wolfgang Pauli and Carl Jung* (New York and London, 2009).

56 Michael V. Berry, 'Exclusion Principle', in *The Fontana Dictionary of Modern Thought*, ed. Alan Bullock and Oliver Stalleybrass (London, 1977), p. 220.

57 See Hendrik B. G. Casimir, *Haphazard Reality: Half a Century of Science* (New York, 1983), pp. 144–5.

58 Jung, *CW*, XI, §967.

59 Thomas S. Kuhn, *The Structure of Scientific Revolutions* (Chicago, IL, 1962).

60 Jung, 'Synchronicity: An Acausal Connecting Principle'; *CW*, VIII, §958.

61 Ibid., §827.

62 See Arthur Schopenhauer, *On the Fourfold Root of the Principle of Sufficient Reason* [1813], trans E.F.J. Payne (La Salle, IL, 1847).

63 For a recent analysis of Jung's diagram in relation to a theory of time, see Angeliki Yiassemides, 'Chronos in Synchronicity: Manifestations of the Psychoid Reality', *Journal of Analytical Psychology*, LVI/4 (September 2011), pp. 451–70.

64 Arthur Koestler, *The Roots of Coincidence* (London, 1972), p. 101. (The comments to which Koestler refers may be found in Jung, *CW*, viii, §964–§965.)

65 See Frank McLynn, *Carl Gustav Jung: A Biography* (London, 1996), pp. 474–5.

66 *Faust II*, lines 8186–7; *Faust*, p. 232.

67 Lacan, *Écrits*, 2 vols (Paris, 1966–71), II, p. 130.

68 See Dylan Evans, *An Introductory Dictionary of Lacanian Psychoanalysis* (London and New York, 1996), pp. 158–9.

69 Jung, *CW*, VIII, §440.

70 Jung, *L*, I, p. 494.

71 Ibid., p. 546.

72 Ibid., II, p. 329.

73 See Jung, *CW*, VIII, §843 and §982.

74 Ibid., §845.

75 See Jung, *RB*, pp. 237 and 271.

76 Jung, *CW*, VIII, §860; cf. Johann Peter Eckermann, *Conversations of Goethe* [1930], trans. John Oxenford, ed. J. K. Moorhead (New York, 1998), p. 234.

77 *Dichtung und Wahrheit*, part 3, book 14; Goethe, *GE*, IV, p. 457.

78 *Wolfgang Pauli und C. G. Jung: Ein Briefwechsel*, ed. C. A. Meier (Berlin, 1993); available in English as *Atom and Archetype: The Pauli/Jung Letters*, ed. C. A. Meier (Princeton, NJ, 2001). This translation contains a helpful introductory essay by Beverley Zabriskie, 'Jung and Pauli: A Meeting of Rare Minds', pp. xxvii–l.

79 H. J. Eysenck, 'Of two minds' [review of *Wolfgang Pauli und C.G. Jung: Ein Briefwechsel*], *Nature*, CCCLXI, no. 6411 (4 February 1993), p. 415.

80 Suzanne Gieser, *The Innermost Kernel: Depth Psychology and Quantum Physics: Wolfgang Pauli's Dialogue with C. G. Jung* (Berlin, 2005); Harald Atmanspacher, 'The Hidden Side of Wolfgang Pauli: An Eminent Physicist's Extraordinary Encounter with Depth Psychology', *Journal of Consciousness Studies*, III/2 (1996), pp. 112–26; and Harald Atmanspacher and Hans Primas, 'Pauli's Ideas on Mind and Matter in the Context of Contemporary Science', *Journal of Consciousness Studies*, XIII/3 (2006), pp. 5–20.

81 Jung, *L*, I, p. 494, n. 4; see ibid., p. 502; and see also *Aion* (*CW*, IX/ii §347–§420).

82 Koestler, *The Roots of Coincidence*, pp. 88–9. For further discussion, see Gino Segré, *Faust in Copenhagen: A Struggle for the Soul of Physics* (London, 2008).

83 The correspondence between Jung and White has been published as *The Jung-White Letters*, ed. Ann Conrad Lammers and Adrian Cunningham (London and New York, 2007).

84 See Jung, *PU*, §354, n. 42.

85 *Goethe: Conversations and Encounters*, pp. 102–3; Jung, *PU*, §353.

86 Jung, *PU*, §353, n. 42.

87 Ibid.

88 Ibid., §356.

89 *The Jung-White Letters*, p. 53.

90 Jung, *CW*, IX/ii, §347–§421; *The Jung-White Letters*, p. 119.

91 Jung, *CW*, IX/ii, §147.

92 Ibid., §146.

93 See the document prepared by the Pontifical Council for Culture and the Pontifical Council for Interreligious Dialogue entitled 'Jesus Christ: The Bearer of the Water of Life: A Christian Reflection on the New Age' (2003).

94 *The Jung-White Letters*, p. 158.

95 Ibid., p. 119; ibid., p. 189.

96 Goethe, *Dichtung und Wahrheit*, part 2, book 8; *GE*, IV, p. 261.

97 Jung, *CW*, XVI, §397; Origen, *Homilies on Leviticus* 5.2; *Patrologiæ cursus completus, Series græca*, ed. J.-P. Migne, vol. XII, *Origenis: Opera omnia*, II (Paris, 1862), col. 449; Jung, *CW*, XVI, §397; Origen, *On the First Book of Kings*, Homily 1, §5, in *Opera Omnia Sanctorum Patrum Græcorum*, vol. XII (Würzburg, 1783), p. 76.

98 Jung, *CW*, XVI, §398; cf. *Faust II*, line 11962; *Faust*, p. 340.

99 For further discussion, see Paul Bishop, *Jung's 'Answer to Job': A Commentary* (Hove and New York, 2002).

100 Jung, *CW*, XI, §718; ibid., §750; *MDR*, pp. 78–9.

101 Joyce Carol Oates, 'Legendary Jung', in *The Profane Art: Essays and Reviews* (New York, 1983), pp. 159–64 (p. 162); interview with Anthony Storr on 4 September 1974; cited in Vincent Brome, *Jung: Man and Myth* (London, 1978), p. 252.

102 See *The Jung-White Letters*, pp. 173 and 181; see Victor White, review of *Jung's 'Answer to Job'*, in *Blackfriars*, XXXVI, no. 420 (March 1955), reproduced in *The Jung-White Letters*, pp. 349–56.

103 *The Jung-White Letters*, p. 6.

104 *The Apocryphal New Testament*, ed. J. K. Elliott (Oxford, 1993), pp. 139–40. See also Jung's discussions of 31 October 1934 and 23

January 1935 in his Nietzsche Seminar (Jung, *SNZ*, I, pp. 217–18 and 323–4); *The Jung-White Letters*, p. 143.

105 Jung, *CW*, XII, §558; *MDR*, pp. 297–8.

106 Jung, 'Analytical Psychology and "Weltanschauung"' (1928/1931); Jung, *CW*, VIII, §737.

107 See Wagner, *Tristan und Isolde*, Act III, Scene 1; Nietzsche, *The Birth of Tragedy*, §21, p. 127.

108 *MDR*, p. 301.

109 Cf. Matthew 10:39; Matthew 16:25; Luke 17:33; *The Jung-White Letters*, p. 240.

110 Goethe, *Dichtung und Wahrheit*, part 2, book 8; *GE*, IV, p. 237; Friedrich Nietzsche, *The Will to Power*, ed. Walter Kaufmann, trans. Walter Kaufmann and R. J. Hollingdale (New York, 1968), §853; cf. *The Birth of Tragedy*, Foreword to Wagner, *Tristan und Isolde*.

111 Jung, 'Psychotherapy and a Philosophy of Life' (1943); *CW*, XVI, §181.

112 Jung, *CW*, VIII, §789. For further discussion, see Sonu Shamdasani, '"The boundless expanse": Jung's Reflections on Life and Death', *Quadrant: Journal of the C. G. Jung Foundation for Analytical Psychology*, XXXVIII (2008), pp. 9–32, in which he suggests that, for Jung, analysis became a modern form of the *ars moriendi* (p. 24).

113 Robert d'Harcourt, *Goethe et l'art de vivre* (Paris, 1935); Angelo Caranfa, 'The Aesthetic Harmony of How Life Should Be Lived: Van Gogh, Socrates, Nietzsche', *Journal of Aesthetic Education*, XXXV (2001), pp. 1–13; John Armstrong, *Love, Life, Goethe: How to be Happy in an Imperfect World* (London, 2006); and Pierre Hadot, *N'oublie pas de vivre: Goethe et la tradition des exercices spirituels* (Paris, 2008).

Conclusion

1 Deirdre Bair, *Jung: A Biography* (Boston, MA, 2003), p. 623.

2 David Luke and Robert Pick, eds, *Goethe: Conversations and Encounters* (London, 1966), pp. 249–50.

3 Vincent Brome, *Jung: Man and Myth* (London, 1978), p. 273.

4 Bair, *Jung*, p. 625.

5 Ibid.

6 See Thomas Arzt, 'Analytische Psychologie und Naturphilosophie', in *Jung heute*, ed. Dieter Klein and Henning Weyerstraß (Cologne, 2008), pp. 14–29.

7 See Bair, *Jung*, p. 617. For the Coleridge source, see Samuel Taylor Coleridge, *The Notebooks*, I: *1794–1804*, ed. Kathleen Coburn (London, 1957), no. [1798].

8 *MDR*, p. 356.

9 For an introduction to this tradition, see Peter Watson, *The German Genius: Europe's Third Renaissance, the Second Scientific Revolution and the Twentieth Century* (London, 2010).

10 Philip Rice and Patricia Waugh, *Modern Literary Theory: A Reader* [1989], 3rd edn (London and New York, 1996), p. 123.

11 Jacques Derrida, 'Structure, Sign and Play', in *Writing and Difference*, trans. Alan Bass (London and New York, 2001), pp. 351–70; see 'The history of metaphysics, like the history of the West, is . . . the determination of Being as *presence* [*présence*] in all senses of this word' (p. 353).

12 Jacques Derrida, 'Différance', in *Margins of Philosophy*, trans. Alan Bass (Brighton, 1982), pp. 1–27 (pp. 7, 15 and 22).

13 Dorn, 'De tenebris contra naturam, et vita brevi', in *Theatrum chemicum*, I; cited in Jung, 'Psychology and Religion: The Terry Lectures' (1938/1940); *CW*, XI, §104, n. 47; cf. 'A Psychological Approach to the Dogma of the Trinity' (1942/1948); *CW*, XI, §180.

14 For an account of 'negative dialectics' as 'non-identity thinking', see Gillian Rose, *The Melancholy Science: An Introduction to the Thought of Theodor W. Adorno* (London and Basingstoke, 1978), pp. 44–6.

15 Jung, *CW*, XI, §180.

16 Ibid.

17 Ibid.

18 Jung, *Psychological Types*; *CW*, VI, §85.

19 Ibid., §202; thus the more generally applicable formulation of a critique made by Richard Sheppard, *New Ways in Germanistik* (New York and Oxford, 1990), p. 1.

20 Jung, *CW*, XI, §180.

21 Ibid., VI, §709. The actual source in Heraclitus is unclear, but the idea of *Enantiodromie* and *Enantiotropie* as things always having a mutual effect on one another is attributed to Heraclitus in *Meyers Konversations-Lexikon*, 4th edn (Leipzig and Vienna, 1885–92), V,

p. 611; on the libido returning to the unconscious, see Jung, *cw*, VI, §314; on the rhizome, see Gilles Deleuze and Félix Guattari, *Milles Plateaux* (Paris, 1980); *A Thousand Plateaus*, trans. Brian Massumi (New York and London, 2004).

22 See Christopher Hauke, *Jung and the Postmodern: The Interpretation of Realities* (London and Philadelphia, PA, 2000).

23 Jung, 'Transformation Symbolism in the Mass' (1942/1954); Jung, *cw*, XI, §417.

24 Ibid.

25 Goethe, *Maxims and Reflections*, ed. Hecker, §115; Jeremy Naydler, ed. and trans., *Goethe on Science: An Anthology of Goethe's Scientific Writings* (Edinburgh, 2000), p. 72; ibid.

26 Jung, *cw*, XI, §417.

27 Ibid.

28 *Faust I*, lines 382–3; Johann Wolfgang von Goethe, *Faust: A Tragedy*, ed. Cyrus Hamlin, trans. Walter Arndt, 2nd edn (New York and London, 2001), p. 12; *Faust II*, lines 12110–11; *Faust*, p. 344.

29 Jung, *The Psychology of the Transference* (1946); *cw*, XVI, §361.

30 See Goethe's letter to Johann Heinrich Meyer of 8 February 1796; Goethe, *Briefe* [*HA*], II, p. 215.

Select Bibliography

Anthony, Maggy, *The Valkyries: The Women around Jung* (Longmead, 1990)

Atmanspacher, Harald, 'The Hidden Side of Wolfgang Pauli: An Eminent Physicist's Extraordinary Encounter with Depth Psychology', *Journal of Consciousness Studies*, III/2 (1996), pp. 112–26

——, and Hans Primas, 'Pauli's Ideas on Mind and Matter in the Context of Contemporary Science', *Journal of Consciousness Studies*, XIII/3 (2006), pp. 5–20

Baeumler, Alfred, *Das mythische Weltalter: Bachofens romantischer Deutung des Altertums* (Munich, 1965)

Bair, Deirdre, *Jung: A Biography* (Boston, MA, 2003)

Barnaby, Karin, and Pellegrino d'Acierno, eds, *C. G. Jung and the Humanities: Toward a Hermeneutics of Culture* (London, 1990)

Barnes, Hazel E., 'Neo-Platonism and Analytical Psychology', *Philosophical Review*, LIV (1945), pp. 558–77

Bendayan, Gertrudis Ostfeld de, *Ecce Mulier: Nietzsche and the Eternal Feminine: An Analytical Psychological Perspective* (Wilmette, IL, 2007)

Bennet, E. A., *Meeting with Jung: Conversations recorded by E. A. Bennet during the years 1946–1961* (London, 1982)

Berry, Ruth, *Jung: A Beginner's Guide* (Abingdon, 2000)

Bettelheim, Bruno, *Freud and Man's Soul* (New York, 1984)

Bishop, Paul, *Analytical Psychology and German Classical Aesthetics: Goethe, Schiller, and Jung*, I: *The Development of the Personality* (London and New York, 2008)

——, *Analytical Psychology and German Classical Aesthetics: Goethe, Schiller, and Jung*, II: *The Constellation of the Self* (London and New York, 2009)

——, *Jung's "Answer to Job": A Commentary* (Hove and New York, 2002)

——, 'Jung's *Red Book* and its Relation to Aspects of German Idealism',

Journal of Analytical Psychology, LVII/3 (June 2012), pp. 335–63

——, *Reading Goethe at Midlife: Ancient Wisdom, German Classicism, and Jung* (New Orleans, LA, 2011)

——, *Synchronicity and Intellectual Intuition in Kant, Swedenborg, and Jung* (Lewiston, NY, 2000)

——, *The Dionysian Self: C. G. Jung's Reception of Friedrich Nietzsche* (Berlin and New York, 1995)

——, ed., *Jung in Contexts: A Reader* (London and New York, 1999)

——, ed., *The Archaic: The Past in the Present* (London and New York, 2012)

Bloom, Harold, *The Western Canon: The Books and School of the Ages* (New York, 1994)

Boyle, Nicholas, *Goethe: The Poet and the Age*, I: *The Poetry of Desire (1749–1790)* (Oxford and New York, 1991)

Brome, Vincent, *Jung: Man and Myth* (London, 1978)

Brooke, Roger, *Jung and Phenomenology* (London and New York, 1991)

Burleson, Blake W., *Jung in Africa* (New York, 2005)

Cambray, Joseph, and Linda Carter, eds, *Analytical Psychology: Contemporary Perspectives in Jungian Analysis* (Hove and New York, 2004)

Carotenuto, Aldo, *A Secret Symmetry: Sabina Spielrein between Jung and Freud*, trans. Arno Pomerans, John Shepley and Krishna Winston (New York, 1982)

Charet, F. X., 'Understanding Jung: Recent Biographies and Scholarship', *Journal of Analytical Psychology*, XLV (2000), pp. 195–216

——, *Spiritualism and the Foundations of C. G. Jung's Psychology* (Albany, NY, 1993)

Dixon, Patricia, *Nietzsche and Jung: Sailing a Deeper Night* (New York, 1999)

Dohe, Carrie B., 'Wotan and the "archetypal Ergriffenheit": Mystical Union, National Spiritual Rebirth and Culture-Creating Capacity in C. G. Jung's "Wotan" essay', *History of European Ideas*, XXXVII/3 (2011), pp. 344–56

Drob, Sandford L., *Reading the Red Book: An Interpretive Guide to C. G. Jung's "Liber Novus"* (New Orleans, LA, 2012)

Ellenberger, Henri F., *The Discovery of the Unconscious: The History and Evolution of Dynamic Psychiatry* (New York, 1970)

——, 'The Story of Helene Preiswerk: A Critical Study with New Documents', *History of Psychiatry*, II (1991), pp. 41–52

Evers, Tilman, *Mythos und Emanzipation: Eine kritische Annäherung an C. G. Jung* (Hamburg, 1987)

ffytche, Matt, *The Foundation of the Unconscious: Schelling, Freud and the Birth of the Modern Psyche* (Cambridge, 2012)

Franz, Marie-Louise von, *C. G. Jung: His Myth in Our Time*, trans. William H. Kennedy (New York, 1975)

Freud, Sigmund, *The Standard Edition of the Complete Works of Sigmund Freud*, general eds J. Strachey and A. Freud, 24 vols (London, 1953–74)

——, and C. G. Jung, *The Freud-Jung Letters: The Correspondence between Sigmund Freud and C. G. Jung*, ed. William McGuire, trans. Ralph Manheim and R.F.C. Hull (Cambridge, MA, 1988)

Gay, Peter, *Freud: A Life for Our Time* (New York and London, 1988)

Gieser, Suzanne, *The Innermost Kernel: Depth Psychology and Quantum Physics: Wolfgang Pauli's Dialogue with C. G. Jung* (Berlin, 2005)

Goethe, Johann Wolfgang, *Briefe*, ed. Kurt Robert Mandelkow, 4 vols (Hamburg, 1962–7)

——, *Faust: A Tragedy*, ed. Cyrus Hamlin, trans. Walter Arndt, 2nd edn (New York and London, 2001)

——, *Goethe's Collected Works [Goethe Edition]*, ed. Victor Lange, Eric A. Blackall and Cyrus Hamlin, 12 vols (Boston, MA, and New York, 1983–9)

——, *Poems of the West and East: West-Eastern Divan – West-Östlicher Divan: Bi-lingual Edition of the Complete Poems*, trans. John Whaley (Bern, 1998)

——, *Werke [Hamburger Ausgabe]*, ed. Erich Trunz, 14 vols (Hamburg, 1948–60; Munich, 1981)

——, *Werke [Weimarer Ausgabe]*, ed. on behalf of Großherzogin Sophie von Sachsen, 4 parts, 133 vols in 143 (Weimar, 1887–1919)

Goodheart, William B., 'C. G. Jung's First Patient: On the Seminal Emergence of Jung's Thought', *Journal of Analytical Psychology*, XXIX (1984), pp. 1–34

Gossman, Lionel, *Basel in the Age of Burckhardt: A Study in Unseasonable Ideas* (Chicago, IL, and London, 2000)

Hannah, Barbara, *C. G. Jung: His Life and Work: A Biographical Memoir* (New York, 1976)

Hauke, Christopher, *Jung and the Postmodern: The Interpretation of Realities* (London and Philadelphia, PA, 2000)

Hayman, Ronald, *A Life of Jung* (London, 1999)

Heidegger, Martin, *Basic Writings*, ed. David Farrell Krell, revised edn (London, 1993)

Homans, Peter, *Jung in Context: Modernity and the Making of a Psychology* (Chicago, IL, and London, 1979)

Hopcke, Robert, *Jung, Jungians, and Homosexuality* (Boston, MA, and London, 1989)

Huskinson, Lucy, *Nietzsche and Jung: The Whole Self in the Union of Opposites* (Hove and New York, 2004)

Hyde, Maggie, and Michael McGuinness, *Jung for Beginners* (Cambridge, 1992)

Jaffé, Aniela, ed., *C. G. Jung: Memories, Dreams, Reflections*, trans. Richard and Clara Winston (London, 1983)

——, ed., *C. G. Jung in Word and Image*, trans. Krishna Winston (Princeton, NJ, 1979)

——, *From the Life and Work of C. G. Jung*, trans. R.F.C. Hull (London, 1972)

Jones, Ernest, *The Life and Work of Sigmund Freud*, I: *The Formative Years and the Great Discoveries 1856–1900* (New York, 1953)

Jones, Raya, 'A Discovery of Meaning: The Case of C. G. Jung's House Dream', *Culture & Psychology*, XIII (2007), pp. 203–30

Jung, Andreas et al., *Haus C. G. Jung: Entstehung und Erneuerung des Wohnhauses von Emma und Carl Gustav Jung-Rauschenbach* (Küsnacht-Zurich, 2009)

Jung, Andreas, 'The Grandfather', *Journal of Analytical Psychology*, LVI (2011), pp. 653–73

Jung, C. G., *Analytical Psychology: Notes of the Seminar Given in 1925*, ed. William McGuire (Princeton, NJ, 1989)

——, *Collected Works*, ed. Herbert Read, Michael Fordham, Gerhard Adler and William McGuire, 20 vols (London, 1953–83)

——, *Letters*, ed. Gerhard Adler and Aniela Jaffé, trans. R.F.C. Hull, 2 vols (London, 1973–5)

——, *Psychology of the Unconscious: A Study of the Transformations and Symbolisms of the Libido: A Contribution to the History of the Evolution of Thought*, trans. Beatrice M. Hinkle, intro. William McGuire (London, 1991)

——, *Seminar on Nietzsche's "Zarathustra": Notes of the Seminar Given in 1934–1939*, ed. James L. Jarrett, 2 vols (London, 1989)

——, *The Red Book: Liber Novus*, ed. Sonu Shamdasani, trans. Mark Kyburz, John Peck, and Sonu Shamdasani (New York and London, 2009)

——, *The Zofingia Lectures*, trans. Jan van Heurck (London, Melbourne, Henley, 1983)

——, *Visions: Notes of the Seminar given in 1930-1934*, ed. Claire Douglas, 2 vols (Princeton, NJ, 1997)

——, and James Kirsch, *The Jung-Kirsch Letters: The Correspondence of C. G. Jung and James Kirsch*, ed. Ann Conrad Lammers, trans. Ursula Egli and Ann Conrad Lammers (London and New York, 2011)

——, and Victor White, *The Jung-White Letters*, ed. Ann Conrad Lammers and Adrian Cunningham (London and New York, 2007)

Kaufmann, Walter, *Discovering the Mind*, vol. I, *Goethe, Kant, and Hegel* (New York, 1980)

Kerr, John, *A Most Dangerous Method: The Story of Jung, Freud, and Sabina Spielrein* (London, 1994)

Kerslake, Christian, *Deleuze and the Unconscious* (London and New York, 2007)

——, 'Rebirth through incest: On Deleuze's Early Jungianism', *Angelaki*, IX/1, 2004, pp. 135–57

Kirsch, Thomas B., *The Jungians: A Comparative and Historical Perspective* (London and Philadelphia, PA, 2000)

——, and George Hogenson, eds, *The Red Book: Reflections on C. G. Jung's "Liber Novus"* (London and New York, 2013)

Laplanche, Jean, and Jean-Bertrand Pontalis, *The Language of Psycho-Analysis*, trans. Donald Nicholson-Smith (London, 1973)

Lehmann, Herbert, 'Jung contra Freud/Nietzsche contra Wagner', *International Review of Psycho-Analysis*, XIII (1986), pp. 201–9

Lewin, Nicholas, *Jung on War, Politics and Nazi Germany: Exploring the Theory of Archetypes and the Collective Unconscious* (London, 2009)

Liebscher, Martin, *Libido und Wille zur Macht: C. G. Jungs Auseinandersetzung mit Nietzsche* (Basel, 2012)

McGrath, S. J., *The Dark Ground of the Spirit: Schelling and the Unconscious* (London and New York, 2012)

McGuire, William, and R.F.C. Hull, eds, *C. G. Jung Speaking: Interviews and Encounters* (Princeton, NJ, 1977)

——, 'Firm Affinities: Jung's Relations with Britain and the United States', *Journal of Analytical Psychology*, XL (1995), pp. 301–26

McLynn, Frank, *Carl Gustav Jung: A Biography* (London, 1996)

Maidenbaum, Aryeh, and Stephen A. Martin, *Lingering Shadows: Jungians, Freudians, and Anti-Semitism* (Boston, MA, and London, 1991)

Main, Roderick, ed., *Jung on Synchronicity and the Paranormal* (London, 1997)

Miller, Arthur I., *Deciphering the Cosmic Number: The Strange Friendship of Wolfgang Pauli and Carl Jung* (New York and London, 2009)

Murphy, Peter, and David Roberts, *Dialectic of Romanticism: A Critique of Modernism* (London and New York, 2004)

Myers, Steve, 'The Cryptomnesic Origins of Jung's Dream of the Multi-Storeyed House', *Journal of Analytical Psychology*, LIV (2009), pp. 513–31

Nietzsche, Friedrich, *Basic Writings*, ed. and trans. Walter Kaufmann (New York, 1968)

——, *Dithyrambs of Dionysus*, trans. R. J. Hollingdale (London, 1984)

——, *Ecce Homo*, trans. R. J. Hollingdale (Harmondsworth, 1992)

——, *Human, All Too Human: A Book for Free Spirits*, trans. R. J. Hollingdale (Cambridge, 1986)

——, *The Will to Power*, ed. Walter Kaufmann, trans. Walter Kaufmann and R. J. Hollingdale (New York, 1968)

——, *Thus Spoke Zarathustra*, trans. Graham Parkes (New York, 2005)

——, *Twilight of the Idols/The Anti-Christ*, trans. R. J. Hollingdale (Harmondsworth, 1968)

——, *Unmodern Observations*, ed. William Arrowsmith (New Haven, CT, and London, 1990)

Noll, Richard, *The Aryan Christ: The Secret Life of Carl Jung* (New York, 1997)

——, *The Jung Cult: Origins of a Charismatic Movement* (Princeton, NJ, 1994)

Onfray, Michel, *Apostille au Crépuscule: Pour une psychanalyse non freudienne* (Paris, 2010)

——, *L'art de jouir* (Paris, 1991)

——, *La puissance d'exister: Manifeste hédoniste* (Paris, 2006)

——, *Le crépuscule d'une idole: L'affabulation freudienne* (Paris, 2010)

——, *Le désir d'être un volcan: Journal hédoniste I* (Paris, 1996)

——, *La construction du surhomme* (Paris, 2011)

Ornton, Darius Gray, ed., *Translating Freud* (New Haven, CT, and London, 1992)

Papadopoulos, Renos K., ed., *The Handbook of Jungian Psychology: Theory, Practice and Applications* (Hove and New York, 2006)

Pauli, Wolfgang, and C. G. Jung, *Atom and Archetype: The Pauli/Jung Letters*, ed. C. A. Meier (Princeton, NJ, 2001)

Pietikäinen, Petteri, *C. G. Jung and the Psychology of Symbolic Forms* (Helsinki, 1999)

Platania, Jon, *Jung for Beginners* (New York and London, 1997)

Portmann, Adolf, 'Jung's Biology Professor: Some Recollections', *Spring: A Journal of Archetype and Culture* (1976), pp. 148–54

Rosen, David, *The Tao of Jung: The Way of Integrity* (New York, 1996)

Rosenzweig, Saul, *Freud, Jung, and Hall the King-Maker: The Historic Expedition to America (1909) with G. Stanley Hall as Host and William James as Guest* (St Louis, MO, and Seattle, WA, 1992)

Rowland, Susan, *C. G. Jung and Literary Theory: The Challenge from Fiction* (Basingstoke and London; New York, 1999)

——, *C. G. Jung in the Humanities: Taking the Soul's Path* (New Orleans, LA, 2010)

——, *Jung as a Writer* (London, 2005)

——, *Jung: A Feminist Revision* (Cambridge, 2002)

——, *The Ecocritical Psyche: Literature, Evolutionary Complexity and Jung* (Hove and New York, 2012)

Ryce-Menuhin, Joel, *Jungian Sandplay: The Wonderful Therapy* (London, 1992)

Saayman, Graham, ed., *Modern South Africa in Search of a Soul: Jungian Perspectives on the Wilderness Within* (Boston, MA, 1990)

Samuels, Andrew, *Jung and the Post-Jungians* (London and New York, 1985)

——, Bani Shorter and Fred Plaut, *A Critical Dictionary of Jungian Analysis* (London and New York, 1986)

Schmitt, Gerhard, *Text als Psyche: Eine Einführung in die analytische Psychologie C. G. Jungs für Literaturwissenschaftler* (Aachen, 1999)

——, 'Vom Übermensch und Übersinn: Nietzsches Metaphorik im *Roten Buch*', in *Recherches germaniques*, special edition, VIII (2011), pp. 117–33

——, *Zyklus und Kompensation: Zur Denkfigur bei Nietzsche und Jung* (Frankfurt am Main, 1998)

Shamdasani, Sonu, 'A Woman Called Frank', *Spring*, L (1990), pp. 26–56

——, '"The boundless expanse": Jung's Reflections on Life and Death', *Quadrant: Journal of the C. G. Jung Foundation for Analytical Psychology*, XXXVIII (2008), pp. 9–32

——, *C. G. Jung: A Biography in Books* (New York and London, 2012)

——, *Jung and the Making of Modern Psychology: The Dream of a Science* (Cambridge, 2003)

——, *Jung Stripped Bare by His Biographers, Even* (London and New York, 2005)

Shelburne, Walter A., *Mythos and Logos in the Thought of Carl Jung: The Theory of the Collective Unconscious in Scientific Perspective* (Albany, NY, 1988)

Spinoza, Baruch de, *Selections*, ed. John Wild (London, 1928)

Stern, Paul J., *C. G. Jung: The Haunted Prophet* (New York, 1976)

Stevens, Anthony, *Jung: A Very Short Introduction* (New York, 2001)

Storr, Anthony, *Jung*, Fontana Modern Masters (London, 1973)

Tacey, David, *How to Read Jung* (London, 2006)

Van der Post, Laurens, *Jung and the Story of Our Time* (London, 1976)

Vergely, Bertrand, *Retour à l'émerveillement* (Paris, 2010)

Watson, Peter, *The German Genius: Europe's Third Renaissance, the Second Scientific Revolution and the Twentieth Century* (London, 2010)

Wehr, Gerhard, *An Illustrated Biography of C. G. Jung*, trans. Michael H. Kohn (Boston, MA, and Shaftesbury, 1989)

——, *C. G. Jung und das Christentum* (Olten, 1975)

——, *C. G. Jung und Rudolf Steiner* (Stuttgart, 1972)

——, *Jung: A Biography*, trans. David Weeks (Boston, MA, 1987)

Wilson, Colin, *C. G. Jung: Lord of the Underworld* (London, 1988)

Ziolkowski, Theodor, *The View from the Tower: Origins of an Antimodernist Image* (Princeton, NJ, 1999)

Zumstein-Preiswerk, Stefanie, *C. G. Jungs Medium: Die Geschichte der Helly Preiswerk* (Munich, 1975)

Acknowledgements

Having undertaken research into the intellectual-historical genesis and conceptual affinities of the thought of C. G. Jung, taught a number of Jung's texts in university courses, and learned much from conferences on Jung organized by academics and clinicians alike, it was a pleasure to have been asked to write this book. It offered me the chance to address myself to the question of Jung's relevance and significance for readers today. For various reasons, however, it proved increasingly difficult to find sufficient time for the introductory or synthesizing writing of the kind intended by this study. (*Quoniam quae perfecisti, destruxerunt: iustus autem quid fecit?*) So I am grateful to the publisher, Michael Leaman, for being so patient as the completion of this project became delayed, and for suggesting improvements to make the manuscript clearer and tighter. (Discussions of Jung's awareness of the problems of autobiography, the genesis of *The Red Book*, and of the institutional legacy of analytical psychology have been omitted for reasons of space.)

During the writing of this book, I have benefited greatly, as in the past, from the resources of Glasgow University Library, but also – a new discovery for me – from the branch of the Deutsche Nationalbibliothek in Frankfurt am Main. I am also indebted to the following individuals for information and assistance: in the first instance, for help with a number of detailed queries about Jung or about Switzerland, to Herrn Ulrich Hoerni and Andreas Jung of the Stiftung der Werke von C. G. Jung, Zurich; to Dr Thomas Fischer, Wissenschaftlicher Mitarbeiter, Stiftung der Werke von C. G. Jung, Zurich; and to Herrn Urs Niffeler, Zentralsekretär of Archäologie Schweiz.

Then, in respect of key pieces of information, I should like to thank Andrew Burniston, for material relating to Jung and Wolfgang Pauli;

Professor Malcolm Pender, for the source of a quotation in a Thomas Mann quotation; and Professor Roderick Main, for a number of conversations around the topic of Jung and synchronicity. I have also learnt much from a number of conversations during conferences and workshops arranged by the Society of Analytical Psychologists, the Guild of Pastoral Psychology, and C. G. Jung Scotland.

As ever I am indebted in more ways than I can say to Helen Bridge.

Photo Acknowledgements

The author and publishers wish to express their thanks to the below sources of illustrative material and/or permission to reproduce it. Some information not given in the captions for reasons of brevity is also given below. Every reasonable effort has been made to trace the copyright owners of anonymous photographs, but sometimes this has proven impossible. The publisher will be glad to receive information leading to more complete acknowledgements in future printings of the book.

Photo Dieter Bachmann: p. 151 (foot); photo German Federal Archives: p. 20; photo F. Hartmann: p. 70; from the *Küsnachter Jahresblätter*, Ausgabe 1961: p. 89 (top); photos Library of Congress, Washington, DC: pp. 91, 112; photo Carl Lutherer: p. 52; Metropolitan Museum of Art, New York: p. 105; Musée Archéologique de Nîmes: p. 43; Musée du Louvre, Paris: p. 162; photos National Library of Medicine, Washington: pp. 23, 76, 156, 159, 216; from *Neue Denkschriften der Schweizerischen Naturforschenden Gesellschaft*, vol. 54 (1918): p. 42; thanks to Urs Niffeler: p. 42; photo Qtea: p. 209; and photo Stadt- und Universitäts-Bibliothek Frankfurt am Main, Schopenhauer-Archiv: p. 57.

Qtea, the copyright holder of the image on p. 209, has published it online under conditions imposed by a Creative Commons Attribution 2.0 Generic licence; Dieter Bachmann, the copyright holder of the image on p. 43, and Philipp Roelli, the copyright holder of the image on p. 151 (foot), have published them online under conditions imposed by a Creative Commons Attribution-ShareAlike 3.0 Unported licence; Philipp Roelli, the copyright holder of the images on pp. 150 and 151 (top), has published